Northern Ireland Since 1969

Northern Ireland Since 1969

Paul Dixon and Eamonn O'Kane

Longman
is an imprint of

Harlow, England • London • New York • Boston • San Francisco • Toronto • Sydney • Singapore • Hong Kong
Tokyo • Seoul • Taipei • New Delhi • Cape Town • Madrid • Mexico City • Amsterdam • Munich • Paris • Milan

PEARSON EDUCATION LIMITED

Edinburgh Gate
Harlow CM20 2JE
United Kingdom
Tel: +44 (0)1279 623623
Fax: +44 (0)1279 431059
Website: www.pearsoned.co.uk

First published in Great Britain in 2011

© Pearson Education 2011

The rights of Paul Dixon and Eamonn O'Kane to be identified as authors of this work have
been asserted by them in accordance with the Copyright, Designs and Patents Act 1988.

Pearson Education is not responsible for the content of third party internet sites.

ISBN: 978-1-4058-0135-5

British Library Cataloguing in Publication Data
A CIP catalogue record for this book can be obtained from the British Library

Library of Congress Cataloging in Publication Data
Dixon, Paul, 1964–
    Northern Ireland since 1969 / Paul Dixon and Eamonn O'Kane.
      p. cm.
    Includes bibliographical references and index.
    ISBN 978-1-4058-0135-5 (pbk.)
    1. Northern Ireland–Politics and government. 2. Great Britain–Foreign
relations–Northern Ireland. 3. Northern Ireland–Foreign relations–Great Britain.
4. Peace movements–Northern Ireland. 5. Northern Ireland–Politics and
government–Sources. 6. Great Britain–Foreign relations–Northern Ireland–
Sources. 7. Northern Ireland–Foreign relations–Great Britain–Sources.
8. Irish question. I. O'Kane, Eamonn. II. Title.
    DA990.U46D597 2011
    941.60824–dc22

2010044153

10 9 8 7 6 5 4 3 2 1
15 14 13 12 11

Set in 10/13.5 Berkeley Book by 35
Printed and bound in Malaysia, CTP-KHL

Introduction to the Series

History is a narrative constructed by historians from traces left by the past. Historical enquiry is often driven by contemporary issues and, in consequence, historical narratives are constantly reconsidered, reconstructed and reshaped. The fact that different historians have different perspectives on issues means that there is also often controversy and no universally agreed version of past events. *Seminar Studies in History* was designed to bridge the gap between current research and debate, and the broad, popular general surveys that often date rapidly.

The volumes in the series are written by historians who are not only familiar with the latest research and current debates concerning their topic, but who have themselves contributed to our understanding of the subject. The books are intended to provide the reader with a clear introduction to a major topic in history. They provide both a narrative of events and a critical analysis of contemporary interpretations. They include the kinds of tools generally omitted from specialist monographs: a chronology of events, a glossary of terms and brief biographies of 'who's who'. They also include bibliographical essays in order to guide students to the literature on various aspects of the subject. Students and teachers alike will find that the selection of documents will stimulate discussion and offer insight into the raw materials used by historians in their attempt to understand the past.

Clive Emsley and Gordon Martel
Series Editors

For Jack and Tom

and

Thea, Niall and Dylan

Contents

Publisher's acknowledgements

We are grateful to the following for permission to reproduce copyright material:

Figures

Figure 1 from *Northern Ireland*, 2nd edition, Palgrave Macmillan (Dixon, P. 2008b) p. 29, reproduced with permission of Palgrave Macmillan; Figure 2 adapted from *Atlas of Irish History*, 2nd edition, Gill & Macmillan Ltd (ed Duffy, S. 2000) p. 129, reproduced by permission of Gill & Macmillan Ltd; Figure 3 adapted from *From Civil Rights to Armalites*, 2nd edition, Palgrave Macmillan (O'Dochartaigh, N. 2004) pp. 330–331, reproduced with permission of Palgrave Macmillan; Figure 4 'Sectarian Map of Belfast', www.wesleyjohnston.com, copyright © Wesley Johnston.

Tables

Table 1.1 from *Northern Ireland: The Politics of War and Peace*, 2nd edition, Palgrave Macmillan (Dixon, P. 2008b) p. 11, reproduced with permission of Palgrave Macmillan; Table 4.1 adapted from 'Is There a Concurring Majority about Northern Ireland?', Richard Rose, Ian McAllister and Peter Mair (Glasgow: University of Strathclyde Studies in Public Policy No. 22, 1978), copyright © GFK NOP Limited.

Text

Quote on page 53 from Margaret Thatcher, House of Commons, Vol 985, Col 250, 20/05/80, © Parliamentary copyright 2010; Quote on page 57 from Margaret Thatcher 1993: 385, copyright © Lady Thatcher; Extract on page 74 from The Downing Street Declaration, 1993, © Parliamentary copyright; Quote on pages 88–89 from Tony Blair, Doc 24. Reproduced by permission of The Labour Party; Quote on page 92 from Tony Blair, *News Letter & Irish News*, Doc 25, 22/05/1998. Reproduced by permission of

The Labour Party; Quote on page 92 from Tony Blair, *The Observer*, 24/05/1998. Reproduced by permission of The Labour Party; Extract on pages 125–126 from 'Extract from minutes of the UK Cabinet's sub-committee on Northern Ireland', GEN 47 (71) 5th Meeting, 6th October 1971, 10.30am, © Parliamentary copyright 2010; Extract on pages 127–128 from *The Long War – The IRA and Sinn Féin*, The O'Brien Press Ltd, Dublin (Brendan O'Brien, 1993) copyright © Brendan O'Brien; Extract on pages 129–130 from *Northern Ireland: Crisis and Conflict*, Routledge (John Magee, 1974) copyright © Taylor & Francis Books, 1974; Extract on pages 130–131 from 'The Future of Northern Ireland: A Paper for Discussion', NIO, London HMSO 1972, Crown Copyright material is reproduced with permission under the terms of the Click-Use License; Extract on pages 132–134 from 'Northern Ireland Constitutional Proposals', CMND 5259, London, HMSO. March 1973 (White Paper), Crown Copyright material is reproduced with permission under the terms of the Click-Use License; Quote on pages 134–135 from Harold Wilson, text of broadcast during the Ulster Workers' Council Strike, also known as the 'Spongers Speech' 25/05/1974. Reproduced by permission of The Labour Party; Extract on pages 136–137 from 'The Glover Report', also known as 'Northern Ireland: Future Terrorist Trends' (Brigadier James Glover). Crown Copyright material is reproduced with the permission of the Controller, Office of Public Sector Information (OPSI); Extract on page 139 from House of Commons Debates, 27 November 1985 Vol 87 Col 912–913, © Parliamentary copyright 2010; Extract on page 141 from a speech by John Hume MP MEP to the SDLP's 18th Annual Conference, 25–27 November 1988. Europa Hotel, Belfast (published by the SDLP), pp.4–5. Reproduced by kind permission of Mr Hume and SDLP; Extract on pages 141–142 from *All Hell Will Break Loose*, The O'Brien Press Ltd, Dublin (Austin Currie 2004) pp. 329–330, copyright © Austin Currie; Quote on pages 142–143 from Peter Brooke, Secretary of State for Northern Ireland 'Whitbread Speech', 09/11/1990, reproduced by kind permission of Lord Peter Brooke; Extract on page 146 from *Report of the International Body on Arms Decommissioning*, NIO (Senator George Mitchell) © Crown Copyright 2010 Northern Ireland Office; Quote on pages 147–148 from Prime Minister Mr. Tony Blair, The Royal Agricultural Society, Belfast, 16/05/1997. Reproduced by permission of The Labour Party; Extract on pages 148–149 from *The Good Friday Agreement*, NIO © Crown Copyright 2010 Northern Ireland Office; Extract on pages 149–150 from *The Principles and Realities of a Settlement: An Alliance Paper*, The Alliance Party of Northern Ireland www.allianceparty.org, copyright © Alliance Party of Northern Ireland; Extract on pages 150–151 from 'Ulstermen march to a new drum', *The Independent* 14/10/1994 (David McKittrick), copyright © The Independent, 1994; Extract on pages 151–152 from David Trimble, Nobel Peace Prize Speech, Oslo, 10/12/1998, http://

nobelprize.org; Quote on pages 152–153 from Tony Blair, 'Belfast Harbour' speech, 18/10/2002. Reproduced by permission of The Labour Party; Quote on page 153 from Tony Blair regarding The British governments' decision to suspend the Assembly elections scheduled for 29th May 2003, 01/05/2003. Reproduced by permission of The Labour Party.

In some instances we have been unable to trace the owners of copyright material, and we would appreciate any information that would enable us to do so.

Picture Credits

Plate 1 © Pacemaker Press International; Plate 2 © PA Photos/TopFoto; Plate 3 © Associated Newspapers Ltd/Solo Syndication; Plate 4 © Kaveh Kazemi/ Getty Images; Plate 5 © Tom Arne Hanslien/Alamy; Plate 6 © The White House/Getty Images; Plate 7 © Alan Lewis; Plate 8 Northern Ireland Office and Bagenal's Castle, Newry; Plate 9 © PAUL FAITH/AFP/Getty Images; Plate 10 © LANDOV/Press Association Images.

Every effort has been made to trace the copyright holders and we apologise in advance for any unintentional omissions. We would be pleased to insert the appropriate acknowledgement in any subsequent edition of this publication.

Chronology

1969

4 January PD civil rights march attacked at Burntollet Bridge near Derry by loyalists

24 January Deputy Prime Minster Brian Faulkner resigns

17 April Civil rights activist, 21-year-old Bernadette Devlin elected as a Westminster MP in a by-election.

28 April Terence O'Neill resigns as Northern Ireland's Prime Minister

12 August Serious rioting begins in the Bogside area of Derry as a loyalist march passes close to the area (the Battle of the Bogside)

14 August British troops deployed in Derry

15 August British troops deployed in Belfast

11 October Constable Victor Arbuckle killed by the UVF on the Shankill Road, first policeman killed during the Troubles

28 December The IRA splits and the Provisional IRA is formed

1970

28 June 500 Nationalist workers are expelled from their jobs at Harland and Wolff shipyard in east Belfast by Protestant colleagues

3 July A 34-hour curfew imposed on the nationalist Lower Falls area of Belfast. Five people are killed and 60 injured (including 15 soldiers)

21 August The SDLP is formed

1971

6 February The Provisional IRA kills Gunner Robert Curtis, the first British soldier to die while on duty during the Troubles

16 March Chichester Clark resigns as Northern Ireland's Prime Minister

19 March Brian Faulkner becomes Prime Minister

9 August Internment without trial introduced

1972

30 January	14 men are shot dead by the British Parachute Regiment during a civil rights march in Derry (Bloody Sunday)
30 March	Stormont parliament is suspended (prorogued) and direct rule introduced
29 May	The OIRA announces a permanent end to its campaign of violence
19 June	Special category status introduced for paramilitary prisoners in Northern Ireland
7 July	Home Secretary William Whitelaw meets Provisional IRA leaders in London
21 July	The Provisional IRA detonates 26 bombs in Belfast, killing 11 and injuring 130 ('Bloody Friday')
31 July	The British army removes the barricades to the 'no go' areas of Derry and Belfast (Operation Motorman)

1973

20 March	Government White Paper, *Northern Ireland Constitutional Proposals*, proposes a Northern Ireland Assembly
22 November	The UUP, SDLP and APNI agree to form a power-sharing executive
6–9 December	Sunningdale Conference agrees to create a Council of Ireland

1974

1 January	Northern Ireland Executive takes office
4 January	Brian Faulkner resigns as leader of the UUP after the party rejects the Sunningdale Agreement (Faulkner remains Chief of the Executive)
28 February	British general election. Anti-Sunningdale candidates (UUUC) win 11 of Northern Ireland's 12 seats
15 May	The UWC calls for a general strike in protest against the Sunningdale deal
17 May	33 people are killed by car bombs in Dublin and Monaghan in the Irish Republic
28 May	Brian Faulkner resigns as Chief Executive leading to the collapse of devolved government
30 May	The Northern Ireland Assembly is prorogued
10 October	British general election. The UUUC win 10 of Northern Ireland's 12 seats
21 November	The IRA kills 21 and injures over 160 in two pub bombings in Birmingham (seven other people had been killed by IRA pub bombs in England in the previous weeks)

1975

9 February   The IRA announces an indefinite ceasefire, seen as marking a truce with the British

12 November   Rees announces the incident centres are to be closed, effectively ending the Truce

5 December   Rees announces the end of detention without trial (internment)

1976

23 January   The IRA officially ends its ceasefire

21 July   British Ambassador in Dublin Christopher Ewart-Biggs is killed by a land-mine under his car

1977

30 August   US President Jimmy Carter calls for a new initiative on Northern Ireland

1978

17 February   12 Protestants are killed by an IRA bomb at the La Mon House Hotel in Castlereagh

17 December   The IRA bombs Liverpool, Manchester, Bristol, Coventry and Southampton

1979

20 February   11 members of the notorious loyalist gang the Shankhill Butchers are convicted of 112 offences, including 19 murders

30 March   Airey Neave, the Conservative Party's spokesman on Northern Ireland, is killed by an INLA bomb under his car in the House of Commons' car park

3 May   Margaret Thatcher's Conservative Party wins the British general election

27 August   Earl Mountbatten and three others are killed by an IRA bomb on their boat off Sligo in the Irish Republic. Later two IRA bombs kill 18 soldiers near Warrenpoint in Northern Ireland

1980

27 October   Seven republican prisoners begin a hunger strike in the Maze prison

8 December   Margaret Thatcher and Taoiseach Charles Haughey hold a summit in Dublin

18 December   The hunger strikes are called off

1981

1 March   The IRA leader in the Maze, Bobby Sands, begins a hunger strike

9 April   Bobby Sands is elected as an MP in a by-election

5 May   Bobby Sands dies. His funeral two days later attracts an estimated 100,000 people

11 June   Two H-Block (Maze) prisoners are elected as members of the Irish parliament

3 October   After ten prisoners have died on hunger strike the protest is called off

6 October   Secretary of State Jim Prior announces that prisoners will be allowed to wear their own clothes at all times

10 October   The IRA bombs Chelsea barracks in London

14 November An IRA bomb kills UUP MP Revd Robert Bradford and a caretaker

1982

20 July   Two IRA bombs in London kill 11 soldiers

20 October   Sinn Féin receives over 10 per cent of the vote in elections to a new Assembly; the first time it has contested a Northern Ireland-wide election

6 December   An INLA bomb kills 11 soldiers and six civilians at the Droppin' Well disco at Ballykelly, Co. Londonderry

1983

11 March   The Irish government announces the creation of the New Ireland Forum

9 June   Thatcher's Conservative Party is returned to power in the general election. Sinn Féin's Gerry Adams is elected as MP for West Belfast

25 September 38 IRA prisoners escape from the Maze prison. One warder is killed

17 December An IRA bomb outside Harrods kills three police officers and three civilians. Over 90 are injured

1984

2 May   New Ireland Forum Report published

29 September Trawler with 7 tons of IRA arms and ammunitions seized by Irish police off the Kerry coast

12 October   The IRA bombs the Grand Hotel, Brighton during the Conservative Party Conference. Five people are killed, including one MP and the wife of the Chief Whip

1985

15 November The AIA signed, granting the Irish government an institutionalised right of consultation over Northern Ireland

23 November Over 100,000 unionists attend a demonstration against the AIA at Belfast City Hall

1986

11 March The US House of Representatives approves a $250 million aid package for Northern Ireland in support of the AIA.

23 June The Northern Ireland Assembly is dissolved.

15 November Up to 200,000 attend an anti-AIA rally at Belfast City Hall

1987

8 May Eight IRA men and a civilian are killed by the SAS when the IRA attacks an RUC station at Loughall, Co. Armagh

8 November An IRA bomb explodes during a Remembrance Day ceremony in Enniskillen, killing 11 and injuring 63

11 November 150 tons of arms and ammunition destined for the IRA from Libya are seized off the French coast

1988

6 March Three unarmed IRA members are shot by the SAS in Gibraltar

16 March In Belfast three mourners are killed and 50 injured by a loyalist at the funeral of the three IRA members killed in Gibraltar

19 March Two soldiers are killed when they are dragged from their car after driving towards the funeral cortege of one of those killed in the loyalist attack three days earlier

15 June Six soldiers are killed when an IRA bomb explodes under their minibus after they return from a 'fun run' in Lisburn

20 August An IRA bomb kills eight soldiers and injures 28 on a bus in Ballygawley, Co. Tyrone

1989

14 September John Stevens appointed to investigate the leaking of intelligence documents to loyalist paramilitaries

22 September Ten army bandsmen killed by an IRA bomb at the Royal Marines School of Music in Deal, Kent

3 November	Secretary of State Peter Brooke suggests that the British might talk to Sinn Féin if the IRA renounces violence

1990

17 May	Stevens Report claims there has been collusion between security forces and loyalist paramilitaries but it was not 'widespread or institutionalised'
30 July	IRA kills Conservative MP Ian Gow
27 November	John Major replaces Margaret Thatcher as leader of the Conservative Party and Prime Minister

1991

7 February	The IRA fires three mortar bombs at Number 10 Downing Street during a Cabinet meeting
30 April	Preliminary talks begin between Peter Brooke and the main political parties in Northern Ireland
3 July	Peter Brooke ends the talks after little progress has been made

1992

4 February	An off-duty police constable shoots three dead inside the Sinn Féin office on the Falls Road, then later kills himself
5 February	Five Catholics are killed by loyalist gunmen in a bookmaker's shop on the Ormeau Road, Belfast
9 April	British general election. John Major's Conservatives are re-elected. Gerry Adams loses his seat to the SDLP
10 April	Two IRA bombs explode at the Baltic Exchange in the centre of London, killing three people
29 April	Political talks restart at Stormont under the new Secretary of State, Sir Patrick Mayhew
10 November	The Mayhew talks end without agreement
16 December	Sir Patrick Mayhew says Sinn Féin could be included in future talks if the IRA ends its campaign

1993

25 March	An IRA bomb in the centre of Warrington kills 3-year-old Jonathan Ball and 12-year-old Timothy Parry
24 April	An IRA bomb at the Nat West Tower in London kills one person, injures over 30 and causes an estimated £1,000 million of damage

23 October   An IRA bomb in a fish shop on the Shankill Road, Belfast, kills nine Protestants and the bomber, 57 are injured

30 October   Seven people are killed in a UFF gun attack on the Rising Sun pub in Greysteel, Co. Londonderry

28 November   *The Observer* reveals the British government have had a channel of communication with Sinn Féin and the IRA for three years

15 December   Joint Declaration on Northern Ireland issued (Downing Street Declaration)

1994

29 January   US President Bill Clinton issues a 'limited duration' visa to Gerry Adams against the stated wishes of the British government

18 June   UVF gunmen kill six men in an attack at the Heights bar in Loughinisland, Co. Down

31 August   The IRA announces 'a complete cessation of military operations'

6 September   Irish Taoiseach Albert Reynolds meets John Hume and Gerry Adams in Dublin

13 October   The CLMC announces it will 'cease all operational hostilities'

1 November   President Clinton announces the US is to increase its contribution to the International Fund for Ireland from $20m to $30m a year

1995

22 February   British and Irish governments publish *Frameworks for the Future* (Framework Documents)

10 May   First official talks between Sinn Féin, led by Martin McGuinness, and a government minister, Michael Ancram

9 July   Confrontation between the RUC and members of the Orange Order at Drumcree after attempts to re-route an Orange march ('the siege of Drumcree')

30 November   President Clinton visits Northern Ireland

1996

9 February   The IRA announces an end to its ceasefire and bombs Canary Wharf, London

30 May   Elections to multi-party talks

10 June   Talks begin at Stormont; Sinn Féin are excluded

15 June   The IRA bombs Manchester city centre

1997

5 March	The multi-party talks are adjourned
1 May	British general election. Labour leader Tony Blair replaces John Major as Prime Minister
3 June	Multi-party talks resume in Belfast
19 July	The IRA announces its ceasefire will be restored the following day
21 July	The DUP and UKUP withdraw from the talks
9 September	Sinn Féin enters all-party talks
27 December	LVF leader Billy Wright is shot dead by the INLA inside the Maze prison

1998

10 April	Belfast Agreement (Good Friday Agreement) is concluded
22 May	GFA endorsed in referendums in Northern Ireland and the Republic
3 June	British government announces an independent commission on the future of policing in Northern Ireland, headed by Chris Patten
25 June	Elections held to the new Northern Ireland Assembly
12 July	Three Catholic boys, the Quinn brothers, are killed in a sectarian arson attack on their home in Ballymoney
8 August	The LVF announces a complete ceasefire
15 August	The RIRA bombs Omagh, killing 29 people and injuring 360
22 August	The INLA announces a 'complete ceasefire'
8 September	The RIRA announces a 'complete cessation of all military activity'
16 October	John Hume and David Trimble are awarded the Nobel Peace Prize

1999

1 April	Multi-party talks at Hillsborough conclude. Two governments issue the Hillsborough Declaration
17 April	An enquiry, headed by John Stevens, is announced into the murder of the solicitor Pat Finucane in 1989
6 September	George Mitchell begins a review to try to break the impasse
29 November	The Executive is successfully created
2 December	Power is devolved to the Northern Ireland Executive

2000

11 February	Secretary of State Peter Mandelson suspends the Assembly as a result of the failure of the IRA to decommission

6 May An IRA statement asserts the organisation is ready to begin a process that will put its arms 'completely and verifiably' beyond use

30 May Power is restored to the Executive

26 June The IRA issues a statement that its arms dumps have been inspected by independent weapons inspectors

2001

7 June British general election. Tony Blair returned as Prime Minister

19 June Loyalist protest at Holy Cross Catholic Girls' School in Belfast (the protests continued until November)

1 July David Trimble resigns as First Minister

18 October The UUP's three ministers resign from the Executive

23 October The IRA announces it has carried out an act of decommissioning, later confirmed by the IICD

24 October Trimble re-nominates the UUP ministers to the Executive

4 November The PSNI replaces the RUC

6 November David Trimble elected First Minister and the SDLP's Mark Durkan becomes Deputy First Minister

2002

8 April The IRA carries out a second act of decommissioning

17 May Sinn Féin wins five seats in the Irish general election. Fianna Fáil leader Bertie Ahern is returned as Taoiseach

4 October Sinn Féin offices at Stormont are raided by the PSNI in relation to allegations of intelligence gathering by republicans

14 October Secretary of State John Reid announces the suspension of devolved government

2003

17 April The Stevens Report finds evidence of collusion between security forces and loyalist paramilitaries in the murder of Pat Finucane

1 May Tony Blair announces Assembly elections in Northern Ireland are to be postponed

21 October Tony Blair announces Assembly elections to be held in November and the IICD confirms a further act of decommissioning by the IRA

26 November Assembly elections. The DUP replaces the UUP as largest party and Sinn Féin replaces the SDLP as largest nationalist party

2004

7 January   British and Irish governments create the IMC to monitor paramilitary activity in Northern Ireland

20 December   Over £20 million is stolen from the Northern Bank in Belfast. The theft is subsequently attributed to the IRA

2005

30 January   Robert McCartney is murdered outside Magennis's Bar, Belfast. The killing is linked to members of the IRA

28 July   The IRA announces the end of its armed campaign

26 September IICD Report confirms that the IRA has 'met its commitment to put all its arms beyond use'

2006

15 May   Assembly sits for the first time since 2002

6 September   An IMC Report states the IRA is no longer involved in terrorist activity

11–13 October Multi-party talks held at St Andrews, Scotland

2007

28 January   A special Sinn Féin *ard fheis* (conference) votes to call for support of police forces on both sides of the border

7 March   Assembly elections

26 March   After a meeting Ian Paisley and Gerry Adams announce the DUP and Sinn Féin will share power in a new Executive

8 May   Northern Ireland Assembly reconvenes. The DUP's Ian Paisley and Sinn Féin's Martin McGuinness are appointed First and Deputy First Ministers

31 July   The British army's operation in Northern Ireland (Operation Banner) officially ends

2008

4 March   Ian Paisley announces he is to stand down as First Minister and DUP leader in May

5 June   New DUP leader Peter Robinson replaces Ian Paisley as First Minister

2009

7 March   The Real IRA shoots dead two British soldiers at an army base in Antrim

9 March   The Continuity IRA shoots dead a PSNI officer in Craigavon

10 March   Sinn Féin's Martin McGuinness calls dissident republicans 'traitors to the island of Ireland'

2010

12 April   David Ford, leader of the Alliance Party, becomes the first Justice Minister of Northern Ireland since 1972

Who's who

Adams, Gerard (Gerry) (b.1948): MP for West Belfast 1983–92, 1997–present, President Sinn Féin 1983–present.

Ahern, Bertie (b.1951): Taoiseach (Irish Prime Minister) 1997–2008.

Atkins, Humphrey (1922–96): Secretary of State for Northern Ireland 1979–81.

Blair, Tony (b.1953): British Prime Minister 1997–2008.

Brooke, Peter (b.1934): Secretary of State for Northern Ireland 1989–92.

Bruton, John (b.1947): Taoiseach 1994–97.

Callaghan, James (1912–2005): British Home Secretary 1967–70, Prime Minister 1976–79.

Chichester-Clark, James (1923–2002): Prime Minister of Northern Ireland 1969–1971.

Clinton, Bill (b.1946): US President 1993–2001.

Craig, William (b.1924): Northern Ireland's Minister for Home Affairs 1966–68, MP 1974–97, created Ulster Vanguard.

Devlin, Bernadette (later Bernadette McAliskey) (b.1947): Independent MP 1969–74.

Donaldson, Jeffrey (b.1963): UUP MP 1997–2004, DUP MP 2004–present.

Durkan, Mark (b.1960): Leader of the SDLP 2001–10, Deputy First Minister 2001–2002.

Faulkner, Brian (1921–77): Prime Minister of Northern Ireland 1971–72 (Northern Ireland's last Prime Minister) and Northern Ireland Chief Executive 1974.

Fitt, Gerry (1926–2005): Leader of the SDLP 1971–79, Westminster MP 1966–83.

FitzGerald, Garret (b.1926): Irish Foreign Minister 1973–77, Taoiseach 1981–82, 1982–87.

Goodall, David (b. 1931): British civil servant, Foreign Office and Cabinet Offices, 1982–87.

Haughey, Charles (1925–2006): Taoiseach 1979–81, 1982, 1987–92.

Heath, Edward (1916–2005): British Prime Minister 1970–74.

Hume, John (b.1937): Leader of the SDLP 1979–2001, Westminster MP 1983–2005, MEP 1979–2004.

Hurd, Douglas (b.1930): Secretary of State for Northern Ireland 1984–85, Home Secretary 1985–89, Foreign Secretary 1989–95.

King, Tom (b.1933): Secretary of State for Northern Ireland 1985–89.

Lynch, Jack (1917–99): Taoiseach 1966–73 and 1977–79.

McCann, Eamonn (b.1949): prominent member of the civil rights movement.

McGuinness, Martin (b.1950): Vice President of Sinn Féin 1983–present, MP 1997–present, Deputy First Minister of Northern Ireland 2007–present.

Major, John (b.1943): British Prime Minister 1990–97.

Mallon, Seamus (b.1936): SDLP MP 1986–2005, Deputy First Minister of Northern Ireland 1999–2001.

Mandelson, Peter (b.1953): Secretary of State for Northern Ireland 1999–2001.

Mason, Roy (b.1924): Secretary of State for Northern Ireland 1976–79.

Maudling, Reginald (1917–1979:) British Home Secretary 1970–72.

Mayhew, Patrick (b.1929): Secretary of State for Northern Ireland 1992–97.

Mitchell, George (b.1933): US Senator 1980–95, Chair of Northern Ireland all-party talks 1996–98.

Molyneaux, James (b.1920): Leader of the UUP 1979–95, MP 1970–97.

Mowlam, Marjorie (Mo) (1949–2005): Secretary of State for Northern Ireland 1997–1999, MP 1987–2001.

O'Neill, Terence (1914–90): Prime Minister of Northern Ireland 1963–69.

Paisley, Ian (b.1926): Leader of the DUP 1970–2008, MEP 1979–2004, First Minister of Northern Ireland 2007–2008.

Powell, Jonathan (b.1956): Tony Blair's Chief of Staff 1997–2007.

Prior, Jim (b.1927): Secretary of State for Northern Ireland 1981–84.

Rees, Merlyn (1920–2006): Secretary of State for Northern Ireland 1974–76.

Reid, John (b.1947): Secretary of State for Northern Ireland 2001–2002.

Reynolds, Albert (b.1932): Taoiseach 1992–94.

Robinson, Peter (b.1948): Deputy Leader of the DUP 1979–2008, MP 1997–2010, Leader of DUP 2008–present, First Minister of Northern Ireland 2008–present.

Sands, Bobby (1954–1981): hunger striker, MP 1981.

Spring, Dick (b.1950): Irish Tánaiste (Deputy Prime Minister) 1982–87, 1993–97, Foreign Minister 1993–97.

Stevens, John (b.1942): senior British police officer who headed several investigations (Stevens inquiries 1989–2003) into allegations of collusion between loyalist paramilitaries and security forces in Northern Ireland.

Thatcher, Margaret (b.1925): British Prime Minister 1979–90.

Trimble, David (b.1944): MP 1990–2005, Leader of the UUP 1995–2005, First Minister of Northern Ireland 1991–2001, 2001–2002.

West, Harry (1917–2004): Leader of the UUP 1974–79.

Whitelaw, William (1918–99): Secretary of State for Northern Ireland 1972–73.

Wilson, Harold (1916–1995): British Prime Minister 1964–70, 1974–76.

Glossary

AIA Anglo-Irish Agreement signed by the British and Irish governments, 15 November 1985.

APNI Alliance Party of Northern Ireland, founded April 1970.

Bloody Sunday 30 January 1972, the Parachute Regiment shot dead 13 people in Derry (another man died later from his injuries).

B Specials Ulster Special Constabulary, disbanded April 1970.

CLMC Combined Loyalist Military Command, umbrella organisation created in 1991 to co-ordinate loyalist paramilitary groups.

Continuity IRA (CIRA) republican paramilitary group, formed from a split in the IRA in 1986.

Dáil Lower house of the Irish parliament.

DCAC Derry Citizens' Action Committee, civil rights group formed in October 1968.

DUP Democratic Unionist Party, formed in September 1971, since 2003 the largest party in Northern Ireland.

Good Friday Agreement (GFA) Alternative name for the Belfast Agreement of 1998.

IGC Intergovernmental conference, created under the AIA as a forum for discussions between the two governments.

IICD Independent International Commission on Decommissioning, established August 1997 to oversee decommissioning of paramilitary weapons.

IMC Independent Monitoring Commission, created September 2003 to monitor actions of paramilitary groups in Northern Ireland.

INLA Irish National Liberation Army, republican paramilitary group, created 1975.

IRA Irish Republican Army, the main paramilitary group, which split in 1969 into two factions – the Official IRA and the Provisional IRA.

LVF Loyalist Volunteer Force, loyalist paramilitary group formed after a split within the UVF in 1996.

NIF New Ireland Forum, conference of the main nationalist parties in Ireland, created by the Irish government in 1983, reported in May 1984.

NILP Northern Ireland Labour Party, socialist party formed in 1924, which lost a significant proportion of its working class support to the DUP and SDLP in the early 1970s.

NORAID Irish Northern Aid Committee, US-based organisation established in 1969 to provide support to republicans in Ireland, closely linked to the PIRA.

Official IRA (OIRA) term used for the rump of the IRA after the split of late 1969/early 1970. The OIRA announced a ceasefire on 29 May 1972.

PD People's Democracy, civil rights group formed by students in October 1968.

Provisional IRA (PIRA) formed from a split in the IRA in December 1969. The PIRA had become the dominant republican paramilitary group by the early 1970s and after 1972 was commonly referred to simply as the IRA.

PSNI Police Service of Northern Ireland, replaced the RUC in November 2001.

PUP Progressive Unionist Party, loyalist political party associated with the UVF.

Real IRA (RIRA) republican paramilitary group formed from a split within the PIRA in November 1997.

RHC Red Hand Commandos, small loyalist paramilitary group associated with the UVF.

RUC Royal Ulster Constabulary, Northern Ireland's police force from 1922, replaced by the PSNI in 2001.

SDLP Social Democratic and Labour Party, nationalist political party, formed in August 1970. The largest nationalist party in Northern Ireland until over-taken by Sinn Féin in 2003.

Sinn Féin Political party linked to the PIRA and formed as a result of the split in the IRA in January 1970.

Taoiseach Title used for the Irish Prime Minister.

TUV Traditional Unionist Voice, political party created out of a split within the DUP in 2007.

UDA Ulster Defence Association, largest loyalist paramilitary organisation, formed in September 1971.

UDP Ulster Democratic Party, loyalist political party, formed in 1989, linked to the UDA.

UDR Regiment of the British army, formed 1 April 1970 (to replace the B Specials), merged with the Royal Irish Rangers in July 1992 to form the Royal Irish Regiment.

UFF Ulster Freedom Fighters, cover name used by the UDA.

UKUP United Kingdom Unionist Party, small unionist party formed by former UUP member Robert McCartney in 1995.

Ulster Vanguard Unionist pressure group created in 1972 (became Vanguard Unionist Progressive Party in 1973).

UUP Ulster Unionist Party, historically the largest party in Northern Ireland, overtaken by the DUP in 2003.

UUUC United Ulster Unionist Council, body created by unionists in 1974 to oppose the Sunningdale Agreement. Included the UUP, the DUP and Ulster Vanguard.

UVF Ulster Volunteer Force, loyalist paramilitary group established in 1966.

UWC Ulster Workers' Council, co-ordinating body for the 1974 Ulster Workers' Strike.

Women's Coalition Northern Ireland Women's Coalition, cross-community party formed in 1996.

The Northern Crisis

1. October 1968: Civil Rights march conflicts with police
2. January 1969: march attacked
3. August 1969: British troops deployed
4. July 1970: Falls Road curfew
5. August 1971: Internment swoop
6. January 1972: 'Bloody Sunday'
7. July 1972: 'Bloody Friday'
8. May 1974: Car bomb
9. January 1976: 10 workmen shot dead
10. August 1976: Peace People movement starts
11. 1978: 'Dirty protest' by prisoners

12. August 1979: 18 paratroopers killed in explosion
13. August 1979: Lord Mountbatten assassinated
14. 1980–81: hunger strikes
15. 1982: 17 people killed in bombing
16. November 1985: Anglo-Irish Agreement signed
17. May 1987: 8 IRA members shot
18. November 1987: 11 killed at War Memorial bombing
19. January 1992: 8 killed in IRA bombing
20. October 1993: Shankill Road bombing
21. October 1993: Grey Steel shooting by Loyalists
22. 1995–98 Orangemen march on Drumcree

Map 1 Northern Ireland showing key events from recent history

Source: After Duffy (1997), p. 129.

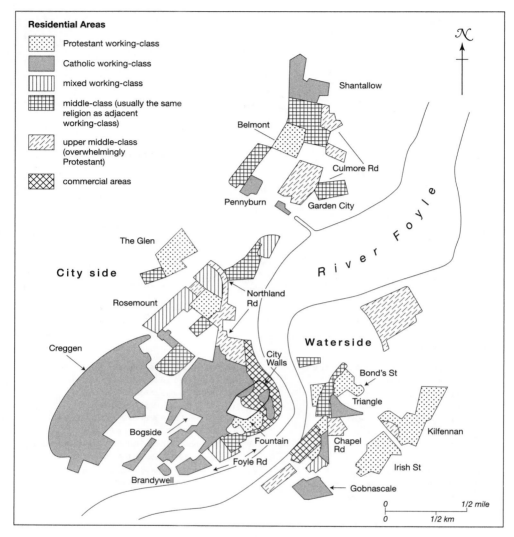

Map 2 The sectarian geography of Derry, late 1960s
Source: Ó Dochartaigh (1997), p. 330.

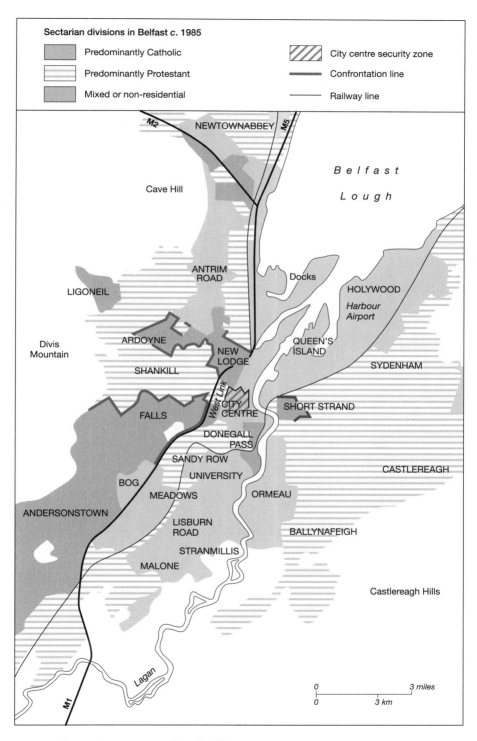

Map 3 The sectarian geography of Belfast

Source: www.wesleyjohnston.com, © Wesley Johnston.

Part 1

ANALYSIS AND ASSESSMENT

1

Perspectives on the Northern Ireland conflict

Since 1969 Northern Ireland has seen remarkable transformations. In the 1960s optimists believed that the economic forces of modernisation were eroding 'tribal' divisions. By 1969 rioting could not be controlled by the police and the British army was deployed onto the streets of the United Kingdom. The worst year for violence was 1972 when 496 people were killed as a result of the violence in Northern Ireland; 258 of these were civilians and 108 were British soldiers, 43 from Northern Irish security forces and 85 paramilitaries. Plate 9, a photograph of Martin McGuinness and Ian Paisley sitting together, sharing a joke, symbolises a dramatic change in the attitudes of the leading political figures. Martin McGuinness, who became Deputy First Minister in 2007, was a leading figure in the IRA who believed in 1972 that they were on the verge of victory. In 1972 Dr Ian Paisley was leader of the recently founded hard-line loyalist Democratic Unionist Party (**DUP**), having made his reputation as an implacable opponent of the civil rights movement. The reputation of these two politicians as hardliners was intact when the **IRA** announced its first ceasefire in 1994. Yet by 1998 McGuinness' party, **Sinn Féin**, had accepted the Good Friday Agreement (**GFA**) which established power-sharing but left Northern Ireland within the United Kingdom. Ian Paisley's DUP opposed the GFA and brought down yet another unionist leader, David Trimble of the Ulster Unionist Party, who tried to reach an accommodation with nationalists. Yet by 2007, the 'Dr No' of Ulster politics was First Minister of Northern Ireland and sharing power with the former Chief of Staff of the IRA in a double act which became known as the 'Chuckle Brothers'.

This book analyses the transformations of Northern Irish politics since 1969. Why did the conflict emerge and intensify? Why did a power-sharing settlement in 1974 fail when it was so similar to the one agreed in 1998? How do we explain the political impasse after 1974? Did the Anglo-Irish

DUP: Democratic Unionist Party, formed in September 1971, since 2003 the largest party in Northern Ireland.

IRA: Irish Republican Army, the main paramilitary group, which split in 1969 into two factions – the Official IRA and the Provisional IRA.

Sinn Féin: Political party linked to the PIRA and formed as a result of the split in the IRA in January 1970.

Good Friday Agreement (GFA): Alternative name for the Belfast Agreement of 1998.

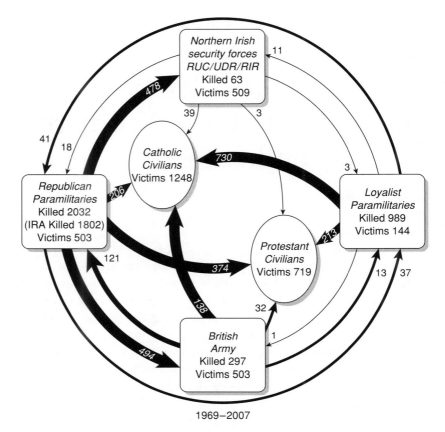

Figure 1.1 Who killed whom during 'the Troubles', 1969–2007
Source: Dixon (2008a), p. 29, fig. 1.2.

Agreement of 1985 have a positive impact on the emerging peace process? Why was the Good Friday Agreement agreed in 1998? What are the prospects for the ongoing peace process?

The interpretation of recent Northern Irish political history is highly controversial partly because of the intensity of the violence. As a result of the conflict, in the period 1966–2006 approximately 3,720 people were killed, out of a population of just 1.6 million. More than half the people in one survey reported that they knew someone who had been killed or injured.

Competing stories are told about the course of events since 1969 in order to justify contemporary bargaining positions and to gain political advantage in the ongoing negotiations of the peace process. This chapter introduces four key perspectives. 'Nationalists' are moderates who would like to see Northern Ireland leave the United Kingdom of Great Britain and Northern

Ireland and join a united Ireland, governed from Dublin, but have attempted to achieve this goal through peaceful means. 'Republicans' favour Irish unity but have advocated 'armed struggle' to achieve this goal. 'Unionists' favour the preservation of the Union between Great Britain and Northern Ireland and tend towards more moderate tactics to achieve this and a greater preparedness to share power with nationalists. 'Loyalists' are more militant defenders of the Union and some have supported violent means to oppose Irish unity; they have tended to be less willing to share power with nationalists.

It is important to remember that these perspectives are *simplifications* of a constantly changing and complex reality. There are also people in Northern Ireland who do not identify themselves as either nationalist or unionist. The term 'republican' has come to be associated with the advocacy of IRA violence to achieve the unity of Ireland, but some republicans would strongly oppose the 'capture' of the term 'republican' by the IRA. The 'republican' perspective has radically changed during the course of the conflict from favouring 'armed struggle' against the British state up until 1994 and from 1996 to 1997, to power-sharing accommodation within it. A key loyalist perspective shifted from opposition to any power-sharing with nationalists to power-sharing with republicans. Within each of these ideological perspectives are different strands. Catholics overwhelmingly voted for left-wing parties but there was a strong conservative strand within nationalism. Protestants tended to vote for right-wing parties although there has been a significant leftist strand within unionism (Edwards, 2009). Table 1.1 on p. 18 shows the electoral performance of the leading political parties throughout the recent conflict in Northern Ireland.

NATIONALISTS AND REPUBLICANS

Nationalists and republicans date Ireland's problems from the Anglo-Norman invasion of 1169 and 800 years of English oppression since then. History is a simple and repetitive story of Irish heroes fighting English oppressors: from Cromwell's massacres in Ireland through the Irish famine of the 1840s, the execution of the leaders of the Easter Rising in 1916 to atrocities perpetrated by the British during the Irish war of independence in 1919–21. The partition of Ireland in 1920 is seen as an undemocratic imposition by the British which created the artificial, gerrymandered state of Northern Ireland. The British could have overcome unionist resistance and created a united, independent state. The British-imposed, unionist-dominated Stormont parliament (1921–71) was responsible for discrimination against nationalists and the oppression meted out by the 'Orange state'.

Nationalists

Nationalists favour the unity of Ireland but advocate the use of non-violent tactics to achieve this goal. The nationalist view of Irish history and the recent conflict tends to be less antagonistic to the British state than the republicans', and this has led to a greater willingness to accommodate unionists. In Northern Ireland nationalists are overwhelmingly 'Catholics' and tend to be more religious and politically closer to the Catholic Church than their more hard-line republican rivals. The party that has dominated the political representation of nationalists in Northern Ireland is the Social Democratic and Labour Party (**SDLP**) and its most famous leader is John Hume. There was sympathy for the nationalist position in the British Labour Party and widely among the political parties in the Republic of Ireland.

SDLP: Social Democratic and Labour Party, nationalist political party, formed in August 1970. The largest nationalist party in Northern Ireland until overtaken by Sinn Féin in 2003.

The SDLP is a centre-left party with working-class support but has performed better than its republican rival among the middle classes [**Docs 7, 18, 19, pp. 129–30, 141, 141–2**]. The party also had the support of the Catholic Church, which shared its non-violent approach to politics. The founding members of the SDLP had been leading members of the civil rights movement although they struggled to contain the violence that followed. Nationalists were critical of the repressive nature of the police force in Northern Ireland and supported its reform. Initially, they welcomed the deployment of British troops but, as violence and repression escalated, became increasingly critical of the army, the Royal Ulster Constabulary (**RUC**) and, particularly, the part-time Ulster Defence Regiment (**UDR**). The SDLP also strongly condemned IRA violence during the conflict. But the party was also critical of the abuse of human rights by the security forces and refused to encourage nationalists to join the RUC.

RUC: Royal Ulster Constabulary, Northern Ireland's police force from 1922, replaced by the PSNI in 2001.

UDR: Regiment of the British army, formed 1 April 1970 (to replace the B Specials), merged with the Royal Irish Rangers in July 1992 to form the Royal Irish Regiment.

In the founding constitution of the SDLP the party committed itself to Irish unity but only with the consent of a majority of the people of Northern Ireland. Unlike republicans, SDLP politicians tended to believe that it was not the opposition of the British government that prevented Irish unity but the resistance of unionists. While British policy, particularly on security issues, could be repressive, the British political elite was not particularly determined to maintain the Union with Northern Ireland. The problem for nationalists, therefore, was primarily in trying to win the consent of at least some unionists, and the acquiescence of most others, for Irish unity.

In its constitutional policy, the SDLP sought to create institutions, such as power-sharing within Northern Ireland and North–South bodies, which, by demonstrating the material benefits of cooperation, would win the support of a majority for Irish unity. The SDLP, therefore, supported and participated in the failed power-sharing experiment with unionists in January–May 1974. After this failure some within the SDLP were drawn towards support for

British withdrawal from Northern Ireland and Irish independence. The principal division within the SDLP was between those around John Hume, who emphasised the importance of the Irish dimension, and those around Gerry Fitt, who prioritised power-sharing and accommodation with unionists within Northern Ireland. From the founding of the SDLP there was significant support for joint authority over Northern Ireland by the British and Irish governments. This would have involved the two governments jointly running Northern Ireland, with unionists in Northern Ireland being represented by the British government and nationalists being represented by the Irish government. The Anglo-Irish Agreement (**AIA**) of 1985 was strongly supported by the SDLP because it gave the Irish government a formal role in the governance of the North. In the wake of the agreement some in the party pushed strongly for its evolution into full joint authority. Secretly, the SDLP leader, John Hume, successfully attempted to get the IRA to declare a cease-fire and enter into a peace process. This resulted in the Good Friday Agreement which, to a considerable degree, reflected the kind of settlement that the SDLP had been pursuing throughout the recent conflict. Ironically, in the period since the agreement the party has been overtaken by its republican rival, Sinn Féin. The SDLP continues to support Irish unity by consent but, at times, has firmed up its 'green' nationalist rhetoric, probably in a bid to shore up electoral support.

AIA: Anglo-Irish Agreement signed by the British and Irish governments, 15 November 1985.

Nationalist solutions

Joint authority/sovereignty
The proposal: the British and Irish governments jointly run Northern Ireland. The British government represents unionist interests while the Irish government represents those of nationalists. This compromise recognises the split loyalties of Northern Ireland's population and is an equitable way of managing the conflict.

Evaluation: while this appears to be a symmetrical solution it is not. Generally, the unionists do not trust the British government to maintain the Union and would have seen joint authority as a major step towards Irish unity. The prospect of the implementation of joint authority could have provoked a widespread, violent revolt among unionists (see unionist reaction to the more modest Anglo-Irish Agreement in Chapter 5). Opinion polls suggest there was practically no unionist support for joint authority and limited support among nationalists. If it had been implemented the Irish government may have become liable for half of the British subvention to Northern Ireland and it is not clear that the Irish government could afford to take on the North in economic terms.

United Ireland by 'consent' (power-sharing and an Irish dimension)

The proposal: the SDLP supported power-sharing with an Irish dimension both in 1974 and again with the Good Friday Agreement in 1998. Power-sharing involves the participation of both unionists and nationalists in the government of Northern Ireland. The Irish dimension refers to institutions that promote cooperation between the North and South of Ireland. The SDLP argued that accommodation within Northern Ireland and cooperation between the North and South would lead to a majority consenting to Irish unity.

Evaluation: unionist support for power-sharing with an Irish dimension was limited for most of the recent conflict. Some unionists did support power-sharing in 1974 but the Irish dimension became the focus of much unionist hostility (see Chapter 3). After the collapse of power-sharing the Irish dimension was off the agenda, but unionists struggled even to support power-sharing within Northern Ireland. For much of the conflict, opinion polls suggested that power-sharing was the solution that held out the most prospect of cross-community agreement. The Anglo-Irish Agreement of 1985 did create an Irish dimension by giving the Irish government a consultative role. During the peace process it became clear that an Irish dimension would be part of any settlement; the question remained whether unionist politicians would be able to sign up to such a deal. In 1998 the Ulster Unionist Party (**UUP**) leader did support power-sharing with an Irish dimension and in 2007 the Democratic Unionist Party entered a power-sharing administration with Sinn Féin. It seems unlikely that power-sharing with an Irish dimension will lead to Irish unity (Chapters 7 and 8). Unionist opinion has not wavered during 'the Troubles' in its opposition to Irish unity, in spite of growing integration within the European Unity and the Celtic Tiger phenomenon. During the course of the conflict unionist opinion has hardened against Irish unity and there is no evidence that increased cooperation on economic and social matters will lead to political unity.

UUP: Ulster Unionist Party, historically the largest party in Northern Ireland, overtaken by the DUP in 2003.

Republicans

Nationalist is the term that is often used to describe all Catholics, including republicans. In the context of Northern Ireland, 'republican' has come to be associated with those who have supported the use of violence to achieve Irish unity and, in particular, the IRA and its political wing, Sinn Féin [**Docs 1, 5, 6, 12, 13, 21, 22, pp. 124, 127–8, 128–9, 135, 136–7, 144–5, 146**]. There are a variety of strands within republicanism including traditional catholic nationalism, Catholic defenderism, democratic socialism, Trotskyism and other varieties of Marxism. The **Provisional IRA** (PIRA) represented a more right-wing, Catholic and militaristic republicanism when it split away from the Marxist **Official IRA** (OIRA) in 1969. The PIRA adopted a more socialist stance in the late 1970s and early 1980s. Sinn Féin, the political wing of the IRA, is overwhelmingly 'Catholic' but more strongly secular than the SDLP and has had an antagonistic relationship with the Catholic Church, which condemned its violence. Gerry Adams and Martin McGuinness, the most prominent Sinn Féin leaders, are, however, both practising Catholics. Sinn Féin originally won support particularly in working-class areas but the IRA's ceasefire and the peace process allowed more sceptical, middle-class nationalists to support Sinn Féin.

Republicans were involved in the founding of the civil rights movement and subsequent development, although this was not under republican control. Republicans sought to exploit the violence surrounding the attacks on the civil rights movement and the deployment of British troops to fight for Irish unity. The Provisional IRA took advantage of growing nationalist alienation from the increasingly repressive policies of the security forces to go on the offensive. The IRA argued that Ireland was Britain's first and last colony and that the British should and would, inevitably, withdraw as they had from the rest of their Empire. As an interim measure the IRA supported the suspension of the Northern Ireland parliament and the introduction of direct rule in 1972. In negotiations with the British government in June 1972 republicans refused to compromise on their goal of a British declaration of its intent to withdraw and the creation of a federal Irish state, based on the four provinces of Ireland, including a nine-county Ulster. The IRA opposed the power-sharing settlement of 1974 and attempted to bring it down because it saw the project as shoring up British rule in Ireland. The SDLP were seen as 'collaborators' for participating in this British-inspired initiative.

Republicans tended to see unionists in two, highly contrasting ways. A civic republicanism would see unionists as an integral part of the Irish nation and emphasise the role that Irish Protestants had played in the anti-imperialist struggle against the 'English' invaders. The artificial partition of Ireland and the 'marginal privileges' that were given to unionists over their nationalist comrades in the North of Ireland had prevented the realisation of a united nation on the island of Ireland. The removal of the English presence would end these 'marginal privileges' and undermine the prop that sustained unionism in Ireland, and Irish Protestants would realise that they were Irish and not British after all. The unionists were the dupes or puppets of a manipulative British government, and freed from the puppet-master, unionists would embrace their future in a united Ireland. Alongside this inclusive strand of republicanism was a more sectarian exclusive variant. According to this perspective the Protestants of Ulster were an illegitimate colonial presence in

Provisional IRA (PIRA): formed from a split in the IRA in December 1969. The PIRA had become the dominant republican paramilitary group by the early 1970s and after 1972 was commonly referred to simply as the IRA.

Official IRA (OIRA): term used for the rump of the IRA after the split of late 1969/early 1970. The OIRA announced a ceasefire on 29 May 1972.

Northern Ireland with all the features of a supremacist, settler mentality. A 'British' withdrawal, for these republicans, would include the British settlers of Northern Ireland. This strand of republicanism was apparent in the offer of the Irish President, Eamonn De Valera, to swap unionists in Northern Ireland for Irish Catholics in Liverpool. Sinn Féin's 1987 document *A Scenario for Peace* stated: 'Anyone unwilling to accept a united Ireland and wishing to leave would be offered resettlement grants to permit them to move to Britain.'

In contrast to the more moderate nationalists, Sinn Féin/IRA saw the British state as an imperialist state determined to hold on to its colony and fully supportive of its unionist allies. The British did have selfish, strategic and economic interests, they argued, in preserving the Union.

During the 1980s the IRA dropped its support for a federal united Ireland in favour of a unitary state. Sinn Féin campaigned for a declaration of intent by the British government to withdraw from Northern Ireland. The party opposed the Anglo-Irish Agreement 1985 as a security initiative directed at the IRA but in 1986 voted to end abstentionism and take their seats in the **Dáil**. The Sinn Féin leadership engaged in public and private debates with leading members of the SDLP and began to moderate its perspective. By the early 1990s Sinn Féin was acknowledging Northern Ireland's economic dependence on Britain, the possibility of a Protestant backlash following a British withdrawal and indicating some sympathy for joint authority. Sinn Féin's support for the Good Friday Agreement in 1998 represented a radical shift in the party's attitude towards Northern Ireland, accepting that for the foreseeable future the North would remain part of the United Kingdom. Even more remarkable was Sinn Féin's endorsement of the Police Service of Northern Ireland and entry into power-sharing with the DUP in May 2007.

Dáil: Lower house of the Irish parliament.

Republican solutions

Republicans have advocated British withdrawal for much of the period since 1969, only flirting with joint authority in the early 1990s, and then endorsing the Good Friday Agreement, which was much more in line with the SDLP's policy.

'Armed struggle' to bring about British withdrawal and Irish unity

Proposal: the IRA probably believed that it was part of the wave of post-war decolonisation that would result in the 'British', perhaps including British unionists in Northern Ireland, withdrawing from the North. The 'armed struggle' was the only way to demoralise English domestic political and public opinion and expel the British. This strategy appeared to meet with early success; opinion polls suggested majorities for withdrawal, some demoralisation of the army and a political elite that was less than determined to maintain the Union (see Chapter 4). Until the mid-1970s the IRA believed the British were about to withdraw. When this did not happen it settled down for the 'long war' until the recent peace process when it accepted power-sharing.

Evaluation: British governments, some Irish governments, unionists, many nationalists and, perhaps, even a few republicans believed that a British withdrawal from Northern Ireland would result in a bloodbath, as it had following British withdrawal from India and Palestine. There was little evidence that once the British government announced its intention to withdraw unionists would suddenly realise that they were Irish after all and peacefully enter a united Ireland. The strength of unionist opposition to Irish unity was apparent in opinion polls throughout the Troubles, in unionist voting behaviour, in the emergence of loyalist paramilitary groups from 1971 and their vicious sectarian murder campaign, in the massive public demonstration against the introduction of direct rule in 1972, in the successful Ulster Workers' Council Strike of 1974, in the widespread opposition to the Anglo-Irish Agreement 1985, in support for Orange parades and, during the peace process, in growing electoral support for the most hard-line parties. The strength of unionist opposition to Irish unity suggested that in the event of British withdrawal unionists were likely to fight to retain as much territory as possible for an independent Ulster. Unionists largely populated the security forces in Northern Ireland and so had access to weapons and had been trained in their use. It was feared that the civil war that was likely to follow British withdrawal could well destabilise the Republic of Ireland and lead to an IRA victory there too. Republican expectations of a British withdrawal reached such a fever pitch in the mid-1970s that even Ruairi O Braidaigh, the President of Sinn Féin, warned the British not to withdraw and leave behind a 'Congo situation' (civil war). During the 1980s Sinn Féin still argued that the British should withdraw from Northern Ireland but it wanted the British army to disarm the RUC and UDR before it left, an unlikely prospect given the chaos that would follow any announcement of British withdrawal.

The key weakness of republican ideology was its understanding of the British state and unionism. The British political elite were generally ambivalent about the union between Great Britain and Northern Ireland. There was no overriding selfish, strategic or economic reason for Britain to retain the region within the Union. Some argued that there were strategic reasons for retaining the Union, but these were not overriding and could probably have been secured in negotiations with the Irish state. The reason the British could not withdraw was that unionist resistance made this policy disastrous. Far from unionists being the dupes of British imperialism, they had demonstrated their independence from the London government and opposition to its policies. Withdrawal would probably have resulted in civil war, ethnic cleansing and could lead as much to an independent Ulster as Irish unity. A civil war would have disastrous destabilising consequences for both the rest of Britain and the Republic of Ireland (the IRA saw the southern state as illegitimate). Republican violence, if anything, deepened sectarianism and reduced the prospects of unionists consenting to a united Ireland and by the mid to late 1980s seemed to be counterproductive to the electoral prospects of Sinn Féin. The decision of the Sinn Féin leadership to enter a peace process was partly the product of the lack of realism in its political strategy.

UNIONISTS AND LOYALISTS

Unionists favour the continuation of the Union between Great Britain and Northern Ireland and tend to regard themselves as 'British' or 'Ulsterfolk'. 'Loyalists' are unionists who use or advocate more militant methods to defend the Union, at times including violence. Loyalists tend to be drawn disproportionately from the working class. Unionists, who are more antagonistic towards nationalists, tend to exaggerate the degree of unionist historical separateness and conflict. Unionists may argue that there are two distinct peoples in Ireland and that unionists have separate economic, ethnic, geographic and religious interests, and this backs their case for partition. Protestants are concentrated in the north-east of Ireland with their origins going back to the settlements of the seventeenth century; some emphasise their 'Scots-Irish' ancestry in particular. Geographically, they argue Northern Ireland has historical ties to Scotland, which lies only about 20 miles away. The north-east of Ireland was part of the British industrial revolution in the way that the more agrarian south was not. Northern Ireland's separateness from the rest of Ireland, unionists may argue, gives it a right to self-determination. Partition did not result in an artificial state but was the logical culmination of a history of cultural, economic, social and political separateness. Subsequently, the Northern Ireland parliament was under threat from republicans both externally and from within. Some argue that this justifies anti-nationalist discrimination during the Stormont era. Others deny discrimination took place, while more moderate unionists have accepted that Northern Ireland was 'a cold house for Catholics'.

The dominant interpretation among unionists of the civil rights movement was, mistakenly, that it was largely republican inspired and controlled.

Unionist politicians called on the British government to implement more repressive security policies against the IRA.

Unionists

'Moderate' unionist opinion is represented by the Ulster Unionist Party, which was the dominant unionist party from partition until 2003 [**Docs 9, 16, 28, pp. 131–2, 139, 151–2**]. The UUP wanted to retain the Stormont parliament and opposed its abolition in March 1972. The party was severely divided over the power-sharing experiment of 1974. The party leader, Brian Faulkner, entered the power-sharing executive but was unable to carry his party with him. A minority of the party supported power-sharing but the majority opposed this constitutional experiment on the grounds that it was designed as a step towards a united Ireland. These unionists preferred the restoration of majority rule and some even flirted with the idea of Ulster independence, most likely in the 'doomsday scenario' of a British withdrawal.

After the collapse of power-sharing with an Irish dimension, unionist opinion shifted away from power-sharing altogether. The UUP was divided in its response to the Anglo-Irish Agreement 1985: some favoured a return to devolved government, with limited safeguards for nationalists, while others argued in favour of integration. In the late 1970s and 1980s there was support in the UUP for integration: making direct rule permanent and running the North as an integral part of the UK like Wales or Scotland (which did not have a devolved assembly).

The integrationist position implied a less hostile attitude towards the British political elite. After all, why give increased power to Westminster if you believe the UK parliament will betray the Union? UUP leaders tended to be closer to and more trusting of the British Conservative Party (with which the UUP has been formally linked) than loyalist politicians. The UUP was, generally, also able to draw a clearer distinction between moderate, non-violent nationalists, with whom it was prepared to negotiate, and violent republicans, with whom it was not. The party was more likely to accept that northern nationalist opposition to the Union was not simply a product of the manipulation of the Irish government in the South but arose out of legitimate grievances.

During the early 1990s the UUP took some steps towards accommodating nationalist demands in a devolved 'responsibility-sharing' assembly. During the peace process the UUP gave little sign that it was prepared to compromise on its position until the final week of negotiations when it endorsed a power-sharing deal with an Irish dimension. The UUP was divided over whether to support the Good Friday Agreement and a section of unionist voters and key unionist political activists defected to the more hard line Democratic Unionist Party, which subsequently became the dominant party of unionism.

During the recent conflict the UUP advocated hard-line security policies – including support for internment and 'shoot to kill' – with little regard to human rights. This position tended to be more hard line than those implemented by successive British governments.

Loyalists

The hard-line Democratic Unionist Party was founded in 1971 by the Reverend Ian Paisley [**Docs 14, 27, 31, pp. 137, 150–1, 153**]. Initially, the party favoured the integration of Northern Ireland into the UK but then shifted to support for majority rule with some safeguards for the nationalist minority. The DUP strongly opposed the power-sharing experiment and played an active role in trying to bring it down. In the wake of its collapse the party successfully manoeuvred to overcome key rivals and establish itself as the dominant, hard-line unionist party. The party took an uncompromising position on unionist majority rule in a devolved assembly until 2007, when it performed a remarkable reversal in its policy stance and entered into a power-sharing government with Sinn Féin (although there were some subtle hints that this might occur). The DUP was more hostile than the UUP to the Irish government's involvement in the affairs of the North, suggesting that nationalist opposition to the Union was largely or partly a product of the South's territorial claim on the North.

The DUP advocated more hard-line security positions than the UUP. The party also had some dealings with loyalist paramilitary organisations (during the Ulster Workers' Strike of 1974, the Loyalist Strike of 1977 and in the wake of the Anglo-Irish Agreement 1985). The DUP was probably more likely than the UUP to consider Ulster independence. In this respect, the DUP tended towards an 'Ulster' identity and was less trusting of perfidious English/British governments at Westminster than the UUP. The DUP was very hostile to the emerging peace process and the Good Friday Agreement. As a result of this stance the party defeated the UUP and emerged as the dominant party of unionism. Its decision to enter into power with Sinn Féin in 2007 led to a new hard-line loyalist party, the Traditional Unionist Voice (**TUV**), which opposed power-sharing.

In the 1990s the parties of the loyalist paramilitary organisations, the Progressive Unionist Party (**PUP**) and Ulster Democratic Party (**UDP**), the political wings of the Ulster Volunteer Force (**UVF**) and the Ulster Defence Association (**UDA**) respectively, did gain some political representation [**Docs 2,**

TUV: Traditional Unionist Voice, political party created out of a split within the DUP in 2007.

PUP: Progressive Unionist Party, loyalist political party associated with the UVF.

UDP: Ulster Democratic Party, loyalist political party, formed in 1989, linked to the UDA.

UVF: Ulster Volunteer Force, loyalist paramilitary group established in 1966.

UDA: Ulster Defence Association, largest loyalist paramilitary organisation, formed in September 1971.

17, 27, pp. 125, 140, 150–1]. These parties critiqued the DUP for its willingness to inspire loyalist paramilitaries in their attacks but then to subsequently distance themselves from the perpetrators. They also attacked the DUP for its conservative policies and abandonment of the loyalist working class.

Unionist and loyalist solutions

Devolved majority rule

Proposal: unionists and loyalists opposed the suspension of the Stormont Assembly in March 1972 as the best way of bringing power to Northern Ireland and safeguarding the Union.

Evaluation: while unionists and loyalists did propose some guarantees to protect nationalists under a restored majority rule system these were inadequate. A return to Stormont could have meant a return to unionist domination and exclusion for nationalists. There was no willingness to consider the cultural rights of nationalists and the unionist parties also pursued approaches to security policy that would have been highly repressive. According to opinion polls, this option had considerable support among unionists but little among nationalists and little prospect of winning their consent. For this reason, the British and Irish governments and international opinion opposed this solution.

Independence

Proposal: that only in an independent state of Ulster could the interests of Protestants be protected. The English/British government was untrustworthy and only by delivering power to the local majority in Northern Ireland could effective measures be taken to root out and destroy the IRA.

Evaluation: this was more of a 'doomsday scenario' for unionists or else a threat to warn British and Irish governments against imposing a united Ireland. Independence has very little support among nationalists and unionists and would probably only gain support among unionists in the event of British withdrawal (Chapter 4). There would be very little international support for such a state.

Integration of Northern Ireland into the UK

Proposal: that a return to devolution in the period from the late 1970s to the late 1990s marked Northern Ireland out as a distinct part of the UK. Direct rule should be extended into integration where Northern Ireland would be ruled like Wales or Scotland from Westminster and the North receive representation there in proportion to its population. It was argued that the integration of Northern Ireland into the UK would end the constitutional question and therefore any incentive the IRA had to use violence. Integrationists also claimed that the UK was a multinational state and that as an integral part of that state nationalists would be fairly treated.

Evaluation: Integration would represent a British-imposed settlement that would give unionism a victory over nationalism. The British concern was that integration would benefit the IRA by undermining moderate nationalism in the North and South of Ireland. There is significant public support for integration among unionists but very limited support among nationalists. Moderate nationalists would have gained nothing from their non-violent approach and this might encourage nationalists to advocate violence as the only route left to influence their political future. Furthermore, integration would have alienated the Irish government and southern nationalism. The British government was hoping to extend cooperation with the Irish government to deal with the cross-border threat from the IRA and to manage nationalist alienation in the North. International, particularly US, opinion would also have opposed integration. Unionists might also object that integration would place too much power in the hands of untrustworthy English politicians.

Power-sharing and an Irish dimension
Proposal: that this would satisfy nationalist and unionist opinion and result in a reasonable, compromise settlement.

Evaluation: the leader of the UUP, Brian Faulkner, tried and failed to make this deal work in the power-sharing experiment of 1974 – he could not bring sufficient unionists behind such an accommodation (see Chapter 3) because they feared it would lead to a united Ireland. There was a faction within the UUP that was prepared to contemplate the sharing of power or 'responsibility-sharing' but not the Irish dimension. For hard-line unionists, the term 'power-sharing' became associated with the failed Sunningdale initiative and what they believed was an attempt to manipulate them into a united Ireland. Nevertheless, a power-sharing settlement with or without an Irish dimension appeared to be, according to opinion polls, the only likely settlement that had the potential to win over a majority of unionist and nationalist public opinion. The problem was how the political parties, with hardening of their negotiating positions during the course of the Troubles, could possibly deliver such a compromise. The peace process saw remarkable shifts by both unionist and nationalist political parties to accept the GFA and then for the DUP to enter power with Sinn Féin in 2007.

THE CENTRE

The most prominent centre parties were the now defunct Northern Ireland Labour Party and the Alliance Party, which won 5.2 per cent of the vote at the 2007 Assembly election. Both parties combined 'Protestants' and 'Catholics' within their ranks and opposed 'tribal' politics. The Northern Ireland Labour Party supported civil rights, favoured the Union and advocated power-sharing. The Alliance Party has championed power-sharing throughout the recent conflict [**Doc. 26, pp. 149–50**].

CONCLUSIONS

Different stories can be told about the history of Northern Ireland since 1969 and they have different implications for how that conflict should be managed. Republicans have highlighted the repressive nature of the British state and its security forces to justify violence and later radical reforms of policing in Northern Ireland. Unionists have emphasised the violence of republican paramilitaries in order to campaign for more repressive security policies and, later, to put pressure on them to abandon their weapons. The British government has told a story that blames 'the two tribes' and absolves itself of responsibility. It is not necessary to agree with these nationalist, republican, unionist and loyalist perspectives on the conflict to understand their logic and to appreciate the sincerity – sometimes a murderous sincerity – with which they were often held.

This does not mean to say that there are no grounds for discriminating between these perspectives. Some stories, based on logical argument and available evidence, are better and more convincing than others. But the debate over the Troubles continues and evolves as new evidence comes to light and new ways of reinterpreting the past are developed. In recent years much evidence has emerged about the 'dirty war' in Northern Ireland between the security forces and the paramilitaries, which involved dirty tricks and collusion. Readers must make their own minds up about which story they find most convincing but should be flexible enough to revise this perspective in the light of new evidence and arguments. This book provides an overview and entry point into many of the recent debates over the history of Northern Ireland since 1969, a story that continues to evolve.

Table 1.1 Election results, 1973–2010 (principal parties, percentage shares)

Election		Unionist parties			Alliance	Nationalist parties	
		Democratic Unionist	Vanguard Unionist 1973–77/ Traditional Unionist Voice 2009–10	Ulster Unionist		Social Democratic & Labour Party	Provisional Sinn Féin
May 1973	L	4.3	2.1	41.4	13.7	13.4	–
Jun 1973	A	10.8	10.5	29.3	9.2	22.1	–
Feb 1974	W	8.2	10.6	32.3	3.2	22.4	–
Oct 1974	W	8.5	13.1	36.5	6.4	22.0	–
May 1975	C	14.7	12.7	25.8	9.8	23.7	–
May 1977	L	12.7	1.5	29.6	14.4	20.6	–
May 1979	W	10.2	–	36.6	11.9	18.2	–
Jun 1979	E	29.8	–	21.9	6.8	24.6	–
May 1981	L	26.6	–	26.5	8.9	17.5	–
Oct 1982	A	23.0	–	29.7	9.3	18.8	10.1
Jun 1983	W	20.0	–	34.0	8.0	17.9	13.4
Jun 1984	E	33.6	–	21.5	5.0	22.1	13.3
May 1985	L	24.3	–	29.5	7.1	17.8	11.8
Jun 1987	W	11.7	–	37.8	10.0	21.1	11.4
May 1989	L	17.7	–	31.3	6.9	21.0	11.2
Jun 1989	E	29.9	–	22.2	5.2	25.5	9.1
Apr 1992	W	13.1	–	34.5	8.7	23.5	10.0
Jun 1993	L	17.3	–	29.3	7.6	22.0	12.4
Jun 1994	E	29.2	–	23.8	4.1	28.9	9.9
May 1996	F	18.8	–	24.2	6.5	21.4	15.5
May 1997	W	13.6	–	32.7	8.0	24.1	16.1
May 1997	L	15.9	–	27.8	6.6	20.7	16.9
Jun 1998	A	18.1	–	21.3	6.5	22.0	17.6
Jun 1999	E	28.4	–	17.6	2.1	28.1	17.3
May 2001	W	22.5	–	26.8	4.8	21	21.7
May 2001	L	21.4	–	22.9	5.2	19.4	20.7
Nov 2003	A	25.6	–	22.7	3.7	17	23.5
Jun 2004	E	31.9	–	16.5	–	15.9	26.3
May 2005	W	33.7	–	17.7	3.9	17.5	24.3
May 2005	L	29.6	–	18	5	17.4	23.2
Mar 2007	A	30.1	–	14.9	5.2	15.2	26.2
June 2009	E	18.1	13.7	17	–	16.1	25.8
May 2010	W	25	3.9	15.2	6.3	16.5	25.5

Notes:

(i)   Type of election is indicated by letter:
       A = Assembly, W = Westminster Parliament, C = Convention, E = European Parliament, F = Forum, L = Local Council Elections.
(ii)   The symbol (–) indicates the party did not exist or did not contest the election.
(iii) Figures do not add up to 100 per cent, as assorted minor parties and independents also contested elections.

Source: As published in Northern Ireland, 2nd edition, (Dixon, P.) Palgrave Macmillan, 2008b, p. 11.

2

The outbreak of the Troubles

Northern Ireland's descent from a comparatively stable, if politically flawed, society, to one wracked by violent and prolonged inter-communal conflict was swift and, for most, unexpected. What had started out as an apparent movement for 'British rights for British citizens' soon spiralled out of the control of both the original protestors and the Stormont government. The civil rights movement exacerbated the deep divisions between nationalists and unionists. As the problems in Northern Ireland increased, Britain found itself forced to re-engage with an issue that it had tried to avoid for many years. The British government hoped to contain the crisis by putting pressure on the Stormont government to deliver reforms that would meet the demands of the civil rights movement. Hard-line loyalists saw these reforms as appeasement of a republican-dominated civil rights movement and resented London's interference in the internal affairs of Northern Ireland. Republicans, however, saw the growing crisis as an opportunity to reopen the question of partition and campaign for a united Ireland. Violence escalated rapidly – in 1969 there were 18 deaths due to the conflict, by 1972 there were 496 deaths.

Westminster's early attempts to seek to bolster the devolved government in Northern Ireland proved unworkable. The hope held in British policy-making circles, that the problems of Northern Ireland could be resolved if the government of Northern Ireland offered reforms that addressed the demands of the civil rights protesters, was to prove unrealistic. Sections of both the unionist and nationalist communities in Northern Ireland were unhappy with the extent and speed of the proposed reform, but for very different reasons. Hardliners within the unionist community saw the civil rights movement as a front to undermine the constitutional position of Northern Ireland within the Union and viewed the pressure the British government placed on Northern Ireland to reform as an unwarranted intrusion into their affairs. Some nationalists felt that the reforms offered by the unionist government did not go far enough in securing key demands and there were republicans who saw in the growing crisis their opportunity to bring about a united Ireland. Along these fault lines 'the Troubles' emerged.

BACKGROUND TO THE TROUBLES

The period immediately before the outbreak of the Troubles in 1969 appeared to be one of improved relations between the governments of the two parts of Ireland. The Irish **Taoiseach**, Sean Lemass, met Northern Ireland's Prime Minister, Terence O'Neill, at Stormont, the Northern Ireland parliament, in January 1965. This was the first meeting between an Irish and Northern Irish Prime Minister since 1925. The visit by Lemass came as a surprise to many, including members of O'Neill's own Cabinet. O'Neill stressed that it was designed to improve relations between the two parts of Ireland, but not undermine the Union with Britain. In London the Labour government, led by Harold Wilson, was pleased by the visible improvement in North–South relations, although Wilson also appeared to have sympathies for Irish unity. This and other apparent moderating gestures from O'Neill were met by serious loyalist resistance, most significantly from the Reverend Ian Paisley, in a stance that was to become a familiar one over the next three decades. Loyalists denounced the visit and demonstrated outside Stormont (throwing snowballs at O'Neill's car) claiming the visit undermined the Union.

The first major sign that the situation in Northern Ireland was deteriorating occurred on 5 October 1968 when some 400–600 civil rights marchers attempted to march in Derry city centre. Although the Northern Ireland Civil Rights Association (**NICRA**) had been formed in January 1967 by a group of republicans and left-wing activists, the first civil rights march had not been held until June 1968. The first march, from Coalisland to Dungannon, was in protest at unfair allocation of housing by unionist councils. It was, however, the Derry march that transformed the situation in Northern Ireland. The march, which had been banned, was attacked by the RUC. The sight of the police beating demonstrators with batons, which the Cameron Commission later stated was without 'justification or excuse', was captured by television crews and beamed around the world (Bew, 2007: 489). The outrage that the attack generated within the nationalist community in Northern Ireland led to a huge swell in support for the civil rights movement and increased pressure on the Northern Ireland government. O'Neill told his cabinet 'we have now become the focus of world opinion' (Dixon, 2008a: 81). There was an awareness among some of the unionist leadership that there were problems in the structure of Northern Ireland's political and social system. Within the privacy of the Cabinet, O'Neill asked his fellow unionist

Taoiseach: Title used for the Irish Prime Minister.

ministers, 'can any of us truthfully say in the confines of this room, that the minority has no grievance calling for remedy?' (Dixon, 2008a: 90). O'Neill was also very concerned that the Wilson government would use Northern Ireland's economic dependence to push for reform. O'Neill told the Cabinet that he 'must remind his colleagues of Northern Ireland's utter financial dependence: in these circumstances a directive from Downing Street could have grave repercussions' (Bew, 2007: 490). The British Prime Minister did threaten to look more critically at the support offered to Northern Ireland if reform was not undertaken or if the moderate O'Neill was ousted by more hard-line elements.

HOW MUCH DISCRIMINATION WAS THERE IN NORTHERN IRELAND?

The extent of discrimination in Northern Ireland is controversial because claims about the past can be used as a political weapon in negotiations over the future. Unionists tended to play down the extent of discrimination and, therefore, the responsibility of the UUP, which had ruled Northern Ireland continuously since partition. Nationalists tended to play up the issue of discrimination as it was a useful tool in the propaganda war during the civil rights struggle and some republicans used it as a justification for their violence. As a result 'judgements on the unionist record in the period 1921–68 vary from the deepest black to purest white' (Whyte, 1983).

While it is generally agreed that there was discrimination against nationalists, its extent and whether they alone suffered discrimination is debated. The right to vote is the one that has attracted most criticism. Given the electoral rules, around a quarter of adults had no vote in Northern Ireland as the franchise was only granted to ratepayers and their spouses. It is not the case that as a result of these rules only nationalists were denied the vote, poor Protestants were also disenfranchised. But nationalists were disproportionately disadvantaged as they were statistically over-represented among the poorest sections of society. A larger problem, though, was that of electoral gerrymandering (the drawing of electoral boundaries in such a way as to give unfair advantage to one party) and its role in unfairly ensuring unionists controlled councils in certain districts despite there being a nationalist majority in the area. The problems of gerrymandering also had a geographical dimension as it was worse in the west of Northern Ireland, which was predominantly inhabited by nationalists. The most blatant example of this was the Londonderry Corporation on which, in 1967, the UUP had 60 per cent of the seats even though it received just 32.1 per cent of the vote.

Linked to the issue of gerrymandering was that of housing. The lack of access to public housing became an important issue during the civil rights period. Given the reluctance of unionists in certain councils to allow any changes to take place that might undermine their control, in certain councils west of the River Bann nationalists were discriminated against in the allocation of housing. In Dungannon, for example, due to unionist reluctance to house nationalists, by 1963 there were over 300 families on the waiting list and no Catholic family had been allocated a permanent house for 34 years (Patterson, 2002: 195), a situation that led to the first civil rights march. Problems also existed in the allocation of public sector jobs where nationalists were notably under-represented, particularly at the higher grades. There is also evidence, though, that nationalist-controlled councils discriminated against Protestants in their areas, but nationalists controlled far fewer councils (and as a result of gerrymandering, less than their 'fair share'). As a result, although some leaders of the civil rights movement, particularly those on the left such as Bernadette Devlin and Eamonn McCann, criticised nationalist as well as unionist discrimination, this was not an issue to which the civil rights movement gave much coverage.

There is very strong evidence of discrimination against nationalists particularly in electoral practices, employment and housing. Debate is focused on the extent and impact of discrimination rather than its existence. There are possible reasons for this beyond simple discrimination (issues that have been suggested include the lower levels of educational achievement among nationalists, a lack of willingness of nationalists to work in certain sectors, notably the police force, and the allocation by Protestants of jobs to their friends, who were also Protestants). Both real and perceived discrimination contributes towards an explanation of why the civil rights movement had such a rapid impact.

THE GROWTH OF THE CIVIL RIGHTS MOVEMENT

The attacks in Derry in October 1968 led to a massive increase in support for the civil rights movement among nationalists and worsened tensions between the two communities. There was unease within sections of the unionist community regarding both the tactics and purpose of the movement. Some prominent unionists felt that the movement was simply a front for traditional republicanism and that the campaign was aimed not, as it sometimes claimed, to secure 'British rights for British citizens' but to destabilise Northern Ireland and break the Union with Britain. This was to some extent understandable as the 'civil rights movement' was something of an umbrella term covering a diverse range of groups from moderate unionists seeking 'British rights for British citizens' to Irish republicans who saw civil rights as a tactic for achieving a united Ireland. The movement was not a united or coherent entity. By highlighting the activities of different groups plenty of 'evidence' could be provided to substantiate incompatible interpretations of the causes and goals of the movement.

Prime Minister Terence O'Neill was disconnected from the Protestant working class and many viewed his reforming agenda as undermining the Union and encouraging the disloyal nationalist community in its attempts to destroy Northern Ireland. Ian Paisley was more in touch with the Protestant working class and emerged as one of the most vocal and influential of O'Neill's critics. Paisley established the Free Presbyterian Church in 1951 and burst onto the political scene in 1963 when he orchestrated protests against the lowering of the Union flag to mark the death of the Pope. In 1964 he led protests against the flying of the Irish tricolour on the Falls Road, which led to rioting. From the mid-1960s he was at the helm of anti-civil rights protests and led the campaign to oust O'Neill for 'selling out the Union'.

In November 1968 O'Neill, under pressure from the British Prime Minister, announced a five-point plan to address some of the most pressing of the civil rights movement's demands. The reforms would create a new system to allocate housing by local authorities, an ombudsman to investigate complaints and a new Development Commission to replace the Londonderry Corporation. A pledge was given to abolish the Special Powers Act as soon as it was safe to do so and the company vote (which gave owners of business premises an extra vote) was to be abolished. However, the contentious system whereby only ratepayers were entitled to vote was not included in the reforms and so one of the key demands of the civil rights movement, one man one vote, was not met. The reluctance of unionism to meet this demand was in part a result of the historical insecurity that unionism felt towards a 'disloyal' nationalist minority. While such apparently blatant discrimination seemed to the outside world a clearly unacceptable and sectarian practice, to many unionists it was a historical necessity to make sure that they could guarantee stability. Indeed O'Neill had only managed to get agreement from his party to introduce the five reforms by promising not to introduce further reform without their consent (Bew, 2007: 491).

Although the reforms did mark a significant victory for the civil rights movement they did not serve to reduce the growing crisis in Northern Ireland, as both O'Neill and the British government had hoped they might. Increasingly the marches of the movement were being met by counter-demonstrations of disillusioned unionists, sometimes led by Ian Paisley. This resulted in violence that the police often struggled to contain. Opposition to the reform process was also growing within O'Neill's own cabinet. Against this backdrop on 9 December 1968 O'Neill went on television to appeal for calm. O'Neill told the people of Northern Ireland, 'Ulster stands at a cross-roads . . . our conduct over the days and weeks will decide our future.' He publicly stressed the precarious position of Northern Ireland given its financial dependence on Britain: 'Ulster's income is £200 million a year but we can spend £300 million, only because Britain pays the balance.' 'What kind of Ulster do you want? A happy and respected province in good standing with the rest of the United Kingdom? Or a place continually torn apart by riots and demonstrations and regarded by the rest of Britain as a political outcast?' (Bew and Gillespie, 1999: 9). The speech was well received and in the wave of support that followed O'Neill felt able to sack William Craig, one of his most critical cabinet ministers. A campaign by the *Belfast Telegraph* to get readers to send in the 'I back O'Neill' coupon it printed led to 150,000 letters of support to Stormont. Yet this support and apparent lessening of inter-communal tensions did not last.

PD: People's Democracy, civil rights group formed by students in October 1968.

While the moderates in the civil rights movement agreed to take action to deflate the situation and announced a suspension on marching, a more radical student-led civil rights group, People's Democracy (**PD**), announced it would march from Belfast to Derry. Although the march itself was relatively small its repercussions were not. The march was seen as provocative by some Protestants because they perceived it as a 'nationalist' and possibly subversive march through Protestant areas. The turning point was the attack on the marchers at Burntollet Bridge, outside Derry, on 4 January 1969, by loyalists with sticks. A large proportion of the loyalists were actually off-duty members of the **B Specials**, a part-time police force whose membership was overwhelmingly Protestant and had a reputation for sectarianism. The failure to provide adequate policing increased nationalist disillusionment with the Stormont regime and further undermined O'Neill. The policing of the civil rights marches increasingly shifted the political agenda from a narrow focus on the original civil rights demands towards the question of policing itself and the constitutional position of Northern Ireland. O'Neill attempted to reassert his authority by calling the 'Crossroads' election in February 1969 but the result highlighted the increasing opposition among unionists to his reforms and leadership. Ian Paisley stood against O'Neill in the Bannside constituency and polled 6,331 votes against O'Neill's 7,745. O'Neill eventually resigned in April and was succeeded by his Unionist Party colleague James Chichester-Clark. One of O'Neill's final acts before leaving office was to grant the key civil rights demand of 'one man one vote'.

B Specials: Ulster Special Constabulary, disbanded April 1970.

As 1969 progressed tensions between marchers, the RUC and counter-demonstrators became increasingly confrontational. The Bogside area of Derry became effectively a no-go area for the RUC (so called 'Free Derry') after barricades were erected. The Derry Citizens Action Committee (**DCAC**) and other moderates in the civil rights movement were losing control of the marches. As one of its leaders, Eamonn McCann, later wrote, it became difficult 'to organize a demonstration which did not end in riot' (1974: 57). The situation finally spiralled out of control into the 'quasi-civil war' of August 1969 (Bew *et al.*, 1995: 156). The Orange Order parades in Derry on 12 August were accompanied by fierce rioting which resulted in the Bogside being under siege. Rioting spread to Belfast and homes in Catholic areas were attacked and burned out, leading a number of nationalists to seek refuge over the border in the Irish Republic.

DCAC: Derry Citizens' Action Committee, civil rights group formed in October 1968.

On 13 August the Irish Taoiseach, Jack Lynch, called for a UN peace-keeping force to be sent to Northern Ireland and stated 'that the Irish Government can no longer stand by and see innocent people injured and perhaps worse'. Irish troops were sent to the border and set up field hospitals to aid those fleeing the violence. Lynch also questioned the existence of Northern Ireland itself, stating, 'the reunification of the national territory can provide the only permanent solution for the problem' (*Irish Times*, 14 August 1969). This may have encouraged rioters to persist in the hope of bringing about a united Ireland (Ó Dochartaigh, 1997). There were also fears among senior unionist ministers that the Irish might invade the North. Given the deteriorating situation and the evident inability of the RUC and B Specials to control the situation, the British government was forced to take a step it had sought to avoid and on 14 August British troops were deployed onto the streets of Northern Ireland.

EXPLAINING THE CIVIL RIGHTS MOVEMENT

Several explanations have been offered for the emergence of the civil rights movement. The most influential early explanation was the *new Catholic middle class* thesis which was supported by the Cameron Commission, set up to investigate the causes of the October 1969 violence. This explanation centred on an increasing Catholic middle class that was believed to have been the creation of the British post-war welfare state and the increased educational opportunity offered by the 1947 Education Act. According to the argument this newly educated and aspirant Catholic elite were no longer willing to accept their second class status in Northern Ireland and were the driving force behind the civil rights movement. This thesis has been undermined in recent years as critics pointed out that while there had been an expansion in the Catholic middle class this predated the emergence of the civil rights movement by at least a decade, and indeed there was 'virtually no change in the social structure of the male Catholic population' between 1961 and 1971 (Bew *et al.*, 1995: 151). Also, the expansion in the number of Catholics attending university was far more a feature of the 1970s than earlier. Moreover, once the movement took to the streets it was largely populated by nationalist youths whom the middle classes found difficult to control.

Some unionists denied discrimination and saw the civil rights movement as a façade for a *republican/communist conspiracy*. While there was republican and communist involvement in the civil rights movement they were not in effective control of the movement and nor did they anticipate or intend the resurgence of communal conflict that followed. For some nationalists the civil rights movement actually represented a shift away from anti-partitionism and towards participation in the state (Dixon, 2008a: 84–5).

A third explanation for the emergence of the civil rights movement is 'bottom up' and centres on the *growth of the state*. The Northern Ireland government was responsible for the provision of growing state resources in public housing, employment and investment. As a result, nationalists and unionists were involved in more intense competition for these resources and the civil rights movement was an expression of nationalist unhappiness with how these resources were allocated by Northern Ireland's (unionist) government. The civil rights movement emerged, therefore, on a wave of anger over the unfair allocation of state-controlled resources. The street protests that became the most visible element of the civil rights movement were the result of the largely spontaneous mobilisation of the nationalist community in protest at what they saw as the failure of the state to grant them their fair share of the resources and their frustration at the failure of constitutional action to address their grievances. There were a number of triggers that help to explain the timing of the civil rights movement. The first trigger was the prospect of the election of a Labour government. The Labour leader, Harold Wilson, was believed to be sympathetic to the plight of nationalists in Northern Ireland and to be in favour of Irish unity. This raised expectations in the nationalist community, and fears among unionists, that Labour would intervene to address some of the discriminatory practices. The second trigger was the growing alienation of nationalists from their traditional elected representatives, the Nationalist Party. This was a 'party' only in the loosest sense of the word and after decades of constitutional protest had achieved little. The final trigger was the intensely hostile reaction of elements of unionism to the civil rights movement, which further fuelled nationalists' sense of injustice and limited O'Neill's ability adequately to meet their grievances.

THE PATH TO DIRECT RULE

The attack on the civil rights march in October 1968 had forced the British Labour government to engage more directly with the problem. While Harold Wilson threatened to suspend the Northern Ireland parliament and introduce direct rule from Westminster he was very reluctant to do this and became sucked into what was seen as an 'Irish bog'. Wilson's government was aware that if it suspended the Northern Ireland government this was likely to further antagonise unionist opinion and it could find itself facing the army's nightmare scenario: a war on two fronts. As the Minister of Defence, Denis Healey, argued, 'we must keep the Protestants quiet' (Dixon, 2008a: 103). The British government still hoped that Northern Ireland's government could stabilise the situation by reform. This was based on the belief that if Northern Ireland's society could be made fairer, and prosperity increased, then the tensions that were evident between the two communities would diminish and the region's politics would be 'normalised' and become focused on left–right divisions instead of religious or national ones. So London supplied Northern Ireland's government with the temporary assistance of the British army to help it deal with the crisis that emerged in August 1969.

Nationalists in Northern Ireland largely welcomed the deployment of troops and the respite from violence that it provided. The Independent Organisation, led by John Hume, who was to become one of the leading nationalist leaders throughout the Troubles, asserted in October 1969 that 'the civil rights movement in this country can be considered to have drawn to a hitherto unbelievably successful conclusion' (Ó Dochartaigh, 1997: 141). However, the deployment of British troops and the granting of the key demands of the movement did not end the violence and the political agenda shifted onto the highly contentious issue of security.

The British government set up an inquiry, under Lord Hunt, into how Northern Ireland was policed. The Hunt Report, published on 10 October 1969, recommended that the RUC become an unarmed police force and that the B Specials should be disbanded and replaced by a smaller military force under the direct control of the British army (what would become the Ulster Defence Regiment). The unionist community provided the majority of those who served in the police forces in Northern Ireland, and loyalists tended to view the RUC (and indeed the B Specials) as doing a fine job in the face of extreme provocation by 'disloyal' nationalists. The Hunt Report was seen as a slur on 'their' police force and threatened to undermine a bastion of the Union. It could be seen as yet another example of unacceptable interference in their affairs by the British government. The result was that far from keeping the Protestants 'quiet' the deployment of the army and the Hunt Report had further antagonised the unionist community and caused friction between the British and Northern Irish governments. The report led to two days of rioting by loyalists on the Shankill Road in Belfast, during which Victor Arbuckle was killed, the first policeman to die in the Troubles. Two other people were also killed and 66 people were injured, including 14 soldiers and three policemen. The reaction to the report highlighted the predicament that the British government faced – to what extent could reform be introduced without producing a serious loyalist backlash?

The Provisional IRA emerged from a split in the IRA in December 1969. The Provisionals, or Provos, were angered by what they saw as the increasingly political, Marxist nature of the IRA and what they believed was a failure by the 'Official' IRA to protect the nationalist community. The Provisionals favoured a more aggressive military stance and later took the offensive against the British army. In 1972 the Official IRA ended its armed campaign and the term IRA became almost exclusively associated with the Provisionals for the remainder of the Troubles. The Labour government began to doubt whether reforms and improved policing could stabilise Northern Ireland. The British Home Secretary, James Callaghan, was fed up with the nationalists 'stringing the British government along, making fresh demands as soon as old ones were met' and questioned whether Britain could solve the crisis (*Sunday Times* Insight Team, 1972: 222). The British army's 'honeymoon' period with the nationalists gradually eroded. Republicans attempted to provoke the British army into confrontation with the nationalists in order to further delegitimise the Northern Ireland state. The army's involvement in 'heavy-handed' operations against nationalists played into the hands of republicans. In April 1970 the British army came into conflict with Catholic civilians for the first time in two generations. The General Officer Commanding in Northern Ireland, Lt-General Sir Ian Freedland, announced that anyone carrying or throwing a petrol bomb was liable to be shot dead after a warning.

The British general election in June 1970 returned a Conservative government led by Edward Heath. The Conservatives were traditionally associated with support for unionism while the Labour Party had sympathies for Irish unity. Nonetheless, the new Conservative Home Secretary, Reginald Maudling, did not relish his task. After his first trip to Northern Ireland he said, 'For God's sake bring me a large Scotch. What a bloody awful country!' (Bew and Gillespie, 1999: 28). The perception that the new Conservative government was pro-unionist appeared to be confirmed by the introduction of the Falls Road Curfew of 3–5 July 1970, which marked a serious deterioration in relations with the nationalists. During these two days the army sealed off the nationalist Lower Falls Road in Belfast in order to search for weapons. Although a significant number of weapons were recovered, five people were killed during the curfew and 1,600 CS gas canisters were fired by the army into the Lower Falls area. There were widespread accusations of intimidation and looting against the soldiers.

The Falls Road Curfew led to such intense anger that there was increased recruitment to the Provisional IRA and the IRA was now able to change its policy and target British soldiers [**Docs 5, 6, pp. 127–8, 128–9**]. According to the IRA's manual, the Green Book, 'In September of 1969 the existing conditions dictated that Brits were not to be shot, but after the Falls curfew all Brits were to the people acceptable targets. The existing conditions had been changed' (quoted in O'Brien, 1993: 292). In February 1971 the first British soldier was killed. The unionist government continued to pressure the British government for more repressive security initiatives as the security situation continued to deteriorate. The Heath government, though, was worried about further antagonising the nationalists and refused to back Chichester-Clark's demands for tougher security measures, leading to his resignation in March 1971. Chichester-Clark's successor as prime minister was Brian Faulkner, a hard-line member of the cabinet who pressed the British government for more aggressive security measures.

The unionist government (and later the British government) was under strong pressure from loyalists to take a more repressive approach to security during 1971–74. The Vanguard group was established as a pressure group within the Ulster Unionist Party to advocate for a tougher line against republicans and to guard against betrayal by the London government [**Doc. 9, pp. 131–2**]. It was also involved in paramilitary-style displays. In September 1971 the loyalist paramilitary group the Ulster Defence Association was formed as an umbrella body for vigilante groups, and in 1972 had about 40,000 members. In 1971 loyalist paramilitaries killed 22 people; in 1972 they killed 116. In July 1972 the UDA was able to put 8,000 on the streets to confront and outnumber the British army. In October 1972 the UDA even declared war on the British army. The British army feared the 'nightmare scenario' of a war on two fronts against both republicans and loyalists. Loyalist strength culminated in the strike that brought down power-sharing in May 1974.

After the British army killed two Catholics in Derry, John Hume declared that the army had become partial and the government's failure to hold an inquiry into the deaths led the SDLP to withdraw from Stormont. On 9 August 1971 the British government gave in to Faulkner's request for the introduction of internment – the detention without trial of suspected terrorists. The policy proved to be the most disastrous security initiative taken in Northern Ireland during the Troubles. Those that were rounded up were exclusively nationalists, further increasing their sense of injustice and victimisation. Out-of-date intelligence was used, resulting in the internment of people who had been involved in earlier IRA campaigns rather than those who were currently active. Internment led to a major upsurge in violence and made less likely any attempt to win nationalist acceptance of a reformed Stormont assembly. In the two years before internment was introduced 66 people were killed, including 11 soldiers. In the first 17 months after internment 610 were killed, including 146 soldiers. Most notorious among these killings was the shooting dead by members of the Parachute Regiment of 13 innocent unarmed protesters in an anti-internment rally in Derry on 30 January 1972, what would become known as **Bloody Sunday** (a fourteenth person subsequently died from their injuries) [**Doc. 4, pp. 126–7**].

Bloody Sunday: 30 January 1972, the Parachute Regiment shot dead 13 people in Derry (another man died later from his injuries).

The controversy over Bloody Sunday centres on responsibility for the massacre: to what extent does it extend up the chain of command from the soldiers deployed on the ground, through their commanding officers to the British government? Bloody Sunday unleashed an intense wave of anti-British sentiment throughout the nationalist community in Ireland, both north and south of the border. The British embassy in Dublin was attacked by 20,000 demonstrators and burnt down. The Irish foreign minister declared that 'From now on my aim is to get Britain out of Ireland' and John Hume stated that many people now believe 'it is a united Ireland or nothing' (Bew and Gillespie, 1999: 45).

Internment had been the final attempt by the British to avoid having to impose direct rule [**Doc. 3, pp. 125–6**]. It was a gamble that spectacularly backfired, leading to an escalation of violence and reducing the prospect of reconciling nationalists to a reformed Stormont. In March 1972 the unionist prime minister resigned rather than grant the British government's request for a transfer of security powers from Northern Ireland to London. On 24 March 1972 Heath announced that the Stormont government was to be suspended temporarily for one year and, on 30 March, power was officially transferred back to Westminster. The British government had finally taken a step that it had long threatened but tried to avoid. The 'temporary' suspension of Northern Ireland's devolved government was, but for a few months in 1974, to last for over a quarter of a century.

CONCLUSIONS

The Northern Ireland state was carved from six of the nine counties of Ulster. This was the maximum territory unionists believed they could hold and sustain a unionist majority over nationalists. This inbuilt majority resulted in a Stormont parliament that was dominated by the Ulster Unionist Party fearful of 'disloyal nationalists' within and a southern government that laid claim to the whole territory of the island of Ireland. There was a considerable degree of discrimination by unionists against nationalists that their political representatives were unable to remedy by representations to Stormont or Westminster. The civil rights movement took politics into the streets in search of justice. This led to communal confrontations and the escalation of violence. The British government continued to try to keep the 'Irish Question' at arm's length and preferred to put pressure on the unionist government to rapidly introduce reforms to meet the grievances of the civil rights movement, and encouraged nationalist participation in government. The British government only reluctantly deployed troops onto the streets of Northern Ireland after the police could no longer cope. It understood the provocation that the presence of British soldiers represented for Irish republicans and hoped to pull them out as soon as possible. Republicans quickly came to see the potential of the growing crisis for delegitimising the unionist government and ending partition. The unionist government insisted on more repressive security policies, such as internment, as the reforms introduced to placate the civil rights movement failed to end the violence. The British army's heavy-handed approach to security issues – most disastrously the Falls Road Curfew and Bloody Sunday – played into republican hands, allowing them to go on the offensive against the British army and escalate their campaign of violence. In March 1972 the British government gave up indirect rule through the unionist government and introduced direct rule from Westminster. The declared intention was for direct rule to be a short-term measure while an accommodation was negotiated among the Northern Ireland parties so that devolution could be restored. The negotiation, implementation and failure of power-sharing in 1972–74 was a precursor of the more successful negotiation of the Good Friday Agreement in 1998.

3

The power-sharing experiment, 1972–74

The introduction of direct rule removed the unionist-dominated Stormont parliament that had run Northern Ireland for 50 years. The move was largely welcomed by nationalists and indeed was seen as something of a victory by the IRA, who saw it as a stepping stone to a united Ireland. Loyalists largely resented direct rule because they saw it as removing 'their' government and further reducing unionist power, appeasing republicans and putting more power into the hands of an untrustworthy British government. The British government saw direct rule as a temporary measure, until a new power-sharing system of government could be devised to replace unionist majority rule. The British had put pressure on the unionist government to reform and devise ways of giving nationalists a share of power. The problem that became increasingly apparent, however, was that just as there had been little agreement over what was wrong with how Northern Ireland was governed pre-1972, there was no consensus over how it should be governed post-1972. Unionists tended to favour a return to majority rule or, if not, the continuation of direct rule from Westminster. Nationalists favoured a united Ireland but by 'consent' of the Northern Ireland people, which was not forthcoming. The only compromise likely to win support from significant numbers of both nationalists and unionists was some kind of power-sharing alongside an Irish dimension. During 1972–74 the British and Irish governments attempted to construct a power-sharing agreement (a deal which is similar in some respects to the Good Friday Agreement 1998). Their ability to do this was hampered by the violence of both republican and loyalist paramilitaries, which did not create a favourable environment for accommodation. The IRA believed that it was winning and declared in January 1972 that this would be its 'Year of Victory'. Loyalist paramilitaries believed that the British government was weak and might capitulate to republican demands. In this environment of constitutional insecurity violence flourished: 1972 was the bloodiest year of the Troubles with 470 people killed and over 10,000 bombs planted.

DEALING WITH THE EXTREMISTS

The attempt to build a consensus among the moderate parties co-existed with an attempt to bring republicans to the negotiating table. In the wake of direct rule the newly appointed Secretary of State for Northern Ireland, William Whitelaw, ordered the army to adopt a 'low profile', to improve the prospects of bringing republicans into a political process. The British conceded 'special category' status to republican prisoners (in effect treating them as prisoners of war; the removal of this status led to the hunger strikes of 1981) and reduced the number of those interned, from 972 in March 1972 to 372 by June. On 25 May the Official IRA murdered William Best, an off-duty member of the British army who was from Derry. The killing caused outrage in the city and there were angry protests by women from the Bogside and Creggan areas of Derry, 400 of whom marched to Official Sinn Féin's office demanding that they cease their violence. The Official IRA did indeed call a ceasefire four days later, stating that 'the overwhelming desire of the great majority of all the people . . . is for an end to military actions by all sides' (Dixon, 2008a: 125). The Provisional IRA (hereafter the IRA), on the other hand, conducted an increasingly violent and bloody campaign in an attempt to undermine Northern Ireland and to force the British to leave Ireland. In June 1972, the IRA declared a ceasefire and its leaders secretly met representatives of the British government in London in July 1972. The meeting only served to highlight the gulf between them. The IRA, perhaps reflecting its belief that it was pushing on to victory, took an uncompromising line in the talks. Its six-strong delegation demanded that the British leave Ireland by 1975. The ceasefire that had enabled the talks to take place was ended by the IRA less than a week after the failed meeting. On 21 July the IRA set off 26 bombs in Belfast, killing 11 people and injuring 130. The scale and indiscriminate nature of what became known as 'Bloody Friday' damaged the IRA's standing within its own community and created the political environment for the British to take a more assertive stance against the IRA. On 31 July the army launched 'Operation Motorman' which employed 12,000 troops using bulldozers and tanks to remove barricades and reassert control over the 'no-go' areas of Belfast and Derry. This was a successful operation and one accompanied by much less violence or death than the security forces had expected. The unrealistic demands made by the IRA and the subsequent escalation in violence meant that the British were further encouraged in their attempts to broker a deal among the moderates, reach out to the 'silent majority' and marginalise the IRA. The British government was pragmatic, it preferred to bring republicans into a political process but if they excluded themselves through unrealistic and intransigent demands then the government would pursue power-sharing without them.

BRINGING IN THE MODERATES

The British government argued that a moderate 'silent majority' existed in Northern Ireland who were more moderate and accommodating than those responsible for the instability and violence. British policy over the next two years sought an accommodation between the elites who represented this 'silent majority' to try to create a new devolved system of government, returning power to Northern Ireland. The British were encouraged by the revival in the fortunes of the non-sectarian Northern Ireland Labour Party (**NILP**) in the June 1970 election, where it had achieved almost 100,000 votes. If a deal could be brokered between what were seen as the moderate parties of the NILP, the liberal wing of the UUP, the newly formed SDLP and the Alliance Party of Northern Ireland (**APNI**), the hope was that the extremes represented by the factions connected to Ian Paisley's DUP, the more hard-line element within the UUP and Sinn Féin would be isolated and undermined. To this end the British held a conference in Darlington in September 1972 attended by the UUP, the NILP and the APNI. The SDLP had been invited but refused to attend while internment continued. But the parties could not agree on what form a future Northern Ireland government should take, which did not bode well for restoring devolved government. These moderate parties, along with the SDLP, were 'moderate' only insofar as they rejected violence. The UUP, NILP and APNI believed that Northern Ireland should remain within the United Kingdom, but differed in many other respects. The SDLP's position was markedly different. Formed in 1970, the SDLP was resolutely nationalist, advocating a united Ireland by 'consent' [**Doc. 7, pp. 129–30**]. Its 1972 policy document, *Towards a New Ireland*, claimed that Northern Ireland was 'inherently unstable', called on the British government to declare itself in favour of Irish unity and advocated a power-sharing government under joint British–Irish sovereignty as an interim solution until full Irish unity could be achieved.

Despite the lack of progress at Darlington the British produced a Green Paper entitled *The Future of Northern Ireland: A Paper for Discussion* in October 1972 [**Doc. 8, pp. 130–1**]. The document reasserted Britain's commitment to uphold Northern Ireland's status as part of the UK as long as that was the

NILP: Northern Ireland Labour Party, socialist party formed in 1924, which lost a significant proportion of its working class support to the DUP and SDLP in the early 1970s.

APNI: Alliance Party of Northern Ireland, founded April 1970.

wish of the majority of the people (rather than its parliament) in Northern Ireland. There was, however, also an assertion by the British that they would not stand in the way of unity if that was the wish of the people of Northern Ireland, which was to be tested by regular referendums. The Green Paper set out the basis for future accommodation: a future assembly would have to receive cross-community support; the minority should have a share in government; any settlement should, as far as possible, be acceptable to the Republic of Ireland.

After a period of consultation with the parties the British government in March 1973 offered more detailed proposals in a White Paper, *Northern Ireland Constitutional Proposals* [**Doc. 10, pp. 132–4**]. It proposed the creation of a devolved assembly and an executive, which was to be based upon power-sharing as 'it is the view of the Government that the Executive itself can no longer be solely based upon any single party, if that party draws its support and its elected representation virtually entirely from only one section of a divided community' (para. 52). More contentious for unionists was the institutionalisation of the Irish dimension via the creation of a Council of Ireland – for which no details were given. The plan was that after the elections to the Assembly 'the Government will invite the Government of the Republic of Ireland and the leaders of the elected representatives of Northern Ireland to participate with them in a conference' to consider the principle of consent and acceptance of the status of Northern Ireland, 'effective consultation and co-operation in Ireland' and security cooperation against terrorists (para. 116). Unionist opponents of British policy argued that it represented the betrayal of the Union and set Northern Ireland on the road to a united Ireland [**Doc. 3, 9, pp. 125–6, 131–2**].

THE POWER-SHARING AGREEMENT

The election to the Assembly on 28 June 1973 damaged the thesis that there was a 'moderate silent majority'. Despite opinion polls suggesting the NILP and APNI would do well in the election, when the votes were counted the NILP received only 2.6 per cent of the vote and secured only one of the available 88 seats. The APNI's share was only 9.2 per cent and eight seats. Although the vote for the UUP was 37.8 per cent, securing 32 seats, the UUP was deeply divided over whether to accept the model proposed in the White Paper and was split between those who ran as pro-White Paper UUP and those standing as anti-White Paper UUP with the antis accounting for 8.5 per cent of the vote and eight of the UUP seats. A new party, the Vanguard Unionist Progressive Party (VUPP), secured 10.5 per cent of the vote and

Ulster Vanguard: Unionist pressure group cre-
ated in 1972 (became
Vanguard Unionist Pro-
gressive Party in 1973).

seven seats. (The VUPP emerged out of what was essentially a pressure group within unionism, **Ulster Vanguard**, which had strong links to the UUP and loyalists groups.) Paisley's DUP achieved 10.5 per cent and eight seats. (The SDLP, however, performed well and secured 22.1 per cent of the vote and 19 seats.)

The result of the election meant that to be viable an executive would have to be made up of the pro-White Paper UUP, the SDLP and the APNI. The difficulty for the UUP leader, Brian Faulkner, was that the UUP manifesto had stated that while the party was not opposed to power-sharing it would not 'be prepared to participate in government with those whose primary aim is to break the union with Great Britain'. This was interpreted by some within unionism as ruling out power-sharing with the SDLP while others could claim that the SDLP's primary aim was not Irish unity and therefore unionists could share power with it. The three parties reached agreement on forming an executive in November 1973. The executive would comprise six UUP members, four SDLP members and one representative from the APNI. The fact that there was a unionist majority was seen as important in helping Faulkner address growing criticism from within his party over the decision to enter the executive with the SDLP. The executive also had four non-voting members, one from the UUP, two from the SDLP and one from the APNI.

Although the parties had agreed to share power the executive could not take office until the parties had agreed on the creation of the Council of Ireland. The three parties and members of the British and Irish governments met at Sunningdale in December 1973 to discuss its creation. There were real differences between the parties over what level of input the Irish government should have in the affairs of Northern Ireland and what guarantees the Irish should provide in return. The unionists wanted the Irish to remove articles 2 and 3 of their constitution, which claimed jurisdiction over Northern Ireland, to provide greater cooperation on security issues and to extradite suspected terrorists from the Republic to Northern Ireland more easily. The unionists believed the Council should be a weak, largely consultative body. The SDLP, however, wanted a strong Council with executive powers, reform of the RUC and an end of internment.

The Irish government refused to remove its constitutional claim to Northern Ireland, largely on the grounds that it would not be able to secure the necessary support from the Irish electorate to remove these articles in the required referendum. This was almost certainly true as Fianna Fáil, the largest and most republican of the political parties, would not have supported the move and without its support it is highly unlikely that the constitution could have been amended. From a unionist perspective, however, the declining support within their community for the White Paper, and deep apprehension over an Irish dimension, meant Faulkner needed to be able to demonstrate that he had made gains in the talks. The Irish government did declare 'that there could be no change in the status of Northern Ireland until a majority of the people of Northern Ireland desired a change in that status' (Dixon, 2008a: 137). Whatever comfort this declaration may have provided to Faulkner was short-lived after the High Court in Dublin ruled that the declaration made in the agreement was 'no more than a statement of policy'.

The status and powers of the Council of Ireland were also problematic. It was agreed that it would have 14 members, seven from the Northern Ireland Executive and seven for the Irish Government; but it could only take decisions unanimously, which effectively gave unionists a veto on its actions. What functions the executive would perform were not defined, although several areas were mentioned as possibilities: natural resources, agricultural matters, cooperation in trade and industry, tourism, public health, sports and the arts. Although these may seem comparatively unthreatening, the agreement also stated that there was 'no limit to the array of functions which could be devolved to the Council of Ireland', the only stipulation being that they had to have the agreement of the Northern Ireland Assembly and the Irish parliament. For many unionists the ambiguity over what its powers would be was alarming and for others it was not the actual functions of the Council that were so problematic but its symbolic importance. The idea of allowing the Republic of Ireland any role in taking decisions relating to Northern Ireland, no matter how apparently benign or limited, was seen as a slippery slope to eventual Irish unity. Loyalist opponents of the deal proclaimed that 'Dublin is only a Sunningdale away'.

The unionist aim of getting an agreement from the Irish to extradite those suspected of terrorist activity to Northern Ireland was also hampered by Ireland's constitution, which did not allow extradition for political offences. The compromise reached was that those accused of committing crimes in Ireland should stand trial wherever they were arrested – so someone suspected of a crime in Northern Ireland could be tried in the Republic if arrested there.

Although Faulkner had agreed to the Sunningdale proposals, he had been placed under enormous pressure by the British and Irish governments to do so, and he struggled to sell the deal to unionists. While he believed that the Council of Ireland was a 'necessary nonsense' needed to achieve devolution, it was not seen as such by large sections of unionism. During the Sunningdale conference, one SDLP delegate, Paddy Devlin, realised that Faulkner was being pushed too far. Devlin told a member of the APNI, 'Look, we've got to catch ourselves on here. Brian Faulkner is being nailed to a cross. There is no way Faulkner can sell this' (White, 1984: 152). But this was a minority view; the priority for the British was to get an agreement and they presumed that if they could get the UUP to sign up to a deal the party would subsequently be able to sell it to its community. Reflecting on the later problems Willie Whitelaw told the Conservative commentator T. E. Utley, 'You always told me that I was driving Faulkner too far. My goodness you were right! But what a damned fool he was to allow himself to be driven' (*The Times*, 7 May 2005).

The SDLP promoted the Council as a real advance for nationalists and some even portrayed it as an all-Ireland government in embryonic form. One SDLP Assembly member declared that it was 'the vehicle that would trundle unionists into a united Ireland' (Bew and Gillespie, 1999: 77). Such statements were unlikely to help Faulkner calm unionist fears.

THE COLLAPSE OF SUNNINGDALE

On 1 January 1974 the power-sharing experiment was launched. Three days later the governing body of the Unionist Party, the Ulster Unionist Council (UUC), voted against the deal and Faulkner resigned the leadership of his party but remained leader of the executive. This undermined his moral authority because he was only chief executive of the power-sharing coalition because he was leader of the largest party in Northern Ireland. The Westminster general election of February 1974 further undermined power-sharing, subjecting the executive to an election before it had the chance to demonstrate that it could provide stability and effective local governance. The anti-Sunningdale parties, the UUP (now led by Harry West), the DUP and Vanguard agreed to divide the constituencies between their candidates to ensure that they did not split the vote by standing against each other and ran

UUUC: United Ulster Unionist Council, body created by unionists in 1974 to oppose the Sunningdale Agreement. Included the UUP, the DUP and Ulster Vanguard.

under the label of the United Ulster Unionist Council (**UUUC**). The pro-Sunningdale parties, however, did not agree an electoral pact. The result was that the UUUC candidates succeeded in capturing 12 of Northern Ireland's 13 Westminster seats with 51 per cent of the vote, demonstrating that a majority of unionists opposed Sunningdale. The British government refused to hold fresh elections to the Northern Ireland Assembly because its members had been elected less than a year before. The government probably hoped that if the Assembly and executive could survive until 1977, when the next elections were due, it may have proved its worth and become acceptable. Indeed, opinion polls at the time showed that 69 per cent of people in Northern Ireland favoured giving the executive and Sunningdale a chance, but this masked deep divisions. Although 72 per cent of Catholics felt the proposed Council of Ireland was a good thing, just 26 per cent of Protestants shared their view and 52 per cent of that community felt it was a bad thing.

The brief period of devolved government in Northern Ireland was finally defeated by the two-week loyalist **UWC** strike, which led Brian Faulkner to resign as chief executive on 28 May. The immediate trigger for the strike was the decision within the Assembly to ratify the Sunningdale Agreement (by 44 votes to 28). The strike began slowly but gathered momentum and succeeded in paralysing Northern Ireland with power-cuts, factories shut, curtailed opening hours for shops and barricades erected by the strikers. *Nationalist accounts* of the strike argue that it could have been broken if the British had deployed the army in the early stages and made sure that essential services (such as electricity and petrol supplies) were maintained. *Unionist accounts* suggest that it was the inevitable and popular reaction to an attempt to force Northern Ireland out of the Union. While there may have been some intimidation by loyalist paramilitaries they would emphasise the popular support for the strike and opposition to Sunningdale, which had been demonstrated in the February election.

> **UWC:** Ulster Workers' Council, co-ordinating body for the 1974 Ulster Workers' Strike.

The period of the power-sharing experiment was marked by increasing violence. The IRA increased its activities in the first part of 1974 and planted several bombs in England in another attempt to break the British will to remain in Northern Ireland. During the UWC strike, on 17 May three bombs exploded in Dublin and one in Monaghan in the Irish Republic, killing 33 people – the highest toll for a single day's violence during the Troubles. Although both of the main loyalist paramilitary groups denied responsibility, it was widely believed they were the work of loyalists – not least as the cars used were stolen from Protestant areas of Belfast. There has also been continued speculation that elements of the British security services colluded in the bombing. On 25 May Harold Wilson made his infamous 'Spongers Speech', expressing 'British' frustration with the impending collapse of power-sharing and with it British policy since 1972 [**Doc. 11, pp. 134–5**].

CONCLUSIONS

The failure of British policy during 1972–74 to establish a successful and stable power-sharing government led to a prolonged and unwanted period of direct rule from Westminster. The attempts to devolve power back to the region after the suspension of the Stormont regime in 1972 proved unworkable. The 'moderate silent majority' on which power-sharing was to be built had not proved as strong as was hoped. Opinion polls may have suggested support for accommodation but these consistently over-estimated the strength of moderate voting and opinion. While unionists had voted for the Ulster Unionist Party in the Assembly elections in June 1973 they had not

necessarily voted for the deal that was to emerge from the subsequent negotiations, particularly on the Irish dimension. This raises the question of
whether a better deal could have been struck that would have given Faulkner
a more realistic chance of delivering sufficient unionist support to a voluntary power-sharing deal. Or was such a deal simply not possible in the
polarised political climate of Northern Ireland in the mid-1970s?

There was a strong perception among unionists that even a British Conservative government was not a strong guarantor of the Union and that
power-sharing was a means by which Northern Ireland would be expelled
from the UK. Brian Faulkner's growing problems with his party culminated
in his resignation from the leadership just after the executive had been established. Loyalist paramilitary groups also exerted a powerful influence on
unionism and, allied with some unionist politicians, brought down power-
sharing. The violent activities of both loyalist and republican paramilitaries
throughout this period exacerbated tensions and were not conducive to the
achievement of political accommodation. The Irish government played an
important role alongside the British in driving forward power-sharing but
was unable to deliver the reassurances unionists wanted about their constitutional position within the UK. The SDLP was radicalised by the repressive nature of British security policy and had to protect its nationalist flank
from the criticism of republicans who viewed the SDLP as 'collaborators'
with the British state. In the years after 1974 power-sharing with some kind
of, perhaps limited, Irish dimension still appeared to be the most obvious
settlement capable of winning both nationalist and unionist support. The
problem remained that the political positions of the parties and, apparently,
their electorates were too far apart to sustain such an accommodation. The
Good Friday Agreement of 1998 was not dissimilar to the deal agreed at Sunningdale. The deputy leader of the SDLP, Seamus Mallon, later called the
Good Friday Agreement 'Sunningdale for slow learners'. This was a dig at
both republicans and unionists who had undermined power-sharing in 1974
and left Northern Ireland without its own devolved government for a further
25 years.

4

Searching for solutions, 1974–82

The failure of the Sunningdale experiment suggested that many of the assumptions on which British policy had been based since the outbreak of the Troubles were wrong. The Ulster Workers' Council Strike and the election of hard-line unionists undermined the British government's claim that there existed a strong 'moderate silent majority' – bringing Northern Ireland up to 'British standards' and modernisation had not served to isolate hardliners. Power-sharing unionists had been unable to win their voters over to both power-sharing and an Irish dimension. After the collapse of the devolved government the British government considered four options:

1. Withdraw from Northern Ireland, leading to a united Ireland or the creation of an independent state.
2. Create an independent Ulster, perhaps with some redrawing of the borders.
3. Integrate the region into the United Kingdom and govern it on the same basis as Wales and Scotland.
4. Continue with direct rule as a temporary measure until some other solution turned up.

After the collapse of power-sharing, Britain seriously considered each of these policies.

EXAMINING NORTHERN IRELAND'S OPTIONS

The new Prime Minister, Harold Wilson, had a history of sympathy for Irish unity going back to at least the mid-1960s. In 1971 he had proposed Irish unity by consent. In opposition, the Labour leadership had discussed British withdrawal under the codename 'Algeria'. Harold Wilson was contemplating the government's options even before power-sharing had collapsed. These included the 'Doomsday scenario' of British withdrawal. There is little doubt that Wilson was sympathetic to the idea of British withdrawal and was the driving force behind its consideration (Bew, 2007: 517–21). Withdrawal would probably have been a popular option with the British public, as polls have consistently shown support for it since the mid-1970s and even during the recent peace process. British support for withdrawal did not indicate sympathy for the IRA however, as polls simultaneously suggested support for a 'tough', or repressive, security policy in Northern Ireland. Withdrawal was seen as extricating the British army and saving the British taxpayer money rather than supporting Irish unity [**Doc. 11, pp. 134–5**]. For example, by August 1972, after Whitelaw's more conciliatory security policy, a poll found that 71 per cent thought the government was 'not tough enough' in its efforts to bring peace to Northern Ireland, 86 per cent thought that 'no-go' areas should not be allowed and only 4 per cent thought the government was 'too tough'. Support for withdrawal went along with a view of the IRA as terrorists: in a 1977 Gallup poll 97 per cent thought the IRA were terrorists rather than freedom fighters. The British had withdrawn from Empire but in doing so had precipitated violent conflict, most particularly in Palestine and India. In Empire the British were able to escape the consequences of this violence; Northern Ireland, by contrast, was much closer to 'home', less than 20 miles off the Scottish coast, and there were large Irish communities in British cities who might become radicalised by a major escalation of conflict in the North. In addition, British withdrawal might have a destabilising effect on the Republic of Ireland, with whom the British enjoyed close links.

The Irish government was alarmed at the prospect of a British withdrawal. While it had long called for a united Ireland there were severe problems in seeking to incorporate Northern Ireland and up to a million hostile unionists into its state. As a result, the Irish Minister of Foreign Affairs, Garret FitzGerald, approached the US Secretary of State and requested that the US government dissuade Britain from withdrawal. The Irish government feared that withdrawal would gravely destabilise the Republic. An internal Irish report suggested that it would need to deploy 60,000 troops to stabilise the North after British withdrawal, at a time when total Irish defence forces numbered just over 11,000 (Bew, 2007: 517). Irish state papers record that the government even rejected calls from the SDLP's John Hume to draw up a plan of action in the event of British withdrawal: as FitzGerald told him, 'If the Irish Government were to indicate it was facing up to the possibility of British withdrawal, this might certainly give the British Government the alibi they almost certainly wanted to get out; in this way we would be letting them off the hook' (*Irish Examiner*, 1 January 2005).

Although Wilson sympathised with Irish unity, the most effective way that the British could extricate themselves and leave behind a less unstable state was probably to leave behind an independent Northern Ireland. Wilson's plan in 1974, which was only circulated to a small number of close colleagues, was to grant Northern Ireland dominion status and transfer power to its government. In reality this would have meant returning Northern Ireland to majority (Protestant) rule. All British funding was to cease within five years. There was some hope within British circles that a new 'Northern Irish' nationalism might develop that would allow Protestants and Catholics to develop loyalty to an independent Ulster.

Ultimately, the British government dropped the plans for withdrawal as it would have further destabilised not only Northern Ireland but the Republic as well, and may have led to violence in those British cities that had a significant Irish population. In December 1975 Northern Ireland Secretary Merlyn Rees concluded that 'A declaration of intent to withdraw was not on; the position of the Army would become untenable immediately such a declaration was made, irrespective of the time-scale given' (Rees, quoted in 'Minutes of meeting between the Secretary of State at the NIO [Northern Ireland Office] and a Conservative Deputation led by Mr Neave'; see Dixon, 2008a: 153). Although Wilson remained supportive of withdrawal, his cabinet colleagues were less enthusiastic (Bew, 2007: 523).

Repartition and full integration of Northern Ireland into the UK were also considered as options for managing the conflict. Repartition would have meant redrawing the border between Northern Ireland and the Republic to allow those areas in the west of Northern Ireland that had significant Catholic majorities to join the Republic. The advantage of this would be that it would result in a Northern Ireland that contained fewer who were hostile to being part of the United Kingdom; the disadvantage was that, unless it was accompanied by large-scale population movement, the largest concentration of nationalists in Northern Ireland, those in West Belfast, would remain, while significant Protestant minorities would find themselves in the Republic. Repartition could aggravate rather than ameliorate violence as paramilitaries attempted to 'cleanse' and claim areas for their community.

The full integration of Northern Ireland into the UK meant that it would be administered directly from Westminster on the same basis as Scotland and Wales. The advantage of this plan was that it might resolve the constitutional uncertainty of its governance. Its proponents argued that integration would end any hope that republicans had of achieving Irish unity and make their 'armed struggle' a hopeless cause. Integrationists argued that the UK is a multinational and multicultural state which would treat the nationalist minority in a fair way. The disadvantage of integration was that it had the consent of neither the nationalist minority nor the government of the Irish Republic. Integration would deliver 'victory' to a segment of unionist opinion and would have to be imposed against the will of Irish nationalists and republicans. This had the potential to radicalise nationalists and increase support for republican violence rather than reduce it. The Irish government was also likely to withdraw political and security cooperation against the IRA in protest and seek the support of the US President.

The only constitutional settlement with a potential to win significant cross-community support in Northern Ireland was a devolved, power-sharing assembly (perhaps with some kind of Irish dimension) but neither the political will nor popular consent appeared to exist for it (see Table 4.1). The least objectionable option was a continuation of direct rule, although successive British governments maintained that this was only a temporary state of affairs. The Labour government and, after 1979, the Conservative government continued to pursue talks with the political parties in the hope that some way could be found to devolve power to Northern Ireland.

Table 4.1 Preferred form of constitutional settlement, Northern Ireland (1974 and 1976 compared)

	Protestant 1976 (%)	Change from 1974 (%) (1974 % in brackets)	Catholic 1976 (%)	Change from 1974 (%) (1974 % in brackets)
Integrate Northern Ireland fully with the UK, just like any other region in England	38	+5 (33)	19	+13 (6)
Continue with direct rule from Westminster	14	+6 (8)	26	+18 (8)
Accept majority rule	36	+3 (33)	4	+3 (1)
Try to impose power-sharing	6	−12 (18)	18	−37 (55)
Encourage an independent Northern Ireland	3	+1 (2)	3	+2 (1)
Encourage a united Ireland	1	0 (1)	23	0 (23)
Don't know/none	2	−4 (6)	7	0 (7)

Source: NOP Market Research 1976, quoted in R. Rose *et al.*, 1978: 20. Question: 'Now that the Convention is over and the Northern Ireland politicians have not reached full agreement on a form of self-government, which of the following policies that the British Government could adopt would you find acceptable and which would be unacceptable?' (4–10 March 1976 compared to 30 March–7 April 1974 (during the power-sharing experiment)).

DEALING WITH THE IRA

The British government's threats that it was considering withdrawal may have encouraged the IRA to negotiate with the British during 1974–75. The dialogue with the government led the IRA to announce a temporary ceasefire in December 1974 and then an indefinite one in February 1975. This was a welcome development for the British as the IRA had been conducting an aggressive bombing campaign in English cities for several months. In October 1974 two IRA bombs had killed five people in pubs in Guildford and injured 54, a month later two people were killed and 26 injured by a pub bomb in Woolwich and 21 people were killed by bombs in two Birmingham pubs, with 160 injured (Bew and Gillespie, 1999: 95–6; McKittrick *et al.*, 1999: 479–500). Under the conditions of the truce, 'incident centres' were set up by Sinn Féin and offered a 'hotline' to the British government to avoid the misunderstandings and confrontations that had caused problems during the 1972 ceasefire. The centres also elevated the status of Sinn Féin, as they indicated the importance that the British placed on the movement. But the centres were not welcomed by the Irish government or the SDLP and caused real anger and concern among unionists that they were to be 'sold out' by London. The truce lasted until November 1975 and the ceasefire limped on into 1976 but had been breached on numerous occasions before that.

The IRA claimed that it was deceived by the British government into expecting a withdrawal from Northern Ireland. It claimed that it had received a message from the government on Christmas Day 1974 saying the government 'wished to devise structures of disengagement from Ireland', but it became clear during the talks that the British were not willing to withdraw. Loyalist fears of a British withdrawal led to an escalation of their violence and between 1974 and 1976 loyalist paramilitaries killed 452 people, 40 per cent of their total victims throughout the Troubles. The IRA leadership carried out reprisal attacks and was under internal pressure to abandon the ceasefire when it appeared not to be bringing the IRA's objectives any closer. The British government used the ceasefire to undermine the IRA's military capacity by compiling intelligence, and over 400 people were charged with violent offences in the first five months of 1976. The respite from IRA violence during the ceasefire also enabled the British to pursue what became known as 'normalisation'. This policy had two components. First, 'Ulsterisation' was designed to reduce the role of the British army by shifting the responsibility for security onto the locally recruited RUC. The second component was 'criminalisation' which meant that those responsible for the violence were not treated as combatants in a 'war' but as 'normal' criminals. This was to be achieved by the removal of the special category status that had been introduced in 1972. In November 1975 Rees announced that anyone convicted after 1 March 1976 would be treated like other criminals. This removed the right of paramilitary prisoners to wear their own clothes, refuse prison work and freely associate with other prisoners. The move was fiercely resisted by republican prisoners and led to one of the pivotal events of the Troubles, the 1981 hunger strikes. Normalisation also enabled the British to end internment in December 1975.

Whether the British government entered into the talks with the IRA and the subsequent truce to 'con' the IRA is not entirely clear (Dixon, 2008a: 159–65). But what is evident is that the period did cause problems within the IRA and was instrumental in leading to the marginalisation of those who ran the IRA during the truce. A younger, more militant 'Northern' leadership led by Gerry Adams and Martin McGuinness began to assert control in the late 1970s. The movement was reorganised into a cellular structure rather than the more open 'army' structure that had been employed before [**Docs 12, 13, pp. 135, 136–7**]. This was an attempt to reduce the likelihood of infiltration by the British. The IRA also realised that it was not on the verge of a victory and that British withdrawal was not imminent. 'One more heave' would not force the British out, so republicans settled down for 'the long war'.

A SECURITY-DRIVEN POLICY

The British government pursued both a ceasefire with the IRA and an attempt to reach a settlement by convening a Constitutional Convention of the political parties to see if agreement could be reached on the devolution of power to Northern Ireland. Although the British hoped that the Convention would succeed, they also believed that if it failed it would 'at least show the world, and give a message to the South of Ireland, that the blame did not all lie with the British' (Rees, 1985: 107). The elections to the Convention in May 1975 produced a strong anti-power-sharing majority, with the UUUC securing 54.8 per cent of the vote, and the Convention made little progress. This was perhaps unsurprising given the inter-communal antagonisms that were evident after the failure of Sunningdale and the anger within the nationalist community over internment and within the unionist community as a result of the fear of British withdrawal and their contacts with the IRA. The UUUC members ensured that the Convention's report demanded a return to Stormont-type majority rule and stated that the inclusion of representatives from the minority community in the executive should not be compulsory, as well as rejecting an institutionalised Irish dimension. The Convention was formally dissolved in March 1976.

These developments meant that by 1976 it was clear that there were no new political initiatives for Northern Ireland that were likely to be successful in the short term. There were no grounds for agreement between unionists and nationalists over how the region should be governed, talks between the British and the IRA had run their course, the ceasefire was over and loyalist violence had escalated (see Table 4.1 on public opinion). Faced with this situation, the British returned to direct rule, attempting to limit the violence, reduce the exposure of the British army and portray the IRA as a criminal organisation [**Doc. 13, pp. 136–7**]. This security-focused policy of 'normalisa-tion' was popular among the unionist community. Unionism's hand was strengthened by Westminster arithmetic after the general election of October 1974, which saw Labour re-elected but with only a three-seat majority, which made the ten unionist MPs a powerful bloc in the Commons. In 1977 the Labour Party came to an agreement with the UUP at Westminster whereby Northern Ireland's representation at Westminster would be increased from 12 to 17 seats at the next election, in return for which the unionists agreed not to oppose the government. This was seen as an integrationist move by the unionists, an approach that was favoured by a significant section of the UUP, notably James Molyneaux, who became UUP leader in July 1979 (and opposed by the SDLP for the same reason).

In January 1976 Labour introduced a package of security measures that included more surveillance operations, increased the number of checkpoints and personal identity checks and marked the official introduction of the SAS into Northern Ireland. The security focus was also strengthened by the appointment of a hardliner, Roy Mason, as Secretary of State in September 1976. The focus on security, the reassurances offered by Mason that 'The myth of British withdrawal is dead forever' (*Irish Times*, 17 September 1977; Loughlin, 1995: 205), and the expansion of Northern Ireland's representa-tion at Westminster were welcomed by unionists. These changes reduced some of unionism's anxieties, which was demonstrated by the 1977 local elections in Northern Ireland when the UUP vote rose to 29.6 per cent while support for Paisley's hard-line DUP fell to 12.7 per cent from 14.8 per cent in the Convention elections of 1975. In May 1977 a loyalist strike involving Ian Paisley's DUP and the UDA to force the British to return majority rule to Northern Ireland collapsed after ten days, having failed to win the support of unionists employed in key industries.

The British government's emphasis on security was far less attractive to nationalists and republicans. Nationalists were still unhappy with the col-lapse of Sunningdale and what they saw as the failure of the British to stand up to unionism by protecting the deal. Divisions emerged within the SDLP and a section of the party favoured seeking to work with loyalists towards British withdrawal and an independent Northern Ireland. A motion calling on the British to declare their intention to withdraw in order to 'give the divided people of Northern Ireland the opportunity to negotiate a final political solution and a lasting peace' was only defeated by 153 votes to 111. Those that opposed the move and remained committed to traditional nationalism argued that withdrawal would lead to civil war because republican and loyalist paramilitaries would use force to seize power. Nationalists who favoured the move towards independence did so on the pragmatic grounds that the British were preparing to withdraw anyway and so independence was a compromise that could enable both republicans and loyalists to give up violence and seek a constitutional settlement. Once the threat of British withdrawal receded in the late 1970s and the British government moved closer to the unionists, the SDLP became more nationalist in its outlook and demands.

The mid-1970s also saw a change in the stance of the United States. Until then the US government had exerted little or no public pressure on Britain over Northern Ireland. After the collapse of the power-sharing experiment and concern over the rising levels of violence, several American politicians increased their interest in the issue. The Irish government, which was concerned about the funds and support that republicans received in the United States, developed very good relations with several leading politicians, notably the speaker of the House of Representatives, Thomas 'Tip' O'Neill, senators Ted Kennedy and Daniel Moynihan, and the governor of New York, Hugh Carey, who collectively became known as the 'Four Horsemen'. They issued a statement on 16 March 1977 condemning the use of violence in Northern Ireland. The Irish government was keen to combat the romantic view that the British were the cause of all Ireland's problems – a view that republicans sought to perpetuate when seeking support and funds from groups such as the Irish Northern Aid Committee (**NORAID**). The Irish government also sought to persuade key American politicians to put pressure on Britain to alter its policy. President Carter issued a statement in August 1977 urging a new initiative in Northern Ireland and promising to seek increased investment in Northern Ireland in the event of a 'settlement'. The role of the British Foreign Office in Northern Irish policy from the late 1970s suggests an acknowledgement of the growing importance of the international dimension (Donoughue, 1987: 135). American criticisms of human rights abuses and the US suspension of arms sales to the RUC were unwelcome to the British government – and it has been suggested that US pressure was instrumental in bringing about the new round of talks organised by Margaret Thatcher's government between Secretary of State Humphrey Atkins and the Northern Ireland parties in 1979–80. The evidence for this is largely circumstantial however, and there were persuasive domestic reasons for the new initiative.

NORAID: Irish Northern Aid Committee, US-based organisation established in 1969 to provide support to republicans in Ireland, closely linked to the PIRA.

THE HUNGER STRIKES

IRA prisoners resisted the British government's strategy of criminalisation by campaigning against the removal in 1976 of special category status for paramilitary prisoners. The first IRA man sentenced under the new rules, Kieran Nugent, refused to wear the prison uniform on the grounds that he was not a criminal but a political prisoner and wrapped himself in a blanket. Many of those who followed Nugent did the same and the policy of refusing to comply with the prison regime became known as going 'on the blanket'. The blanket campaign became a stand-off between republicans and prison authorities. When the prisoners were refused the right to use the wash or toilet facilities without wearing a uniform, the blanket protest escalated and the prisoners smeared the walls of their cells with excrement rather than wear the clothes. This led to naked prisoners (except for blankets) living in filthy conditions in what was claimed to be one of the newest and best-equipped prison facilities in the UK.

Although the prisoners' situation was an emotive issue within sectors of the nationalist community, it had little resonance outside of nationalist areas of Northern Ireland. This was, however, dramatically altered with the decision of the prisoners to escalate their protest by embarking upon a hunger strike. In October 1980 seven republican prisoners in the Maze prison (commonly known as the H Blocks because of the shape of the prison buildings) began a hunger strike to secure 'political status'. The prisoners issued a statement defining political status by five demands: the right to wear their own clothes, to refrain from prison work, to associate freely with one another, to organise recreational facilities and have one letter, visit and parcel a week, and to have remission that had been lost as a result of previous protests restored. The demands were rejected by the British government. Margaret Thatcher (who had become prime minister the previous year) claimed that granting the demands would give the prisoners 'a kind of respectability, even nobility' (1993: 390). This hunger strike was called off in December with one of the prisoners, Seán McKenna, near death. The prisoners believed that the government had agreed to make concessions on prison conditions, particularly over the clothing issue, but in order to save McKenna's life called off the hunger strike before the document outlining the changes arrived from the Northern Ireland Office. The government, for its part, denied that concessions had been offered and the document that appeared was rather ambiguous, but the prisoners believed it could form the basis of an agreed settlement. The failure of prisoners to be given their own clothes after the dispute ended caused fury in the Maze. The prisoners believed they had been duped by the British and began a second hunger strike in March 1981, which was to have far greater repercussions.

The second hunger strike was led by the IRA's Bobby Sands, who was to be the first of ten republican prisoners to die. This hunger strike had a profound impact upon Northern Ireland and attracted widespread international attention. The British again publicly took a hard line against the prisoners' demands: 'Crime is crime is crime, it is not political', Thatcher declared (*Irish Times*, 22 April 1981). The difference in 1981 was that during his fast Bobby Sands was elected to Westminster as an MP. Sinn Féin, the political wing of the IRA, had long refused to contest elections because this would be to recognise the legitimacy of British rule. When, during the hunger strike, the sitting MP for Fermanagh and South Tyrone died, a decision was made to put Sands up as a parliamentary candidate standing on an 'Anti-H Block' ticket. When Sands won the election it increased both international interest in the hunger strikes and divisions between nationalists and unionists. Sands died on 5 May 1981 and over 100,000 people attended his funeral. For unionists, the fact that over 30,000 people were willing to vote for a convicted IRA terrorist and that such a huge proportion of the nationalist community would turn out for his funeral suggested a great deal of underlying support for the IRA's violent campaign against their community. During the hunger strikes 22 members of the RUC and the UDR were killed by the IRA.

Nationalists interpreted events differently. The support for Sands at the election and the turnout at the funeral were not seen as indicating support for violence but as registering opposition to the British government's handling of the hunger strikes and treatment of the prisoners. The majority of nationalists did not support violence, but neither did they accept that IRA prisoners were 'normal' criminals, as they were fighting to achieve a united Ireland. The British had, implicitly, accepted this in the past when they gave republican prisoners special category status and tried those charged in non-jury courts. In nationalist circles it was believed that it was justifiable to vote for Sands and attend his funeral in the hope that this would increase pressure on the British and force them to settle the dispute. This distinction was probably lost on many unionists.

INLA: Irish National Liberation Army, republican paramilitary group, created 1975.

The hunger strikes continued throughout the summer of 1981, with a succession of IRA and **INLA** men joining the fast at staggered intervals, which created a series of crises as each neared their death. Sands was replaced as an MP by his electoral agent Owen Carron, who won the by-election in August, and two hunger strikers secured seats in the Dublin parliament in the Irish general election in June. The British government was concerned at the level of international attention. There were protests in Paris, New York and Milan, a minute's silence by the opposition party in the Indian parliament, the Iranian government renamed the street behind the British Embassy in Tehran after Bobby Sands and the USSR was highly critical of the government. The British were more concerned to avoid criticism from the governments of traditional allies, particularly the United States. While Irish-Americans did put pressure on the British to make concessions to end the dispute, the Reagan administration did not publicly criticise Britain. The Irish Taoiseach, Garret FitzGerald, alarmed by the impact that the dispute was having in the Republic, wrote to Reagan asking him to 'use his influence with the British Prime Minister' to persuade her to implement what he believed was a possible settlement (based on the work of the Irish Commission for Justice and Peace, which had sought to mediate in the dispute). Despite this Reagan did not get involved (O'Kane, 2007: 26).

Neither was the British government under much pressure domestically. The opposition parties at Westminster generally supported the government's stance of not making concessions to republicans. British opinion outside Northern Ireland was strongly supportive of Thatcher's approach; a poll in England and Wales after Sands' funeral showed that 89 per cent of people had no sympathy with the hunger strikers and only 4 per cent supported their demands.

Publicly the British government refused to make concessions to 'terrorist' prisoners but behind the scenes there were negotiations to resolve the strike. In a book published in 2005 one of the leaders of the IRA inside the Maze at the time, Richard O'Rawe, claimed that an offer was made via an MI6 agent, Michael Oatley, after four hunger strikers had died. The offer was accepted by the prisoners but rejected by the external leadership, perhaps, O'Rawe suggests, because they wished to prolong the strike in order to secure Carron's election, a claim that the republican leadership rejected. The hunger strike was finally called off at the end of October 1981.

At one level the hunger strikes could be seen as a 'victory' for the British government: it did not bow to republican demands and made no concessions to the prisoners during the strike. In her memoirs Thatcher claimed it 'was a significant defeat for the IRA' (1993: 393). The reality, however, was that the hunger strikes were a huge propaganda victory for the IRA and had a profound and lasting impact. After the strike ended the British brought in changes to the prison regime: the prisoners were allowed to wear their own clothes, the rules on remission and association were changed and there was a redefinition of prison work. The British government made a major mistake by not making these concessions after the 1980 strike and defusing the issue. The hunger strikes delivered a major propaganda victory to Sinn Féin, which was able to portray its struggle as a legitimate one of freedom fighters battling against British imperialist intransigence. Sinn Féin had also been launched successfully into electoral politics. At the end of October 1981 a senior republican, Danny Morrison, asked the Sinn Féin conference, 'Who here really believes we can win the war through the ballot box? But will anyone here object if, with the ballot paper in one hand and the Armalite in the other, we take power in Ireland?' (Bew and Gillespie, 1999: 160). The British now found themselves fighting on two fronts, militarily and politically, against the IRA's 'ballot box and Armalite' strategy. In the 1983 general election Sinn Féin polled 13.4 per cent of the vote against the SDLP's 17.9 per cent. In West Belfast, Gerry Adams was returned as a Sinn Féin MP but refused to take his seat at Westminster. The impact of the hunger strikes galvanised the British and Irish governments into action, resulting in the Anglo-Irish Agreement of 1985. The reaction of nationalists to the hunger strikes dismayed unionists and the polarisation of politics in Northern Ireland showed little sign of diminishing.

CONCLUSIONS

By the mid-1970s politics in Northern Ireland were at an impasse. The British government threatened and considered withdrawal from Northern Ireland. This speculation seems to have encouraged an increase in loyalist paramilitary violence as the loyalists fought for power in a post-UK future. The truce with the IRA provided the British with some respite from IRA violence and allowed them to proceed with a policy of normalisation which comprised both Ulsterisation and criminalisation. The Labour government considered its options but fell back on the continuation of direct rule. The IRA successfully resisted criminalisation during the hunger strikes and this allowed Sinn Féin a promising launch into the electoral arena. Inter-communal relations, which had been damaged by the failure of Sunningdale, were also under great strain as a result of the hunger strikes. It is hardly surprising then that attempts by the British to restore devolved government to Northern Ireland in the early 1980s, the Atkins Initiative and, in 1982, 'Rolling Devolution' – based upon structures that required cross-community support and cooperation – were unsuccessful. By the early 1980s the situation in Northern Ireland was stagnant, the two communities were divided, the violence was still pronounced, the economy weak and the political wing of the IRA was seriously challenging the constitutional SDLP for the leadership of nationalism.

5

The Anglo-Irish Agreement 1983–85

T he Anglo-Irish Agreement (AIA), which was signed on 15 November 1985, was an intergovernmental agreement that recognised the right of the Irish Republic to be consulted by the British government over the running of Northern Ireland [**Doc. 15, pp. 138–9**]. It had a significant impact on the conflict, but probably not one that those who negotiated it intended or anticipated. This chapter examines the background to the AIA, explains its content, evaluates the different explanations as to why the agreement was signed and explains the impact of the deal.

THE BACKGROUND TO THE AIA

The signing of the agreement in some respects went against what had been publicly stated by the two governments in the early 1980s. When the Irish government had claimed in 1980 that it had a right to be consulted over Northern Ireland, Margaret Thatcher rejected the claim. She told the House of Commons that 'The future of the constitutional affairs of Northern Ireland is a matter for the people of Northern Ireland, this Government and this Parliament, and no one else' (Hansard, HC Deb., 20 May 1980, vol. 985, col. 250). In 1981 Garret FitzGerald stated, 'We have always understood that the future of Northern Ireland will not be shaped by politicians or civil servants in London and Dublin aiming mirrors at Belfast and Derry. Ultimately it will be decided by Irishmen and women acting together in Ireland' (*Irish Times*, 1 July 1981). Yet these two leaders signed an agreement that gave the Irish government an institutionalised right to be consulted by the British over Northern Ireland. It was negotiated by the two governments in secret with all the leaders of Northern Ireland's political parties excluded from the process except John Hume, the SDLP leader, who was consulted by the Irish government throughout the negotiations.

The two governments had cooperated in the negotiation of the power-sharing experiment during the period 1972–74. After its collapse the prospects for reviving power-sharing even without an 'Irish dimension' were dim and the overt involvement of the Irish government in Northern politics would have been a provocation to unionists. The British government became frustrated by the lack of progress in the North and after 1980 initiated a British–Irish process that resulted in the AIA 1985.

In 1983 the Secretary of State for Northern Ireland, Jim Prior, complained about the negativity of the Ulster Unionists, who 'were making no overtures whatsoever to the SDLP', at a time when the SDLP was under pressure from the rise of Sinn Féin (Northern Ireland Committee of the Conservative Party, 10 November 1983). Frustration with this lack of progress did not mean that the British had to cooperate with the Irish government. London could have continued with direct rule without an Irish dimension. The problem with this was that it was easier for the British to manage the conflict if they had the cooperation of the Irish government to deal with the issue of security and the problem of the alienation of Northern nationalists. The Irish government sought to contain the rise of Sinn Féin and, perhaps, to put pressure on unionists to share power with nationalists.

In 1980 Thatcher launched a joint initiative with the Irish Taoiseach, Charles Haughey, leader of Fianna Fáil. Two summits were held in 1980 and the two governments agreed to establish 'joint studies to consider citizens' rights, security matters, economic cooperation and possible new institutional arrangements' (*Irish Times*, 9 December 1980). This cooperation was emphasised by the formation of an Anglo-Irish Intergovernmental Council which should have led to regular meetings at ministerial and official levels. The positive relationship between the two leaders was, however, short-lived. Thatcher felt that the Irish had 'oversold' the December 1980 summit by allowing the perception to emerge that changes to the constitutional status of Northern Ireland were under consideration (Arnold, 1993: 155). The relationship was strained further by the 1981 hunger strikes and the Irish government's opposition to Britain's action during the Falklands War in 1982. By 1983 Haughey was out of power and Garret FitzGerald, the leader of the more moderate party, Fine Gael, was returned to office in a coalition government with Labour. FitzGerald was concerned by the electoral rise of Sinn Féin and talks began that led to the 1985 Anglo-Irish Agreement.

The negotiations, which began in 1983, were led by the cabinet secretaries of the two states, Robert Armstrong for the British and Dermot Nally for the Irish. That year also saw the creation of the New Ireland Forum (**NIF**) in Dublin, which comprised all the main political parties in the Republic and the SDLP in 'consultation on the manner in which lasting peace and stability can be achieved in a New Ireland through the democratic process' (*Irish Times*, 12 March 1983). At one level the NIF did not mark a major change

NIF: New Ireland Forum, conference of the main nationalist parties in Ireland, created by the Irish government in 1983, reported in May 1984.

in the Republic's policy towards Northern Ireland (the report, published in May 1984, came out in favour of Irish unity). The NIF did, however, suggest an increasing willingness in the South to re-examine the issue and move away from primarily focusing on the question of Northern Ireland's constitutional status to examining how Northern Ireland could be stabilised (Fitzgerald, 1991; O'Kane 2007). The AIA was also primarily concerned with this objective. The original discussion in 1983 considered a much wider agreement than that which eventually emerged in 1985. The Irish pushed for shared sovereignty or joint authority over Northern Ireland in return for the removal from their constitution of the claim to Northern Ireland and a combined British–Irish police force in border areas and joint courts to try terrorist suspects. This was too ambitious for the British, who wanted to scale it down.

A key reason for a move to a more modest agreement was a result of bureaucratic conflict within the British government. The Cabinet Office and the Foreign Office favoured a far-reaching deal but the NIO, which was directly responsible for the government of Northern Ireland, scaled back the plans. Sir David Goodall, a British civil servant who carried out much of the negotiation with the Irish, noted that the NIO 'were always more cautious about what they would agree to and acted . . . as a sort of brake on the thing, because they had responsibility for actually running the Province and they, I think rightly, thought that too many bright ideas by people who weren't responsible for running it would land them in a mess which they would then have to deal with' (O'Kane, 2007: 48). Douglas Hurd, who became Secretary of State for Northern Ireland in 1984, also felt that the Foreign Office and Cabinet Office were in danger of seeking too wide an agreement that would cause problems for the unionists. He recalled that, 'The Foreign Office . . . would have gone further in meeting different Dublin points and I had often to say, "Look, this isn't going to run, it's not going to move like that, we must take into account this or that Unionist feeling"' (O'Kane, 2007: 48). The Irish were frustrated by this scaling down of the ambition of the agreement though it is doubtful whether FitzGerald's governments could have secured the necessary support in the South to pass the referendum needed to remove the constitutional claim on Northern Ireland. Also, given the angry response that greeted the eventual AIA from unionists, the reaction to one that granted Dublin joint authority over Northern Ireland would have been far more destabilising.

THE CONTENT OF THE AIA

The agreement that was signed in 1985 institutionalised the Irish dimension with the creation of an Intergovernmental Conference (**IGC**) and the assertion that Britain 'accept that the Irish Government will put forward views and

IGC: Intergovernmental conference, created under the AIA as a forum for discussions between the two governments.

proposals on matters relating to Northern Ireland' via the IGC. The new role for Dublin was limited: the British retained sovereignty and the Irish could not force them to change policy. However, the agreement stated that 'In the interest of promoting peace and stability, determined efforts shall be made through the Conference to resolve any differences.' This pledge allowed the Irish to argue that they had secured a real role in Northern Ireland or, as FitzGerald claimed in the Irish parliament, one that went 'beyond a consultative role but necessarily, because of the sovereignty issue, falling short of an executive role' (Dáil Éireann, Debates, 19 November 1985, vol. 361, cols 2562–3). The AIA created a permanent secretariat staffed by Irish and British civil servants based in Belfast to assist the IGC.

The creation of the IGC and the secretariat were the most tangible aspects of the AIA, but there were other pledges and undertakings in the document, primarily related to the security agenda. Extradition of suspected terrorists from the South to the North had long been a subject of unhappiness for the British, who felt that the record of the Irish courts in this regard was unsatisfactory (there had been a series of high profile cases in the early 1980s where the courts had refused to extradite suspects back to Northern Ireland). The Irish for their part rejected this criticism, claiming that their record on extradition was good, with 87 of 103 requests met since 1971 (*Financial Times*, 16 November 1985). Whatever the reality, the issue remained a source of friction. Under the AIA the two governments agreed to examine, 'policy aspects of extradition and extra-territorial jurisdiction as between North and South' (Art. 8). Cross-border police cooperation was also highlighted as an area to be examined by the IGC in an attempt to bring about improvements, 'in such areas as threat assessments, exchanges of information, liaison structures, technical co-operation, training of personnel and operational resources' (Art. 9).

THE OBJECTIVES OF THE AIA

There are several different explanations offered as to why the AIA was signed. These include accounts that see the AIA as being designed to increase security cooperation between London and Dublin, reduce nationalist alienation, impel the two communities to agree to share power, remove international criticism over Britain's handling of the problem (particularly from the United States) or to enable Britain to withdraw from Northern Ireland.

For Thatcher the primary consideration was the security environment and the desire to enlist the help of the Irish government in dealing with the IRA.

As she recorded in her memoirs, 'I started from the need for greater security, which was imperative. If this meant making limited political concessions to the South, much as I disliked this kind of bargaining I had to contemplate it' (Thatcher, 1993: 385). Her advisor Charles Powell underlined this, claiming 'it was security, first, second and third' (Mallie and McKittrick, 2001: 18–19, 43–5). This led to the question of what 'price' the British should pay to Dublin for increased security cooperation. Thatcher believed that the price should be minimal, but others in her government, notably Foreign Secretary Geoffrey Howe, appreciated that the Irish government could not enter into an agreement with Britain that was primarily (and certainly not exclusively) security-related. Howe noted that if Britain wanted increased security co-operation the Irish government 'had to be able to demonstrate an enhancement of their political role in the affairs of the Province' (1994: 417). David Goodall recalled that the task fell to Howe and British officials to get Thatcher to understand that it would be 'suicide for an Irish Government to enter into a security arrangement with the British Government which had no political content, which would simply make the Irish Government in the eyes of their own electorate appear to be supporting British military and security activity in Northern Ireland, without any political benefit for it' (ICBH, 1997).

Both the British and Irish governments were concerned with the rise of republicanism in the early 1980s. If Sinn Féin replaced the SDLP as the voice of nationalism in Ireland it would be harder to broker an accommodation between the unionists and nationalists in Northern Ireland and this in turn was likely to worsen the security situation. While the British government saw the threat of republicanism as largely a security problem that was best addressed by security measures, preferably with assistance from Dublin, the Irish government saw the rise of Sinn Féin as a symptom of nationalist alienation and the AIA as a chance to gain a role as protector of nationalist interests and, it was hoped, shore up support for the SDLP. The Irish hoped that their role as spokesperson for northern nationalism and their institutionalised right of consultation would demonstrate that progress could be made through non-violent means and that this would stem the surge in support for Sinn Féin. The British were less convinced that 'alienation' was applicable. Douglas Hurd does not believe that 'we ever accepted the phrase alienation because there were a lot of Catholics, a lot of nationalists, who were actually co-operating perfectly well', though he acknowledged that the British were trying to 'bring the nationalist community more into the actual daily working of the Province' (O'Kane, 2007: 59). The British were also sceptical about whether granting Dublin an increased role in Northern Ireland would reduce nationalist alienation and undermine support for Sinn Féin. But granting Dublin a consultative role in Northern Ireland became the price that London was willing to pay in order to achieve greater security cooperation from the Irish government.

It had been an objective of the British government since the abolition of Stormont in 1972 to devolve power back to Northern Ireland. Some have argued that the AIA was designed to coerce power-sharing. A major obstacle to achieving this was the refusal of unionists to agree to share power with nationalists in any deal that had an Irish dimension. The AIA institutionalised an Irish dimension, which caused fury among unionists. Under the agreement, if there was no devolved government in Northern Ireland, the Irish government would act as spokesperson for the concerns of Northern nationalists. According to the AIA, 'the Irish Government may, where the interests of the minority community are significantly or especially affected, put forward views on proposals for major legislation and on major policy issues' (Art. 5). However, the agreement also stated that the IGC could only discuss matters not devolved to a Northern Ireland government. This was seen by some as a tool to coerce unionists into agreeing to share power with nationalists. By doing so they would be able to reduce the extent of the hated Irish dimension (though not remove it entirely as the IGC would continue to exist). However, the argument that the AIA was an exercise designed to 'force' unionists into agreeing to share power in order to reduce the areas that Dublin could comment upon in the IGC is not persuasive. Key players in the British government, including Thatcher, Hurd, Howe and Goodall, did not believe it was possible to achieve power-sharing in the short term. While they would have been happy to see such an outcome, this was not the purpose of the AIA. In March 1985, eight months before the agreement was signed, Northern Ireland minister Nick Scott told Conservative backbenchers that devolved government for Northern Ireland was 'ruled out by the opposition of some parties in Northern Ireland' (Dixon, 2008a: 196). Indeed it was accepted that the anger caused by institutionalising the Irish dimension would make power-sharing harder to achieve. The primary objective for Dublin was to try to reduce nationalist alienation in Northern Ireland, not least because of the fear that continuing conflict there could undermine the stability of the South. Speaking of the Irish government's reasoning behind the AIA in 1993, FitzGerald explained the key was to create a structure that gave the South a level of influence in the North 'sufficient to engage the emotions of the nationalist community' as without this Northern nationalists would not 'settle down in a Northern Ireland which will for an indefinite future be part of the UK. And our objective has to be to get the Nationalist population to settle down to that, because there isn't any other answer, Northern Ireland is part of the UK' (ICBH, 1997). If this could be combined with devolved government in Northern Ireland, all the better, but for Dublin the main purpose of the AIA was to address nationalist alienation.

There is little doubt that the British government, and particularly the Cabinet and Foreign Office, was keen to reduce the international embarrassment that Northern Ireland could cause Britain. In this regard the AIA could serve a useful function. If London could demonstrate that it was working with Dublin to deal with the problem, this would offer some protection from international criticism, particularly in the United States. This has led some commentators to suggest that the AIA was primarily a response to international pressure. The former British Conservative politician Enoch Powell, who was an Ulster Unionist MP in 1985, went so far as to state that the AIA 'had been done because the United States insisted that it should be done' (Shepherd, 1997: 484). There is little evidence to support this argument and while the British wanted to avoid international criticism the domestic considerations offer a more convincing explanation as to why Britain signed the AIA. The British found the level of international pressure bearable and outright criticism from allies was unusual. Foreign Secretary Geoffrey Howe recalled in his memoirs that 'only rarely were we under direct pressure from the other side of the Atlantic specifically to change our policies' (1994: 43).

Some loyalists saw the AIA as a move towards British withdrawal from Northern Ireland. The DUP's deputy leader, Peter Robinson, told the House of Commons that 'the agreement is intended to trundle Northern Ireland into an all-Ireland Republic' (Kenny, 1986: 114). There is little evidence that the British government signed the AIA to force Northern Ireland out of the Union because, as in the mid-1970s, such a move was more likely to inflame than ameliorate conflict.

The AIA was primarily about improving security cooperation for the British and reducing nationalist alienation for the Irish; it was not about achieving British withdrawal for either. The AIA was carefully phrased so it did not abandon British sovereignty in Northern Ireland and it repeated the commitment to uphold the principle of consent (the assertion that the constitutional status of Northern Ireland would not be altered without the agreement of a majority of the people in Northern Ireland). If power-sharing resulted from the AIA, then this would be an unintended but favourable consequence.

REACTION TO THE AIA

The reaction to the AIA in Britain and the Republic was generally favourable. The British press was largely positive; even 'pro-unionist' newspapers like the *Daily Telegraph* were supportive, although it regarded the AIA as 'an extraordinarily dangerous document' because while the Republic could comment on issues related to Northern Ireland in the IGC, the British could not comment on events in the Republic. Nevertheless, the agreement demonstrated that both governments were equally opposed to the IRA and so it was a 'worthy objective, for which some risks are justified' (*Daily Telegraph*, 16 November 1985). Most other newspapers were more enthusiastic. Political support in parliament was also clear, with the House approving the AIA by 473 votes to 47 – an outcome that illustrated the lack of sympathy for Ulster Unionism among British MPs at Westminster. In the Republic the Irish parliament voted 88 to 75 in favour; opposition was stronger here because Fianna Fáil, the largest party in the Republic, objected to the recognition of British sovereignty in the North. Nevertheless, public support for the AIA rose from 55 to 69 per cent within three months and Fianna Fáil did not oppose the AIA when it formed the government in 1987.

In Northern Ireland the reaction was far more divided. Nationalists were generally supportive, with polls showing 72 per cent of Catholics in favour and only 12 per cent opposed (*Irish Times*, 12 February 1986). This was a welcome outcome given that the AIA was at least in part designed to deal with nationalist alienation. If the nationalist community had rejected the agreement at the outset it would have led to serious concerns over both the purpose and likely outcome of the initiative. Sinn Féin, however, publicly rejected it, arguing that it was a security-driven exercise designed to put a 'diplomatic veneer on British rule' and shore up the SDLP's support (Patterson, 1997: 198).

Although the AIA proved relatively popular in Britain, the Republic and among the majority of nationalists in the North, unionists reacted with anger. They launched a campaign against the agreement which led to a complete breakdown in relations between unionists and the British government. The British government claimed that unionists misunderstood the nature of the agreement and had nothing to fear from a document that clearly stated that the 'current status' of Northern Ireland could not be altered without the agreement of a majority of its people. Such assurances, however, offered no comfort for unionists. The majority community noted that the AIA did not define what that status was. The 1973 Sunningdale Agreement had clearly stated that 'The present status of Northern Ireland is that it is part of the United Kingdom.' But this assurance was not included in the AIA. The reason for its omission was to ensure that it would not violate the Irish constitution if challenged in the Republic's courts. Two unionist brothers, the McGimpseys, subsequently took a case to the High Court in Dublin arguing that the agreement contradicted Articles 2 and 3 of the Irish constitution (which claimed that the North was part of Ireland). Although their case was rejected the Court ruled that Articles 2 and 3 were 'a claim of legal right' over Northern Ireland and that Northern Ireland was not recognised as part of the UK. This ruling was seen by unionists as undermining claims that the AIA actually strengthened the position of unionists. Thatcher had told the House that the agreement was 'the most formal commitment to the principle of consent made by any Irish Government' (Hansard, HC Deb., 18 November 1985, vol. 87, col. 19).

Unionist objections to the agreement were not solely legalistic: they regarded it as capitulating to nationalism's agenda. Despite assurances that sovereignty had not been altered, unionists believed that undertakings to make 'determined efforts' to resolve differences and the fact that the IGC would continue to exist even if devolved government were created in Northern Ireland indicated that there had been a change in Britain's commitment to upholding the Union. The fact that unionists had been excluded from the negotiations while the Irish government had kept the SDLP informed throughout also heightened unionist suspicion that it represented something beyond what the two governments were claiming. One unionist MP declared in the House of Commons that he 'never knew what desolation felt like until I read this agreement' [**Doc. 16, p. 139**].

There was a powerful unionist reaction against the AIA. A march against the agreement in Belfast on 23 November attracted a huge turnout with estimates suggesting over 100,000 people attended (Bew and Gillespie, 1999: 194). The rally was later described by a British minister at the NIO as 'the biggest rally of the Protestant people since . . . 1912' (Needham, 1998: 76–7). A petition against the agreement in early 1986 gathered 400,000 signatures and polls suggested over 80 per cent of Protestants opposed it. But how were unionists to bring down the AIA, which differed from Sunningdale in a fundamental way: it did not require their participation. Indeed, largely as a result of the Sunningdale experience, the AIA was designed to be 'fireproofed' from unionist opposition. The key to the Sunningdale initiative was unionists and nationalists sharing power in a devolved government; thus, if unionists refused to participate or if public pressure could force their political leaders to withdraw from government, the plan would become unworkable and collapse, as happened in 1974. The AIA, however, was purely intergovernmental in focus: so long as the two governments were willing to work the new arrangements there was little opportunity to bring it down. This led to increased anger and frustration among unionists.

Unionist opposition to the agreement originally took the form of mass protest and demands that it be abandoned. When the British government refused to put the AIA to a referendum in Northern Ireland all unionist MPs resigned their seats to provoke by-elections in which the unionist anti-AIA candidates received 418,230 votes. At local government level unionist-controlled councils refused to set rates and were fined. The protests escalated with a one-day strike against the AIA on 3 March 1986, which succeeded in bringing Northern Ireland to a standstill. It also brought widespread intimidation, rioting and attacks on the RUC, with shots fired at the police on 20 occasions and 47 RUC officers injured. The UUP leader, James Molyneaux, and the DUP's Ian Paisley had sought to cooperate in their opposition to the AIA and had initially supported the strike. Molyneaux, however, was 'horrified, shocked and disgusted' by the violence that occurred on the day and announced that his party would not support any further strikes (*Irish Times*, 4 March 1986). The DUP criticised this stance, arguing it gave up a tool to protest against the agreement. The Secretary of State for Northern Ireland, Tom King, was critical of the relationship between politicians and paramilitaries in opposition to the AIA: 'The House will have seen elected Members of this House making common cause with people in paramilitary dress' (Hansard, HC Deb., 4 March 1986, vol. 93, col. 151).

Paisley and Molyneaux struggled to keep control of unionist protests. After an initial meeting with Thatcher in February 1986 to discuss the AIA, the two leaders agreed in a joint statement with the government that they would 'reflect on the various suggestions' raised at the meeting and all pledged to meet again 'shortly'. Yet, after the leaders returned to Belfast and met unionist workers and party members, they issued a statement stating they were pulling out of future talks and could find 'no comfort' from the meeting with the Prime Minister a few hours earlier (*Irish Times*, 26 February 1986). Both leaders were concerned that they would be marginalised by the anger among the unionist people if they were seen to take too accommodating a stance towards the AIA or the government. Molyneaux argued that 'the reality is that Mr Paisley and I . . . have been overtaken by the people of Northern Ireland' (*The Times*, 11 April 1986, quoted in Owen, 1994: 73). There is some debate as to whether the two leaders sought to act as a moderating force within unionism to persuade their community to channel its opposition along constitutional lines or were guilty of stirring up unionist opposition and encouraging it onto the streets, which resulted in violence (which nationalists generally believed to be the case). What is not in doubt is that the anger within the unionist community towards the AIA was genuine and widespread. Ultimately, though, the unionists were unsuccessful in their campaign to force the government to abandon it, although the strength of their protest served to warn the British and Irish governments of the consequences of taking actions that were perceived by unionists as pushing them out of the Union.

THE IMPACT OF THE AIA

The impact of the AIA is difficult to assess. The differences that existed between the two governments over the objectives of the agreement, coupled with the problems of dealing with the unionist reaction, meant that in some respects the AIA was not as successful as its architects had hoped. While both governments were concerned with the security situation in Northern Ireland, they had different prescriptions for improving it. For the British the key was tackling the threat posed by the paramilitary groups, particularly the IRA, by actions such as increased cross-border security cooperation and making the extradition process easier. To this end the British were keen for the Irish to sign up to the European Convention on the Suppression of Terrorism (ECST), which made it harder for suspects to avoid extradition by claiming their actions had been politically motivated. The Irish, however, felt that the security situation was closely linked to the issue of nationalist alienation and believed that it could be improved if the aspects of policing and the criminal justice system that were seen as problematic by the nationalist community were reformed. These included the end of army patrols that were not accompanied by police officers, the reform of the one-judge, no-jury court system used in terrorist cases in Northern Ireland (to one using three judges) and a new code of conduct for the police. While the objectives of the two states were not necessarily incompatible, the Irish were reluctant to ratify the ECST until progress had been made on the areas they identified as necessary to tackle nationalist alienation, but the British, concerned that such measures would be seen as a further concession to nationalism by unionists, would not agree to the reforms. The British government wanted to downplay the role of the AIA and the IGC in order to avoid further inflaming unionist anger. The Irish government sought to demonstrate that the new agreement could secure improvements for nationalists by constitutional methods that republicans could not provide by violent means. Little progress was made on several of the issues that had been highlighted as areas for future consideration in the AIA. The Irish did eventually ratify the ECST in 1987. This was linked to the change in mood in the Republic after the IRA bombed a Remembrance Day parade in Enniskillen in 1987, killing 11 people. As a result of these issues both governments were disappointed with aspects of the agreement. Violence actually increased in the immediate aftermath of its implementation and, not for the first time, the RUC found itself under attack not only from republicans but from loyalists as well.

Thatcher was evidently unhappy with the AIA. She recorded in her memoirs that the concessions the British had made to the Irish in the agreement 'alienated the Unionists without gaining the level of security co-operation we had a right to expect' (Thatcher, 1993: 415). This view was not universally held among the British. David Goodall claimed that security cooperation 'had significantly improved' as a result of the agreement (O'Kane, 2007: 84). Given the secrecy that surrounds this issue it is difficult to know which view is correct. Certainly the Irish rejected the charge that they did not provide adequate assistance to the British in fighting the IRA.

Although there is ambiguity about the record of the AIA in certain areas, there were some successful reforms in the immediate post-1985 period. In his memoirs Garret FitzGerald listed a string of its 'successes': the routing of contentious marches, legislation on fair employment issues, rebuilding of certain poor housing complexes in nationalist areas, establishing a Police Complaints Commission and improvements in how the RUC treated the nationalist community. According to him, its achievements have been 'under-estimated', which may be linked to the desire to avoid unnecessarily further antagonising unionists by trumpeting the advantages of the deal (FitzGerald, 1991: 573–5). The AIA also succeeded in stopping the rise of Sinn Féin in the years immediately following 1985. Sinn Féin's vote fell and the SDLP's rose in the 1986 by-elections caused by the resignation of the unionist MPs and in the 1987 general election, and in the 1989 European election the SDLP reasserted its dominance among the nationalist electorate. The agreement also went some way to constructing a new arena through which the two governments could try to deal with differences and reduce the likelihood of 'megaphone diplomacy', though public disputes between London and Dublin were far from eradicated by the AIA.

CONCLUSIONS

The various political actors in Britain and Ireland who negotiated the AIA came with different objectives. Thatcher proclaimed herself disappointed with a deal that failed to anticipate the extent of unionist alienation and deliver significant security benefits. The AIA may have delivered significant reform and reassured nationalists but there appeared to be political polarisation, and power-sharing seemed to be a more distant prospect as a result. The agreement was instrumental in creating the conditions that would enable the peace process to emerge and develop in the 1990s. The agreement forced all sides to re-examine their tactics, if not their objectives. Republicans began to question some of their long-held beliefs that unionists were merely a tool of the British or that the British would not go against the wishes of Ulster unionists. Both assumptions were harder to sustain after the AIA. Republicans were also concerned about being marginalised if the two governments improved their relationship and the SDLP's position was strengthened. Unionists were greeted with the spectre of an increasing role for the Irish government in the affairs of Northern Ireland if they did not reach some sort of accommodation with nationalism. The AIA had illustrated to unionists the limits of their ability to prevent the British government from imposing change over their heads. These changes to the political landscape in Northern Ireland were not the ones that the two governments had necessarily intended to bring about when they negotiated the agreement, but these unanticipated results were, as we shall see, important in creating the conditions under which the peace process was to emerge in the early 1990s.

6

The origins of the peace process, 1985–94

In the late 1980s the situation in Northern Ireland appeared to be one of stagnation and stand-off. The unionist protest against the AIA, which led them to withdraw from aspects of political life until the agreement was abandoned, had made wider political progress more problematic. The two governments continued to work the agreement, but London was disappointed with progress on security while Charles Haughey, the new Taoiseach, argued that it entrenched partition. Loyalist violence had increased due to fears regarding the constitutional future and the emergence of a younger, more violent, leadership at the top of the Ulster Defence Association. Republicans escalated their violent campaign. The IRA was concerned about possible marginalisation due to the AIA and a faction believed that 'one last push' would drive the British army out. No progress had been made towards devolving government although there was power-sharing on some local councils. The Assembly that had been created in 1982 as part of the Rolling Devolution plan was closed in 1986 as it had simply become a vehicle for unionists to register their anger at the AIA.

The situation was, however, more dynamic than it appeared and there was a good deal of action 'behind the scenes', as governments and parties attempted to wind down the violence and take steps towards a political settlement. By the early 1990s unionists had been persuaded to re-engage politically and they entered talks with the SDLP and British and Irish governments. The British government was also in secret talks with Sinn Féin and began to pursue a policy designed to persuade the IRA to end its violence and enter into negotiations. It also sought to make progress on a deal among the 'constitutional' parties of unionism and nationalism, while attempting to bring Sinn Féin into the political process along with the loyalist paramilitaries. The US President and constitutional Irish nationalists also worked to end the IRA's 'armed struggle' and embed the movement in constitutional politics, but they also recognised the importance of meeting loyalist fears that they were being forced out of the Union.

BRINGING THE UNIONISTS BACK IN

By the late 1980s it was evident that unionism's campaign was not going to bring down the AIA. The structures that were created in 1985 proved resilient; the unionists were hampered by the fact that their participation was not necessary for the system to function. As they came to appreciate the comparative weakness of their position, they also became concerned that their opposition could be counterproductive. Part of the reason that the British government had sought to cooperate with Dublin was due to its frustration at the perceived inflexibility of the Ulster unionists. Further non-cooperation by unionists might cause the British to seek even greater cooperation with the Republic's government and so lead to a greater role for the Irish in Northern Ireland. This was the slippery slope to a united Ireland that the unionists had longed feared. Yet unionist anger at the AIA was formidable and the extent of their resistance may have served as a warning to the two governments that a *peaceful* political settlement would require their consent. Given their position that they would not deal with the British while the agreement existed, a way needed to be found to allow them to re-engage and save face [**Doc. 17, p. 141**].

In a speech to businessmen in Bangor in January 1990, the Secretary of State for Northern Ireland, Peter Brooke, argued that there existed common ground between the parties in Northern Ireland. He pledged to operate the AIA sensitively and talked of the 'three relationships': within Northern Ireland, between the North and South of Ireland and between East and West (Ireland and Britain). The Irish government also began to suggest that it might be possible to replace the AIA through agreement between the parties. Charles Haughey told the Irish parliament that 'Nobody has ever suggested that the Anglo-Irish Agreement is there for all time. It is an international agreement between two governments and can always be substituted by agreement' (*The Times*, 22 January 1990). In March 1991 the two governments announced that there would be a ten-week gap between IGC meetings in order to allow talks among all the constitutional parties and the two governments. The Combined Loyalist Military Command (**CLMC**), an umbrella group representing loyalist paramilitaries, announced a ceasefire for the duration of the talks (*The Times*, 18 April 1991). However, the 'Brooke talks' wound up in early July having failed to move from discussing constitutional arrangements for governing Northern Ireland onto considering Strands 2

CLMC: Combined Loyalist Military Command, umbrella organisation created in 1991 to co-ordinate loyalist paramilitary groups.

and 3 (North–South and East–West relations). The process was undermined by wrangling between the parties over who should chair Strand 2 sessions and where these talks should be held. Unionists were widely blamed for the failure of the talks in 1991, being portrayed as intransigent and opposed to both power-sharing and a meaningful North–South dimension.

After the British general election of April 1992, which saw the Conservatives returned to power, a second round of talks was launched under the new Secretary of State, Sir Patrick Mayhew. These talks were more substantive than the Brooke talks and although they did not achieve agreement on new institutions or systems for government, they did demonstrate some real progress. The 'Mayhew talks' managed to progress to considering Strand 2 and all parties, including the DUP, attended the talks in London in July 1992. This was seen as a breakthrough and was the first time that all the main unionist parties had sat down with the Irish government to discuss Northern Ireland. This move was unpopular with elements of the DUP as it seemed to suggest that the party recognised that the Irish government had a legitimate right to be consulted over Northern Ireland. On 21 September, in a symbolic move, James Molyneaux led a UUP delegation to Dublin for talks on Strand 2. He was the first unionist leader to negotiate with the Irish government in Dublin for over seventy years. The DUP, however, refused to attend.

The Mayhew talks were wound up on 10 November 1992 without achieving any agreement. However, unionists were seen as having taken a more accommodating stance in their proposals for devolution of power. The unionists had entered the talks with the stated objective of getting rid of the AIA but the two governments would only consider its replacement, not its destruction. The Irish saw the AIA as an important advance and were not willing to give it up lightly. In its opening submission to the Strand 2 talks the Irish government argued the AIA was 'a formal acceptance that the Irish Government have both a concern and a role in relation to Northern Ireland. We would expect that any broader agreement, which might be reached, would incorporate these elements in full measure' (Irish Government Opening Statement, 6 July 1992). Yet the UUP had stated in its submission that 'the replacement of the neo-colonialist Anglo-Irish Agreement with a treaty which addresses the totality of relationships within our islands is absolutely crucial' (Ulster Unionist Party Submission, 7 July 1992) . The talks were not without significance: the three-strand structure would underpin the talks that would lead to the Good Friday Agreement, and they brought unionism back into the political process after its self-imposed exile. The SDLP may also have been restrained in its willingness to compromise during the Brooke–Mayhew talks because John Hume was engaged in behind-the-scenes talks with Gerry Adams and trying to get the IRA to rethink its 'armed struggle'. Meanwhile, the British government used its secret 'back channel' to keep

Sinn Féin informed of developments during the talks. It was hoped that the progress of these all-party talks could put pressure on Sinn Féin to 'come in from the cold' before a settlement was negotiated without it (Dixon, 2008a: 223–5).

RETHINKING THE ARMED STRUGGLE

There is evidence that by the mid to late 1980s sections of the republican movement were beginning to re-evaluate the armed struggle. The IRA appeared to be in a stalemate with the British security forces. Its campaign of violence, which it had prosecuted since the early 1970s, appeared no nearer to driving the British from Ireland and its electoral support had stagnated. It was still an 'effective' paramilitary organisation and carried out 'spectaculars' such as the 1984 bombing of the Conservative Cabinet at the Grand Hotel in Brighton. It also massacred seven Protestant workers at Teebane Cross and bombed Remembrance Day commemorations in Enniskillen in 1987, killing 11 and wounding over 60. The military stalemate and fear of further marginalisation appears to have provoked debate within republicanism, partly stimulated by engaging in discussions with the SDLP (1988), the Catholic Church and nationalists in the South [**Docs 18, 19, pp. 141, 141–2**]. Sinn Féin had made a major move in 1986 by ending its abstentionism and resolving to take up its seats in the Irish Dáil. In June 1992 a Sinn Féin speaker claimed at a republican commemoration that British withdrawal 'must be preceded by a sustained period of peace and will arise out of negotiations' (Patterson, 1997: 240), which was a reversal of the previous position that violence would not end until the British agreed to withdraw. In the same year Sinn Féin issued a policy document, *Towards a Lasting Peace in Ireland*, which noted Northern Ireland's economic dependence upon Britain and the possibility of a unionist backlash after a British withdrawal (Dixon, 2008a: 218). This was another departure from republican tradition, which had either ignored unionist opinion or assumed that once the 'British prop' had been removed the unionists would realise that they were Irish after all and accept the inevitability and desirability of a united Ireland.

It is difficult to ascertain how widespread or deep this apparent reconsideration within republicanism was in the late 1980s/early 1990s. It may be that such thinking was limited to just elements of the leadership. The rank and file of the IRA were less enthusiastic about rethinking fundamental principles and there was the constant concern that too rapid movement towards a more political approach and the abandonment of the armed struggle could lead to further splits within the IRA. Gerry Adams spoke in February 1992 of his fear of the 'emergence of an undisciplined, breakaway group from the IRA if a premature ceasefire is called in Northern Ireland' (*Daily Telegraph*, 24 February 1992). Such claims tended to elicit little sympathy from the unionist community, who believed that republican leaders used the threat of a split to try to secure concessions from the British government – concessions which should not be offered to 'terrorists' who were killing and maiming the people of Northern Ireland. But some in the British government accepted that republican leaders did face internal opposition. Speaking in 1995, the Chief Constable of the RUC, Sir Hugh Annesley, called the IRA ceasefire of 1994 'a very considerable achievement'. Annesley argued that 'if Adams and Co. had tried it in 1989, '90, '91, then they would have been unable to carry the leadership with them' (*The Guardian*, 6 September 1995). The secretive nature of the IRA means that it is very difficult to know exactly what discussions took place, how real the opposition within the rank and file was and to what extent such fears were exaggerated for political ends. Nonetheless the two governments, and SDLP leader John Hume, believed that overtures from the republican leadership were at least worth investigating.

TALKING TO THE ENEMY: THE BACK CHANNEL

British governments have historically taken the *public* stance that they would not negotiate with terrorists for fear of giving 'criminals' and 'psychopaths' legitimacy. *Privately*, the British government had dealings with the IRA throughout most of the conflict. The Conservative government met with representatives of the IRA in 1972, a Labour government 'engaged' with republicans during the IRA's 'ceasefire' in 1975–76 and there had been indirect contact with the organisation during the hunger strikes in 1981. Publicly, for most of period of the Troubles, attempts at resolving the conflict had been based upon the exclusion principle. Exclusion rested on the belief that the way to make progress in Northern Ireland was to try to broker an agreement between the moderate constitutional parties and to exclude from the political process those who used violence. The hope was that once agreement was achieved between the constitutional parties support for the extremes would deteriorate and their importance and impact decline. Privately, British governments had encouraged both loyalist and republican parties to become involved in the political process and there was recognition that they had the ability to disrupt negotiations among the moderate parties. The issue was not so much inclusion of paramilitary groups versus exclusion, but on what conditions they would be admitted to all-party talks. At some point during the conflict moderate Irish nationalists and unionists, British and Irish governments expressed concern that to admit the paramilitary organisations to all-party talks would give them legitimacy and undermine moderate parties and democracy. For most of the conflict, even had the British government admitted paramilitary participation, the moderate parties would have walked away. Unionist opposition to the 'betrayal' of the AIA was impressive and barely contained. Arguably, if the British government had openly negotiated with the IRA then the fears of betrayal would have been greatly enhanced, leading to further destabilisation. Britain's refusal to allow Sinn Féin (and the smaller parties associated with loyalist paramilitaries) to participate in talks was based upon its connection to violence, not its political ambitions. The British government argued that Sinn Féin excluded itself from negotiations by continuing its violence.

There is some debate as to whether it was Sinn Féin or the British government that 'blinked first' and shifted its policy in the 1980s. Sinn Féin has claimed that it entered negotiations in response to a dramatic shift in British policy. In November 1989 the Secretary of State for Northern Ireland, Peter Brooke, suggested that it was 'difficult to envisage' the military defeat of the IRA and that the British government would be 'flexible' and imaginative if the IRA stopped its violence (Irish Times, 4 November 1989). On 9 November 1990, Brooke made a famous declaration: 'The British Government has no selfish strategic interest in Northern Ireland; our role is to help, enable and encourage' [Doc. 20, pp. 142–3]. Brooke's speeches were a restatement of British policy since the early 1970s but their timing reinforced the SDLP's argument that, particularly after the AIA, the British were now 'neutral' on the constitutional position of Northern Ireland (Dixon, 2008a: 226–7).

There is evidence that a 'back channel', which involved secret, indirect contacts between the British government and the IRA, existed throughout the conflict. Peter Brooke claimed that this back channel, last used during the hunger strikes, was reactivated in 1990. The British and Sinn Féin used the back channel to build confidence and they exchanged speeches so responses could be prepared in advance. Publicly, Prime Minister John Major denied that the British government needed to talk to republicans, stating: 'If the implication of his remarks is that we should sit down with Mr. Adams and the Provisional IRA, I can say only that that would turn my stomach and those of most hon. Members; we will not do it' (in reply to question from Dennis Skinner MP, Hansard, HC Deb., 1 November 1993, vol. 231, col. 35). Several weeks later the 'back channel' was exposed in the Observer newspaper. Although strictly speaking Major did not mislead the House – he had not met republican leaders – once the contacts between the British and Sinn Féin were revealed such distinctions seemed little more than a technicality.

The British had kept contacts with republicans secret because they did not want to give the IRA legitimacy by being seen to negotiate with it, were concerned that unionists would see this as betrayal and react violently, and that British domestic opinion would not understand why their government negotiated with people who were bombing its streets and killing its civilians.

The Sinn Féin leadership was also concerned that it might be seen by its rank and file as betraying their struggle and surrendering to the British state. According to Sinn Féin's account of the back channel, the running had been made by the British, not republicans, and London had initiated contact in 1990. Indeed up to February 1993 London had sent 19 messages to republicans but had received only one reply (Mallie and McKittrick, 1996: 246). Sinn Féin's version suggested that the British were seeking to persuade republicans that there was 'no longer' any need for the armed struggle. The conclusion that could be drawn from this is that it was the situation in Northern Ireland that had altered, not Sinn Féin. This enabled Sinn Féin to portray itself as being courted by the British, who were keen to do a deal, rather than seeking the best deal it could secure due to the relative weakness of its position. While this account may have served to insulate the republican leadership from criticism from its supporters that it had 'sold out' by dealing with the British on conditions short of negotiations for British withdrawal, it also can be seen as undermining the argument that the peace process was the result of pan-nationalist pressure.

'Pan-nationalism' was a term that was used in the early 1990s to suggest that a shared interpretation of the Northern Ireland situation was emerging among Sinn Féin, the SDLP and the Irish government, and that this could potentially draw on support from the US, the EU and elements of the British Labour Party. The nationalist argument was that this pan-nationalist front forced a reluctant British government into dealing with republicans, which created the conditions for the peace process. Some accounts claim the peace process 'was spawned from within nationalism and the British government was only involved at a point which the participants of the pan-nationalist alliance deemed necessary' (O'Donnell, 2007: 102). Sinn Féin's own account tends to undermine this view because it suggests that the British played an active part in the origins of the peace process.

As well as attempts by both sides to seek to portray the contacts in a manner that presented their actions in the best possible light, there also appears to have been an element of choreography at play in relation to how the British and Sinn Féin cooperated to achieve what were perceived (or hoped) to be shared goals (Dixon, 2002). The distinction between the public rhetoric and private overtures and exchanges of correspondence is clear. While publicly taking a strong stance against Sinn Féin the British were privately offering Sinn Féin advice on how to manage public opinion and even on how it should criticise the British. London advised Sinn Féin to emphasise how the British were dragging their feet on the peace process and suggested, 'Sinn Féin should comment in a major way as possible on the PLO/Rabin deal [in the Middle East] . . . Sinn Féin should be saying "if they can come to an arrangement in Israel, why not here? We are standing at the altar, why won't you come and join us"' (Sinn Féin, 1993: 41). Republicans were assured that the government was expecting a very critical publicity offensive by Sinn Féin against it and had contingencies in place to deal with it. Such exchanges illustrated that the British were aware that Sinn Féin needed to be able to defend its position once it became known that it was dealing with the British and perhaps contemplating an end to violence. Britain had also taken steps to make sure its own position was defensible when the link was exposed.

THE DOWNING STREET DECLARATION

The British and Irish governments signed the Downing Street Declaration (DSD) on 15 December 1993. It was an attempt to persuade republicans to abandon violence. The initiative originated partly in the Hume–Adams talks and the attempt by constitutional nationalists to find a formula that would get the IRA to announce a ceasefire and enter a peace process. In October 1991 John Hume had given the Irish government a document, which had already been seen by Adams, that he believed held out the prospect of securing an IRA ceasefire. The Irish government worked on the document and passed it to the British in January 1992 (Mallie and McKittrick, 1996: 123). These early drafts of the declaration sought to deliver republican demands in order to bring them into a peace process. The British government, on the other hand, had responsibility to see that any final declaration would not unnecessarily antagonise the unionist audience. An early draft, drawn up by John Hume, Charles Haughey and Irish officials in October 1991, noted that it was the 'wish' of Britain to see the people of Ireland 'live together in unity'. A subsequent draft written by Sinn Féin in early 1992 went even further and stated 'The British government, consequently, commits itself to such unity (within a period to be agreed) and to use all its influence and energy to win consent for this policy' (Mallie and McKittrick, 1996: 373–4). Britain's position had long been that while it would accept a united Ireland if that was the wish of a majority of people in Northern Ireland, it would not state that it desired such an outcome or seek to persuade the people of Northern Ireland that they should agree to it. A successful peace process would involve both republicans and unionists negotiating a settlement, and the challenge was how to entice republicans into the process without alienating unionists.

The process of achieving a joint declaration was aided in large part by the two leaders in office at the time. Albert Reynolds, who succeeded Charles Haughey as Irish Taoiseach in February 1992, was a key advocate of the joint declaration approach. Reynolds, like John Major, was a pragmatist, unencumbered by ideological baggage and willing to take risks for peace. As Reynolds' press secretary, Sean Duignan, explained, 'Many, many people in Irish politics have strong beliefs about all this. Reynolds is just a business guy, I don't think he would have a republican bone in his body and indeed not even a nationalist bone really' (O'Kane, 2007: 102). That did not, however, mean that they would do a deal at any price. Both governments were still limited by what was acceptable to the key players in Northern Ireland and by the domestic constraints that operated within their respective states. During the negotiation of the DSD there were periods when the British came close to abandoning the initiative. The period from June to December 1993 was particularly fraught. Elements of the British government remained sceptical as to whether the IRA would abandon violence. Home Secretary Kenneth Clarke recalled that when he was informed of the plans to try to engage republicans and seek to persuade them to enter the political process, 'I was deeply suspicious . . . I found myself spelling out what seemed to me the obvious very very high risk in this and that it was not something that John [Major] should embark upon' (*Endgame in Ireland*, BBC1, 1 July 2001).

The British government was taking risks because it was conducting 'negotiations' with Sinn Féin while the IRA was still bombing and killing British citizens. Although the Joint Declaration arose out of the Hume–Adams discussions and was designed to secure an IRA ceasefire, unionists would be alienated from any process that was seen to originate with, or have input from, Sinn Féin. The British government, therefore, believed it was imperative that the declaration be viewed as an intergovernmental one. The task of distancing the intergovernmental initiative from the Hume–Adams talks was made more difficult in September 1993 when Hume linked the two by announcing that he had passed a 'Hume–Adams document' to the Irish government. This announcement caused annoyance in both London and Dublin. It is unclear that there was such a document: Sean Duignan claims that Reynolds' advisor on Northern Ireland, Martin Mansergh, 'used to say to me that Hume–Adams didn't exist. It was somewhere on the back of an envelope that Hume jotted down . . . You could never pin it down, they could never get their hands on the damn thing' (O'Kane, 2007: 107). Major was angered by Hume's announcement as it meant the 'ball was placed publicly in our court; and yet the prospect of securing Unionist agreement to anything emanating from Adams and Hume was nil' (Major, 1999: 450). As a result the British made it clear to Dublin that 'they would have no truck whatever with any document that had Gerry Adams' fingerprints on it'

(Finlay, 1998: 194). After consulting the UUP leader over the Irish government's draft of the joint declaration the British introduced their own draft, to
the consternation of Dublin. The Irish Cabinet Secretary, Dermot Nally,
expressed his anger to Albert Reynolds arguing, 'It's unforgivable . . . Who
do these people think you are – the prime minister of Tongo? They can't be
allowed to ignore months of detailed negotiation, and tell us we have to start
all over again just because they click their fingers!' (Finlay, 1998: 201). The
issue was resolved in a heated conference in Dublin on 3 December 1993
during which the two leaders met in private. Major recalled that he 'had the
frankest and fiercest exchanges that I had with any fellow leader in my six
and a half years as prime minister' (Major, 1999: 452). Reynolds put the
exchange a little more colourfully, observing, 'He chewed the bollix off me,
but I took a few lumps out of him!' (Finlay, 1998: 203). The result was that
the British allowed their draft to be quietly withdrawn, but the resulting
agreement demonstrates a considerable movement from the earlier drafts
and is a far more balanced document. The two governments made efforts to
secure unionist acquiescence by consulting unionist politicians and paramilitaries, to avoid repeating the alienation of unionism that had followed
the Anglo-Irish Agreement 1985.

The Downing Street Declaration needed to reassure republicans that a
united Ireland could be achieved by the consent of the majority of people in
Northern Ireland while reassuring unionists that they would not be forced
into a united Ireland. In order to reconcile the principles of consent and self-
determination the document stated that: 'The British Government agree that
it is for the people of the island of Ireland alone, by agreement between the
two parts respectively, to exercise their right of self-determination on the
basis of consent, freely and concurrently given, North and South, to bring
about a united Ireland, if that is their wish' (para. 4). Britain also restated that
it had 'no selfish strategic or economic interest in Northern Ireland'. On the
other key republican demand that Britain should act as persuaders for unity,
the DSD deployed subtle language. Britain's 'primary interest is to see peace,
stability and reconciliation established by agreement among all the people
who inhabit the island, and they will work together with the Irish Government to achieve such an agreement, which will embrace the totality of relationships. The role of the British Government will be to encourage, facilitate
and enable the achievement of such an agreement' (para. 4). So the British
were to be facilitators for peace and agreement rather than persuaders for
unity. The DSD also makes it clear that once violence is ended Sinn Féin can
enter the political process.

Paragraph 5 of the DSD sought to reassure unionists. The Irish government asserted that 'it would be wrong to attempt to impose a united Ireland,
in the absence of the freely given consent of a majority of the people of

Northern Ireland', undertook to examine the 'life and organization of the Irish State' for aspects that may be seen as a threat to the unionist 'way of life and ethos' (para. 6) and pledged to remove articles 2 and 3 of its constitution (the claim of jurisdiction over Northern Ireland) 'in the event of an overall settlement' (para. 7).

Albert Reynolds told the Irish parliament that the DSD 'makes clear that the British Government is in no sense an enemy to the rights of the National-ist tradition, and the Irish Government is in no sense an enemy to the rights of the Unionist tradition' (Dáil Éireann, Debates, 15 December, 1993, vol. 437, col. 742). Nationalists in Ireland, North and South, largely reacted positively to the declaration. The SDLP welcomed it and an opinion poll published on 18 December suggested that 97 per cent of southerners believed the IRA should end its violence (*The Observer*, 19 December 1993). Sinn Féin did not endorse the agreement and called for 'clarifications'. Unionists were less impressed: the UUP neither endorsed nor rejected it, but Molyneaux argued that it did not represent a sell-out of the Union. The DUP openly rejected it: the party's deputy leader, Peter Robinson, asked 'What has Ulster done wrong to have this further betrayal visited on us? It seems it is only the final act of separation for which their consent will be required' (*The Guardian*, 16 December 1993). Opinion polls suggested that the unionist community was more apprehensive about it than the UUP leadership. While 56 per cent of people in Northern Ireland were in favour of the DSD, there was a significant imbalance in support between the two communities: 87 per cent of nationalists were in favour, but only 43 per cent of unionists (*The Guardian*, 22 December 1993). The British took steps to reassure unionists and announced the creation of a Northern Ireland select committee at West-minster (a move long favoured by unionists as it brought Northern Ireland more in line with the other parts of the UK such as Wales and Scotland). The Secretary of State for Northern Ireland, Patrick Mayhew, also stated that the IRA would have to decommission its weapons before taking part in all-party talks (*The Guardian*, 17 December 1993). The decommissioning issue was to cause huge problems for the peace process over the coming years but was not a major bone of contention in 1993.

CEASEFIRE

The DSD did not result in an immediate ceasefire by the IRA. The British initially refused Sinn Féin's requests for the document to be clarified but later explained that it was not necessary to accept the declaration in order to enter the process, but that parties must 'declare and demonstrate a permanent end to violence, and to abide by the democratic process'. If this was done, the British would enter into exploratory talks with Sinn Féin within three months (*The Guardian*, 20 May 1994). Events on the ground seemed, however, to indicate that the IRA was not about to end its campaign. The IRA carried out three mortar attacks on Heathrow Airport in a week in March and continued to carry out sporadic attacks in Northern Ireland. After a special Sinn Féin conference in Letterkenny in July it appeared that republicans were not about to call a ceasefire. Adams stated that the 'declaration does not deal adequately with some of the core issues and this is crucial' (*The Times*, 25 July 1994). Patrick Mayhew, greeted the reports of the conference with 'disgust' and stated 'We are not going to wait for Sinn Féin' (*The Independent*, 26 July 1994). The political journalist Andrew Marr concluded that 'The republicans had their moment of history, and they blew it. The failure of Sinn Féin to grasp the opportunity given by the Downing Street Declaration sends the province back to the mire of murder and hopelessness' (*The Independent*, 26 July 1994).

Although the public pronouncements of Sinn Féin and the actions of the IRA may have appeared negative, behind the scenes republicans were debating a ceasefire. During the summer the movement was discussing what became known as the 'TUAS' document [**Doc. 21, pp. 144–5**]. Demonstrating that republicans could also use the tool of creative ambiguity, TUAS was an acronym that could be defined in two ways: at first it was reported that it stood for 'Totally UnArmed Strategy'; later it was suggested that it stood for 'Tactical Use of Armed Struggle' (Moloney, 2002: 423). Ambiguity was needed because the move to abandon armed struggle was unpopular with large sections of the IRA's rank and file. By one reading, TUAS could suggest that a ceasefire was likely to be only temporary – a politically expedient act to try to win concessions from the British. The alternative interpretation could be used to demonstrate to those outside republicanism that the IRA was moving to permanently abandon violence and enter a peace process. The debate within republicanism was not over the moral acceptability of the armed struggle (the movement had long viewed the use of violence to bring about a united Ireland as legitimate) but about its effectiveness. The argument being made by the leadership in 1994 was that due to the 'pan-nationalist' front republicans could gain more by pursuing peaceful methods than via the armed struggle. However, the other nationalist parties in Ireland (the SDLP and the Republic's political parties) and potentially important actors in the US, EU and Britain would not cooperate with Sinn Féin while IRA violence continued. The TUAS document claimed 'It is the first time in 25 years that all the major Irish nationalist parties are rowing in roughly the same direction. These combined circumstances are unlikely to gel again in the foreseeable future.' Despite its previous public rhetoric and action, on 31 August

1994 the IRA announced that from midnight 'there will be a complete cessation of military operations. All our units have been instructed accordingly' (English, 2003: 285).

THE INTERNATIONAL DIMENSION

The role played by the international dimension in the emergence and development of the peace process has been a subject of debate. Nationalist accounts have tended to see the role of external actors, in particular the US, as instrumental in creating the conditions for the process and driving it forward. Nationalists argue that the end of the Cold War reduced the importance of the 'special relationship' between Britain and the United States. This allowed President Clinton, elected in 1992, to exert pressure on the British government to shift its policy towards a more inclusive approach. The peace processes in South Africa and the Middle East also put pressure on the IRA to reassess its anti-imperialist struggle. The growing integration of Europe broke down distrust between the British and Irish governments and provided a model for overcoming conflict (Cox, 1997; Cox *et al.*, 2006; O'Clery, 1996). This interpretation was important because it provided nationalists in Ireland with a powerful argument to persuade republican hardliners to give up the 'armed struggle'.

Critics of the nationalist account of the international dimension claim it deliberately over-emphasises the importance of the international dimension in winning over republicans and so should not be taken so seriously. Certainly the US President played a much more active role in Northern Ireland than his predecessors, but this may have been because it was apparent that the conflict was moving towards a settlement and it would benefit him to be associated with a diplomatic success. While the British government was publicly critical and even hostile to Clinton's support for visas for members of Sinn Féin, this may be seen as part of the choreography of the peace process in which it was important to show republican hardliners that the pan-nationalist front could push the British back. There is evidence that the British were prepared to play their role in the staging of this performance (Dixon, 2006). British policy towards Northern Ireland from the mid-1970s is marked by continuity and tactical adjustment and international influence did not markedly shift British policy. Key developments in the peace process – shifts in republican thinking, contacts between the British government and Sinn Féin – pre-date the end of the Cold War. In addition, the nationalist perspective on the international dimension does not consider its adverse influence on unionists, who considered external intervention to be interference and biased towards nationalism. While the US played an important role in the peace process, it is important not to overstate that role.

CONCLUSIONS

There is a temptation with the benefit of hindsight to see the emergence of the peace process as inevitable. However, in the run up to the IRA's 1994 ceasefire there was a deterioration of the security situation and reason to believe that the conflict was about to get worse rather than better. The cease-fire did appear to reflect a re-evaluation within republicanism of the effect-iveness of the armed campaign but it was not clear to the British government or unionists whether this was a 'tactical' ceasefire to win political advantage or a 'totally unarmed' strategy to negotiate a compromise settlement. Union-ists were unsure what the ceasefire actually signified and whether the British had sold out the Union in a secret deal with the IRA. An opinion poll pub-lished on 2 September 1994 suggested that 56 per cent of people believed the ceasefire was the result of a secret deal, and only 30 per cent believed it was permanent (quoted in Bew and Gillespie, 1999: 295). This interpret-ation was partly fuelled by the euphoric scenes in republican areas when the ceasefire was announced. In this climate of suspicion and distrust it was far from clear that unionists would even sit down in negotiations with repub-licans let alone agree on a political settlement.

Plate 1 Father Edward Daly waves a blood-stained white handkerchief as he seeks help for a victim on Bloody Sunday
© Pacemaker Press International

Plate 2 Unionist jubilation at the collapse of power-sharing in 1974

© PA Photos/TopFoto

Plate 3 Ian Paisley with loyalist paramilitaries during the Ulster Workers strike in 1974

© Associated Newspapers/Solo Syndication

Plate 4 Loyalists burn an effigy of Margaret Thatcher to protest against the signing of the Anglo–Irish Agreement 1985

Plate 5 A wall mural depicting a Hunger Striker
© Tom Arne Hanslien/Alamy

Plate 6 President Bill Clinton photographed with Gerry Adams in the White House on St Patrick's Day 2000
© The White House/Getty Images

Plate 7 The son of a murdered police constable grieves at his father's funeral just two months before the IRA's ceasefire in July 1997
© Alan Lewis

Plate 8 The Belfast or Good Friday Agreement which was sent to every household in Northern Ireland

Source: Northern Ireland Office and Bagenal's Castle, Newry

Plate 9 First Minister Ian Paisley and Deputy First Minister Martin McGuinness had been enemies throughout much of the conflict since 1969, but in May 2007, they found themselves in power together and 'the chuckle brothers' appeared to enjoy their experience to the astonishment of many people in Northern Ireland
© PAUL FAITH/AFP/Getty Images

Plate 10 So-called 'Peace Walls' in Belfast continue in spite of the power-sharing agreement
© LANDOV/Press Association Images

7

From ceasefire to the Good Friday Agreement, 1994–98

The end of the IRA campaign removed one of the major hurdles to negotiating an inclusive all-party agreement among the parties in Northern Ireland, although there was concern as to whether this was a 'permanent' ceasefire or a tactical one that might be ended when it suited the IRA's purpose. The other formidable obstacle was that it was difficult to envisage an agreement that could be acceptable to all parties because their publicly stated positions were so far apart. Republicans had to be reassured that they would not be deceived by the perfidious British and could fruitfully pursue their objective of a united Ireland through politics. Unionists also needed to be reassured that they would not be manipulated out of the Union by what they saw as an untrustworthy British government. The British government had to play a dual role: to make concessions to underpin the fledgling ceasefire while acting as champion of the Union to keep unionists on board. This was a difficult role to play because concessions to republicans tended to inflame unionists while reassuring unionists antagonised republicans. The Irish government also performed a dual role, but was more concerned to play its part in the 'pan-nationalist' front. A 'senior British source' argued, 'It is the job of the British Government to push the Unionists to a line beyond which they will not go; it is the job of the Irish Government to pull the Republicans to a line beyond which they will not come. What was left in the middle, the limits of potential agreement, would be left for discussion between the parties' (*The Observer*, 5 February 1995).

REACTIONS TO THE CEASEFIRE

There was a marked difference in London and Dublin in reactions to the ceasefire. The Irish government was keen to demonstrate to republicans that the IRA ceasefire would bring immediate benefits and so Gerry Adams was publicly received in Dublin within days of the ceasefire. In November 1994 the first republican prisoners were released from jails in the Republic. The reaction of the British government to the ceasefire was more restrained. The prime minister reassured unionists by arguing that 'We need to be sure that the cessation of violence is not temporary that it is not one week or one month but permanent. Once we have that we can move forward.' When this was achieved the government would enter into talks with Sinn Féin about how to bring them 'into the democratic process'. But this could not happen 'under the possible duress of them returning to violence unless they get their own way'. (*The Times*, 1 September 1994). The DUP was even more sceptical than the UUP of the IRA's ceasefire, suggesting that it was a tactical ploy to win concessions. The British, keen to reassure unionists, announced on 16 September that any agreement resulting from talks would be subject to a referendum in Northern Ireland. On 13 October the CLMC, speaking on behalf of three loyalist paramilitary groups, the UDA, the UVF and Red Hand Commandos (**RHC**), declared their own ceasefire.

RHC: Red Hand Commandos, small loyalist paramilitary group associated with the UVF.

DECOMMISSIONING

The issue of when and how the IRA was to dispose of its weapons became highly destabilising for the peace process until the IRA prepared a 'final' act of decommissioning in July 2005. The republican version is that the decommissioning issue was not raised prior to the ceasefire and was only raised later by the British government as a barrier to stop Sinn Féin entering all-party talks. The British version is that it had long been clear that decommissioning would have to be dealt with as part of the peace process and Sinn Féin was aware of this. The problem is that the issue, like so much in the peace process, was discussed in ambiguous terms. The British and Irish governments had raised the issue of decommissioning prior to the IRA's ceasefire. The Secretary of State for Northern Ireland, Patrick Mayhew, stated the day after the DSD was signed that while the government would meet Sinn Féin once the violence ended, it would not be allowed to enter all-party talks until all its arms had been handed over (*The Guardian*, 17 December 1993). The Irish Tanaiste (Deputy Prime Minister), Dick Spring, linked decommissioning to the permanency of the ceasefire: 'Questions were raised on how to determine a permanent cessation of violence. We are talking about the handing up of arms and are insisting that it would not be simply a temporary cessation of violence to see what the political process offers' (Dáil Éireann, Debates, 15 December 1993, vol. 437, col. 77) In June 1994 (two months before the ceasefire) Spring went even further. When pressed in the

Dáil on whether it was possible for Sinn Féin to participate in all-party talks 'without clear, unequivocal and demonstrated disarmament by the IRA', Spring replied, 'It is not possible' (Dáil Éireann, Debates, 1 June 1994, vol. 443, cols 1021–3). Gerry Adams, in an interview with the *Irish News*, acknowledged that decommissioning had been raised by the British government (8 January 1994) [**Doc. 22, p. 146**]. Nonetheless, no one had made decommissioning a major issue prior to the IRA's ceasefire.

The RUC and the British army appeared to place less stress on decommissioning than their political masters. They seemed to believe that the IRA could subsequently rearm even if it had decommissioned; they focused instead on the intentions and actions of those who had the arms (*The Guardian*, 16 November 1995). Privately, senior soldiers and police officers were concerned that the increasing focus on decommissioning could be counterproductive as it might increase the pressure on the leadership and undermine discipline within the IRA (*The Economist*, 11 March 1995; *The Observer*, 1 January 1995).

So why did the British government take a comparatively hard stance on the issues of decommissioning and the permanency of the ceasefire after the August declaration? The issue of permanency was important: if the IRA declared that the violence was over for good then it could not use the threat of a return to violence as a negotiating tactic in future talks and the issue of decommissioning might be less important. Decommissioning would indicate to the British government and unionists whether the republican leadership's ceasefire was permanent and whether it would be able to deliver the republican movement to democratic politics. The negotiations on decommissioning also symbolised for unionists the British government's resolve to defend the Union. If the government reneged on its insistence that the IRA must decommission before it would be allowed into all-party talks, what faith could unionists have in guarantees regarding consent and constitutional change?

Republicans were unwilling to claim unequivocally that the violence was over because they saw this, and decommissioning, as tantamount to surrender and they were conscious of what they saw as Britain's untrustworthy behaviour during the 1975 ceasefire. A few weeks after the ceasefire was announced Adams suggested that the end of the violence was contingent on progress in the peace process: 'None of us can say two or three years up the road that if the causes of conflict aren't resolved that another IRA leadership won't come along because this has always happened' (Bew and Gillespie, 1996: 70).

There is controversy over the British stance on decommissioning. Quentin Thomas, the British civil servant who was head of the NIO at the time, suggested that once the ceasefire was declared there was a 'strange psychological flip' by Major, who wanted 'to show he was not a patsy and he couldn't be conned that easily'. While this may not have been 'wrong' Thomas argued that it was 'tactically inept' as it put pressure on the Sinn Féin leadership to confront those in the IRA who were sceptical about the peace process (O'Kane, 2007: 127). Others have argued that John Major was constrained by his dwindling majority at Westminster and problems with his back benchers but nonetheless managed to push the peace process forward (Dixon, 2008b: 251–4). Prior to the ceasefire both governments had demanded decommissioning and the British were under pressure from unionists to maintain their position. By June 1995 the Irish government recognised that the British government did not have the power to persuade unionists to engage in dialogue unless there was decommissioning (Mallie and McKittrick, 1996: 356).

There was tension between the British and Irish governments over decommissioning. After the ceasefire, the Irish government had argued that the IRA should decommission, but this position had shifted by October 1994, when it argued that decommissioning could only take place once all-party talks were underway (*Irish Times*, 22 October 1994). The British, on the other hand, wanted not only to underpin the IRA's ceasefire but to pave the way for unionists to enter all-party talks, and therefore insisted on decommissioning. In January 1995 Mayhew told an audience of sixth-formers: 'To some extent we have got to help Mr Adams carry with him the people who are reluctant to see a ceasefire, who believe they might be betrayed by the British Government. If the hard men say, "What did Gerry Adams do? We have called a ceasefire but got nothing sufficient in return", then Mr Adams will take a long walk on a short plank and be replaced by someone much harder' (*Irish Times*, 9 January 1995).

THE FRAMEWORK DOCUMENTS

In early 1994 the British and Irish governments agreed to work on another intergovernmental initiative. Progress was delayed by the fall of Albert Reynolds' government in November 1994 and its replacement by a Fine Gael/Labour coalition led by John Bruton, who had a reputation for being more sympathetic to unionists than Reynolds. The Labour leader, Dick Spring, provided some continuity by remaining as tanaiste. The new government continued negotiating with the British and the 'Framework Documents' were published on 22 February 1995. The documents were designed to be 'an illustrative draft of a possible outcome of the [peace] process' (Major, 1999: 462). There were two documents: one, drawn up by the British, dealt with new institutions that may be created within Northern Ireland; the other, an intergovernmental one, outlined possible new arrangements for North–South and East–West cooperation. The documents were designed to serve as a basis for future negotiations. Nationalists welcomed the Framework Documents and the British government had hoped that the Irish government's pledge to withdraw its constitutional claim on the North in the event of an agreement would appease unionists. The key problem for unionists lay with the proposed North–South body tasked to 'discharge or oversee delegated executive, harmonising or consultative functions'. The fear was that this body would evolve into the government of a united Ireland and this was exacerbated by paragraph 47, which stated that if a future agreement collapsed the two governments would introduce 'other arrangements' 'to ensure that the co-operation that had been developed through the North/South body be maintained'. The suspicion among unionists was that if devolved government in Northern Ireland ceased to exist the North–South bodies would become the vehicle for Irish unification.

John Major later claimed that the unionist perception of the Framework Documents as 'nationalist' was inaccurate: 'the language was more "Green" than the substance' (Major, 1999: 469). He also noted that from the 'zero-sum' perception of Northern Irish politics, 'If one side was happy I knew I had probably got it wrong' (Major, 1999: 469). The 'nationalist' tenor of the document may simply have been a miscalculation caused by the failure of the two governments to consult the unionists in the way they had consulted over the DSD. Or the two governments may have decided that it was vital to deliver a nationalist-oriented document in order to help shore up the Sinn Féin leadership and entrench the IRA ceasefire. The Framework Documents were instrumental in undermining Molyneaux's leadership of the UUP and in August 1995 he resigned. He had staked his leadership on his 'inside track' to the British government and his ability to quietly influence the Prime Minister, but he failed to get Major to drop the initiative or to persuade the NIO to allow him to see the negotiating documents (Major, 1999: 465–6).

There were other signs that unionism was unhappy with the direction of the peace process. At a by-election in June 1995 Robert McCartney of the United Kingdom Unionist Party (**UKUP**) defeated the UUP candidate on an anti-Framework Documents ticket. In July there was a confrontation between Orange marchers and nationalist residents at Drumcree in Portadown. The local UUP MP, David Trimble, negotiated the successful passage of the march through a nationalist area but was perceived to have danced a provocative, triumphalist 'jig' with Ian Paisley, much to the annoyance of nationalists. This episode bolstered Trimble's hard-line image in his successful bid for the leadership of the UUP; a victory that was not welcomed by the British and Irish governments (*The Guardian*, 9 September 1995).

UKUP: United Kingdom Unionist Party, small unionist party formed by former UUP member Robert McCartney in 1995.

DECOMMISSIONING AND THE END OF THE CEASEFIRE

The Framework Documents were supposed to sketch the basis for all-party agreement but this could only be achieved through all-party negotiations, which depended on overcoming the issue of decommissioning. The British insisted that all-party negotiations could only begin after IRA decommissioning. Sinn Féin insisted that IRA decommissioning was an unacceptable demand for surrender. On 7 March 1995, Patrick Mayhew announced in Washington three preconditions for Sinn Féin to enter all-party talks: 'a willingness in principle to disarm progressively; a common practical understanding of the modalities, that is to say, decommissioning – what it would actually entail; and in order to test the practical arrangements and to demonstrate good faith, the actual decommissioning of some arms as a tangible confidence-building measure and to signal the start of a process' (*The Guardian*, 8 March 1995). This was a softening of the British government's position, as it had previously insisted upon substantial progress on decommissioning before Sinn Féin could meet British ministers; now it was willing to meet Sinn Féin if there were a start to decommissioning. The IRA continued to oppose any decommissioning, while Irish nationalists argued that what was important was that the guns were silent.

Britain's unwillingness or inability to abandon the demands for some decommissioning prior to all-party talks was the result of several factors. Unionists argued that democracy was being corrupted if 'terrorists' were allowed to sit in negotiations with elected parties while keeping their guns under the table. They were also suspicious of the intentions of the British government and feared a 'sell out'. These unionists had some allies on the Conservative government's back benches and even some sympathy in the Cabinet, including the Home Secretary, Michael Howard (*The Independent*, 3 August 1995). The bloc of UUP MPs at Westminster, when combined with Conservative back-bench sympathy, threatened the Conservative government's slender parliamentary majority. The problem for the UUP was that if it did bring down the Conservative government it would most likely be replaced by a Labour government, with its traditional sympathies for Irish nationalism.

Remarkably, correspondence sent by Dick Spring to John Bruton indicates the Irish government's *private* understanding of the British government's dilemma.

> The essential difficulty as I see it is that the British Government, already in a vulnerable position, is afraid of movement away from its Washington tests, because there is nothing to protect its flank. On the other hand, those who believe that the British Government has the power to persuade

the Unionists to engage in dialogue in the absence of progress on decommissioning are suffering from a delusion. And our own best assessment suggests that the Sinn Féin leadership is powerless to force the issue with their hardliners, even assuming they want to.

(Quoted in Mallie and McKittrick, 1996: 356)

Nonetheless, the two governments disagreed on how much pressure could be safely exerted on the Sinn Féin leadership to decommission. The Irish government feared that too much pressure could push the IRA 'back to war' and had to be seen to be playing its role in the 'pan-nationalist front'. The British had to support unionism in public and argued that 'The Irish have buckled in the face of a Sinn Féin gun' (*Irish Times*, 5 September 1995).

The two governments announced the details of an international commission on decommissioning at 10 pm on 28 November 1995, the night before President Clinton arrived in London for his trip to Britain and Ireland. US Senator George Mitchell headed an advisory commission whose purpose was to 'provide an independent assessment of the decommissioning issue' and report to the two governments by January 1996. When the Mitchell Report was published on 24 January 1996 it did not support the British calls for prior decommissioning and claimed 'paramilitary organisations will not decommission any arms prior to all-party negotiations'. Mitchell was convinced by the Chief Constable of the RUC, Hugh Annesley, that Gerry Adams could not deliver decommissioning prior to negotiations (Mitchell, 1999: 30). The report called for parallel decommissioning and recommended that 'some decommissioning take place during the process of all-party negotiations rather than before or after'. The report also outlined what became known as the 'Mitchell Principles', a set of pledges committing parties to democracy and non-violence, which all parties had to endorse before they could enter the talks [**Doc. 23, p. 146**]. The Mitchell Commission did accept the suggestion from unionists for elections: 'If it were broadly acceptable, with an appropriate mandate, and within the three-strand structure, an elective process could contribute to the building of confidence.' When the report was published the British focused on the reference to an election and selected this as the route that would be used to allow parties into the talks. Major declared that 'such an elective process offers a viable alternative direct route to the confidence necessary to bring about all-party negotiations. In that context, it is possible to imagine decommissioning and such negotiations being taken forward in parallel' (Hansard, HC Deb., 24 January 1996, vol. 270, col. 354).

Although the unionists were pleased with the compromise of an election before parties could enter the process, republicans were furious at the move and portrayed it as another unforeseen and unjustified barrier to Sinn Féin's entry into talks, even after 16 months of IRA ceasefire. The move also antagonised the Irish government. Dick Spring argued that the 'real danger is that we will send out a message that as soon as we have got over one hurdle we have another one to cross' (*The Guardian*, 26 January 1996). At 6 pm on 9 February the IRA announced, 'with great reluctance' it was ending its ceasefire. The explosion at Canary Wharf in London an hour later killed two people, injured over 100 and caused damage totalling over £100 million (Bew and Gillespie, 1999: 321). The IRA ceasefire was over.

VIOLENCE AND RECRIMINATIONS

The end of the IRA's ceasefire was interpreted in contrasting ways by the various parties. For the British and unionists it indicated that they were correct to have been sceptical of the IRA's commitment to non-violence. The bomb indicated that the ceasefire had been 'no more than a tactic' (Major, 1999: 488) that could be abandoned when it was judged to be no longer producing the desired results. Major told the Commons a few days after the Canary Wharf explosion that 'we never lost sight that the IRA commitment had not been made for good . . . I regret to say that the events of last Friday showed that our caution about the IRA was only too justified' (quoted in Bew and Gillespie, 1999: 324). This view gained credibility when evidence emerged that the bombing had been planned for months, perhaps even before the Mitchell Commission was created (Patterson, 1997: 285). Nationalists and the Irish government, however, saw the end of the IRA ceasefire as a vindication of their warnings that republicans were being placed under too much pressure and that the failure to move to substantive talks risked the ceasefire. This was not to argue that the bombing was inevitable or justified, but that the pressures on Sinn Féin's leadership were real and had undermined those in the leadership keen to pursue the political path.

The end of the ceasefire did not end attempts at an inclusive peace process. Publicly, the two governments had to play their role as defenders of unionist and nationalist interests; privately, there is evidence that each understood the constraints that the other laboured under. On 28 February the two governments announced 'that an elective process would have to be broadly acceptable and lead immediately and without further preconditions to the convening of all-party negotiations with a comprehensive agenda'. It was also announced that all that was needed for parties with an electoral mandate to join the talks was to sign up to the Mitchell Principles and 'address' the proposals on decommissioning. This suggested that once the IRA restored its ceasefire, as long as Sinn Féin signed up to the principles, they could enter the talks process regardless of whether the IRA had begun decommissioning. This led to allegations that the IRA had successfully bombed concessions from the British government (*The Independent*, 3 March 1996).

The Forum elections, held in May 1996 as a route into the talks, were the first elections to be held in Northern Ireland since the 1994 ceasefire. Sinn Féin achieved its best result to date in a Northern Ireland election, polling 15.5 per cent of the vote (against the SDLP's 21.4 per cent). This was interpreted in different ways, but could be seen as a vote to restore the ceasefire. The UUP vote declined to 24.2 per cent from 34.5 per cent in the 1992 general election, while the DUP vote rose to 18.8 per cent from 13 per cent in 1992. This apparent shift from the UUP to the more hard-line DUP reinforced the impression of a growing unease within unionism towards the peace process and this was underscored by a major confrontation over the Drumcree march in July 1996. Nationalist opposition to the annual march along the Garvaghy Road in Portadown, by Orangemen returning from the church service at Drumcree, had intensified after what they viewed as Trimble and Paisley's triumphant jig the previous year. Orangemen argued that they were simply exercising their civil and cultural right to walk the 'Queen's highway'. The demographics of the Garvaghy Road area that the Drumcree parade passed through had altered in recent years and had become overwhelmingly nationalist, and nationalists argued that the march was intimidating and unacceptable. As well as reflecting the polarisation in Northern Ireland, the conflict at Drumcree in 1996 also contributed to it. The RUC decided to re-route the march but the Orangemen refused to comply with the order and a stand-off followed, during which there was widespread rioting across Northern Ireland; a Catholic taxi driver was killed by the UVF in nearby Lurgan. The RUC was under increasing pressure and additional troops had to be deployed to deal with the increasing violence. Believing that thousands more Orangemen were about to descend on Portadown, on 11 July, five days after the stand-off began, the RUC Chief Constable reversed his earlier decision and allowed the march down the Garvaghy Road. This led to serious and sustained rioting in republican areas. It was estimated that over 600 Protestant and Catholic families moved during the 'Siege of Drumcree', believed to be the largest such movement in 25 years. An estimated £50 million of damage was done to properties (*Irish Times*, 28 December 1996).

The Forum elections and the Drumcree confrontation in the summer of 1996 suggested that the IRA's 1994 ceasefire and the peace process had not produced 'a moderate silent majority' seeking a compromise settlement. Support for hard-line politics appeared to be rising rather than falling. Unionists demonstrated their power to bring Northern Ireland to a standstill. The IRA's Canary Wharf bomb, on the other hand, appeared to demonstrate the effectiveness of violence in securing nationalist demands.

RECONSTRUCTING THE PEACE PROCESS

The IRA, unwilling to reinstate its ceasefire in order to allow Sinn Féin to enter the talks, detonated a large bomb in the centre of Manchester just five days after the talks began. Major later wrote that the process needed an election to restart it and so the victory of Tony Blair's Labour Party on 1 May 1997 with a 177-seat majority (and the election of a new coalition led by Fianna Fáil, headed by Bertie Ahern, in the Republic a month later) offered new opportunities. Sinn Féin also fared well in the election, securing 16.1 per cent of the vote and two Westminster MPs (the SDLP secured three seats with 24.1 per cent and the UUP did well against the DUP, outpolling them 32.7 to 13.6 per cent). The 'new' Labour government did not, however, embark upon a markedly different policy than that pursued by the Major government. What Blair was able to bring was a new dynamism with his huge majority without the baggage that had weighed down the Conservatives after 18 years in power.

Tony Blair sought to restart the peace process in Northern Ireland. In a speech in Belfast he attempted to assuage unionist concerns by declaring his commitment to 'the principle of consent. And I am committed to peace . . . My agenda is not a united Ireland . . . Unionists have nothing to fear from a new Labour government. A political settlement is not a slippery slope to a united Ireland. The government will not be persuaders for unity' [**Doc. 24, pp. 147–8**]. He argued that 'none of us in this hall today, even the youngest, is likely to see Northern Ireland as anything but a part of the United Kingdom'. To appeal to nationalists, he stressed the importance of an Irish dimension and stated that 'the Joint Framework Document sets out a reasonable basis for future negotiation'. He warned Sinn Féin that it needed to move quickly to remain involved in the search for peace: 'My message to Sinn Féin is clear. The settlement train is leaving. I want you on that train. But it is leaving anyway, and I will not allow it to wait for you.' The IRA restored its ceasefire on 20 July; Sinn Féin signed the Mitchell Principles and took its seats at the all-party talks on 9 September 1997.

The entry of Sinn Féin led to the permanent withdrawal from the talks of Paisley's DUP and the smaller UKUP. On 17 September Trimble led the UUP, accompanied by the leaders of the smaller parties connected to loyalist groups, the UDP and the PUP, into the negotiations that included Sinn Féin.

THE GOOD FRIDAY AGREEMENT (GFA)

UFF: Ulster Freedom Fighters, cover name used by the UDA.

The talks that took place from September 1997 until April 1998 were not without incident. Sinn Féin and the UDP were each temporarily excluded from the process in early 1998 when the IRA and the **UFF** were linked to murders. The talks, which were chaired by Senator George Mitchell, adopted the three-strand approach that had been used during the Brooke–Mayhew talks. At times the process appeared close to collapse from disagreements over the status and powers of the North–South body and what form the new institutions in Northern Ireland should take.

The talks were timed to culminate by Easter weekend in April 1998. A draft of a proposed agreement introduced by Mitchell to the parties only a few days before the deadline outraged unionists as it proposed a wide-ranging North–South Council with over 50 areas of cross-border cooperation identified. Although this was known as the 'Mitchell document' the two governments drew it up and asked the Senator to present it as his own. The Irish government subsequently allowed the proposed North–South structures to be scaled back. The unionists made concessions on Strand 1 and agreed to allow the creation of a power-sharing executive rather than the weaker committee system that they had originally favoured. What is interesting about the negotiations is that Sinn Féin was not particularly active in the talks. It played little part in Strand 1 discussions (on the proposed institutions for the government of Northern Ireland) as it claimed that any 'partitionist' structure (i.e. one that created separate governing structures for Northern Ireland rather than uniting it with the South) was unacceptable (Hennessey, 2000: 120). However, in the early hours of Good Friday, Sinn Féin produced a list of 78 points that required clarification, which led an exasperated Tony Blair (who along with Bertie Ahern attended the final few days of the talks) to declare 'Ah for Jesus' sake . . . this is impossible' (Godson, 2004: 347). Sinn Féin was particularly concerned with issues related to prisoner releases and decommissioning. It argued that prisoners should be released as soon as possible and decommissioning should not be a barrier to the party taking seats in the new governing structures (Godson, 2004: 347–8).

The British agreed to reduce the timescale for all prisoners to be released from within three years to within two, but decommissioning was more problematic. David Trimble thought he had secured an assurance from Tony Blair two weeks before Good Friday that there would be a clear linkage between decommissioning and taking seats in government. When the final draft was presented that clear linkage was not there: it stated that the parties were committed to the decommissioning of all paramilitary organisations and would 'use any influence they may have, to achieve the decommissioning of all paramilitary arms within two years following endorsement in referendums North and South of the agreement and in the context of the implementation of the overall settlement' [**Doc. 25, pp. 148–9**]. This was ambiguous as Sinn Féin always claimed it was separate from the IRA and the text did not explicitly state that the IRA must decommission before Sinn Féin could enter government. The UUP representatives almost left the talks at that stage but were persuaded not to when Tony Blair assured them it was the government's view that the phrasing in the agreement meant 'that the process of decommissioning should begin straight away'. This may have saved the agreement and given the UUP leader the support he needed to accept the deal. The ambiguity surrounding the issue created problems in the future when it became clear how the agreement was going to be implemented. Nevertheless, Jeffrey Donaldson MP walked out of the negotiations over the failure to achieve clarity on decommissioning and he was to become a thorn in the side of the UUP leader because he represented a significant section of opinion.

The GFA had several components:

- *Northern Ireland.* Devolved government was to be returned to Northern Ireland with the creation of a 108-member Assembly sitting at Stormont and elected by proportional representation (using the single transferable vote (STV) system). The Assembly was to operate with safeguards to ensure that one community could not dominate the legislative process. Members of the Legislative Assembly (MLAs) had to designate themselves as unionist or nationalist (or 'other'). Key decisions needed to have either *parallel consent*, where a majority of both unionists and nationalists present must support a proposal, or *weighted majority* whereby 60 per cent of MLAs, including at least 40 per cent of nationalists and unionists, must be in support of a measure. There was to be a 12-member Executive drawn from the Assembly, headed by a First Minister (subsequently David Trimble of the UUP) and Deputy First Minister (Seamus Mallon of the SDLP) elected by a procedure that required cross-community support. The other ten members of the Executive (Ministers) were allocated in relation to party strength in the Assembly.
- *North–South.* A North–South Ministerial Council was to be established with a cross-border body that brought together those with executive responsibility in 12 subject areas from the Republic and Northern Ireland. This covered six areas of cooperation (Transport, Agriculture, Education, Health, Environment and Tourism) and six implementation bodies (Inland Waterways, Food Safety, Trade and Business Development, Special EU Programmes, Language, Aquacultural and Marine Matters). Decisions on the Council were to be taken by agreement on both sides, with each side being accountable to their respective parliaments.
- *East–West.* A new British-Irish Council and Intergovernmental Conference was to bring together representatives of all the assemblies in Britain and Ireland. In addition to the structures designed to reflect the three strands, the GFA also contained proposals for dealing with equality, human rights and victims issues, including the creation of a Human Rights

Commission, an Equality Commission and a Victims Commission. There would also be a wide-ranging review and reform of policing and the criminal justice system.

GETTING AGREEMENT ON THE AGREEMENT

The SDLP's Seamus Mallon called the Agreement 'Sunningdale for slow learners', pointing to the similarities between it and the failed 1973–74 agreement: power-sharing, devolved government, North–South institutions and so on. However, there were fundamental differences, not least the involvement of Sinn Féin in the negotiations. Also, the system agreed under the GFA for allocating seats in the Executive (the d'Hondt procedure) gave all parties with enough support a guarantee of seats in the cabinet, whereas in 1974 power-sharing was the result of a voluntary coalition of nationalist and unionist parties.

The Good Friday Agreement was deliberately ambiguous so that it could be interpreted in different ways by different audiences. This was thought to be necessary because of the political gap between what Sinn Féin and the UUP wanted from the negotiations, but this ambiguity became destructive over time as the implications of the deal became apparent (Dixon, 2008b; Powell, 2008). The UUP could argue that the GFA strengthened the Union: a return of devolved government in Northern Ireland, the entrenchment of consent, the removal of the Irish claim on Northern Ireland once the deal was implemented, and the establishment of the British-Irish Council. Republicans could argue that it helped hasten the reunification of Ireland through the new North–South Council, which could be portrayed as an embryonic all-Ireland government that could be extended and developed in the years to come. The treatment of nationalists in Northern Ireland would also improve as a result of guaranteed power-sharing, the equality agenda and proposed police and justice reforms. Republicans would also see the imminent release of the prisoners and their participation in government without any IRA decommissioning. The agreement was criticised by the DUP and UKUP, who argued that the UUP had sold out the Union, and by critics within the UUP, such as Jeffrey Donaldson, who believed that there were insufficient guarantees on IRA decommissioning. Dissident republicans (such as those republican groups that did not follow the Provisional IRA into the peace process, the INLA and **Continuity IRA**, and the newer **Real IRA** that emerged from a split in the IRA during the talks) argued that Sinn Féin had abandoned the fight for unity and had signed up to a

Continuity IRA (CIRA): republican paramilitary group, formed from a split in the IRA during the peace process.

Real IRA (RIRA): republican paramilitary group formed from a split within the PIRA in November 1997.

partitionist settlement (highlighting the same issues that the UUP used to sell the agreement to unionists).

The GFA had to be ratified by separate referendums in Northern Ireland and in the Republic. The governments and pro-agreement parties campaigned vigorously for a 'Yes' vote in the referendum. Opinion polls suggested that there was little problem in securing the support of a majority of nationalists for the agreement but unionists were far less supportive. The release of IRA prisoners to campaign for a 'Yes' vote highlighted the GFA's proposals to release paramilitary prisoners and this led to a dip in 'Protestant' support for a 'Yes' vote. Paul Dixon (2008b) has argued that Tony Blair deceived voters in Northern Ireland into believing that decommissioning would have to take place before paramilitary prisoners were released and before Sinn Féin could take its seats in an Executive. On the morning of the referendum Tony Blair wrote in the unionist *News Letter* and nationalist *Irish News*:

> There can be no accelerated prisoner releases unless the organizations and individuals concerned have clearly given up violence for good – and there is no amnesty in any event.
>
> Representatives of parties intimately linked to paramilitary groups can only be in a future Northern Ireland government if it is clear that there will be no more violence and the threat of violence has gone. That doesn't just mean decommissioning but all bombing, killings, beatings, and an end to targeting, recruiting, and all the structures of terrorism. . . .
>
> There can be no fudge between democracy and terror. The people of Northern Ireland will not stand for this. . . .
>
> I urge you to trust me, as your prime minister, to deliver what the agreement promises.
>
> (*Irish News*, 22 May 1998) [cf. **Doc. 25, pp. 148–9**]

The 'Yes' campaign was successful and the referendum was passed in Northern Ireland by 71.1 per cent to 28.8 per cent, with a high turnout of 81 per cent. The referendum in the Republic was passed overwhelmingly, by 94 per cent to 6 per cent but with a much lower turnout of 56 per cent. Yet the endorsement of the deal in Northern Ireland masked a real split between the two communities. Polls suggested that while a bare majority of Protestants had voted in favour, over 90 per cent of Catholics had done so (*The Independent on Sunday*, 24 May 1998; *Sunday Times*, 24 May 1998). Blair himself noted the unease within the unionist community over the agreement: 'The people of Northern Ireland have shown courage and vision. I know some have voted with deep misgivings. I accept my duty to answer those misgivings' (*The Observer*, 24 May 1998). The GFA had been endorsed and attention now turned to the difficult task of implementing the deal.

CONCLUSIONS

The signing of the GFA was a major achievement, all the more remarkable given that there did not appear to be any major moderation of party or public opinion in the run-up to it (Dixon, 2008b). The 1993 DSD and the 1995 Framework Documents had indicated on what ground a constitutional settlement could be reached, but the issues of marching, decommissioning and releasing prisoners hampered the progress of the peace process. The GFA did not represent the abandonment of traditional goals by unionists and nationalists, and disagreements continued over the long-term constitutional future. Nevertheless, the GFA did represent a significant degree of agreement on how the people of Northern Ireland could govern themselves without giving up their political aspirations. But much was left open to negotiation, most notably policing. 'Constructive ambiguity' was deliberately used in the GFA in order to allow nationalist and unionist politicians to present the deal in ways that were most attractive to their particular audiences. For republicans it was a step towards Irish unity, for unionists it strengthened the Union. This ambiguity was probably necessary in order for agreement to have been achieved on Good Friday in April 1998 – and for a 'Yes' vote in the referendum. But problems were to emerge once the agreement began to be implemented and it became clear exactly what the implications of the GFA were for the people of Northern Ireland.

8

The endgame? Implementing the agreement, 1998–2010

The Good Friday Agreement was supposed to achieve a moderate, power-sharing settlement based on the moderate parties of the UUP and SDLP. It was probably hoped that the hard-line parties would be increasingly drawn into operating the political structures set up by the agreement and that Northern Ireland would achieve a 'normalisation' of politics. Sinn Féin supported the GFA and this helped to prevent the IRA from going back to all-out war. The DUP, on the other hand, rejected the agreement outright and campaigned to bring down what they saw as the latest threat to the Union. There was much unfinished business left over from the GFA and the referendum campaign: disputes and negotiations continued over the implementation of the agreement and other issues that had not been fully tackled, such as decommissioning and the highly sensitive issue of policing. In the post-agreement period power was devolved for three substantial periods between December 1999 and October 2002 but twice faltered on the rock of decommissioning and an alleged spying campaign by republicans. Support for the moderate parties continued to decline and by 2003 it was clear that they had been overtaken in elections by their hard-line rivals. The rise of the DUP in particular, with its apparently uncompromising opposition to the GFA, threatened to end the peace process. Then, in a breathtaking reversal, the DUP entered into negotiations with Sinn Féin and in May 2007 power was once again devolved – but with the hard-line parties in control. Ian Paisley, the 'Dr No' of Ulster politics who had made his political career accusing others of selling out to nationalism, let alone republicanism, became the First Minister of Northern Ireland. The Deputy First Minister was Martin McGuinness, allegedly the former Chief of Staff of the IRA. This chapter explains how the hard-line parties came to dominate Northern Irish politics after the signing of the Good Friday Agreement.

CHANGING ATTITUDES TO THE GOOD FRIDAY AGREEMENT

Despite the euphoria that greeted the GFA and its endorsement in the referendum in Northern Ireland, there were signs that the agreement was under severe pressure from the outset. Dissident republicans launched a limited but vicious 'armed struggle' which they hoped would rally disaffected republicans to their cause, particularly those active in the IRA. On 15 August 1998 they carried out the worst single atrocity of the conflict by bombing Omagh, where they killed 29 people and injured 360. While they have since maintained a low level of violence they have failed to win significant electoral support among nationalists. In the post-agreement period the two governments had to try to assess how far Sinn Féin could move in the ongoing negotiations of the peace process without causing further significant splits in the IRA, which could lead to a more substantial republican campaign of violence.

Among unionists, there was more popular opposition to the GFA. The British Prime Minister's suspected deception during the referendum campaign suggested that the British government was, on some level, aware of the threat to Trimble's pro-agreement unionists from both within his own party and the DUP (Dixon, 2008b). Unionists became increasingly disillusioned with the peace process as fears grew that their own Prime Minister had deceived them and that IRA decommissioning would not have to take place before prisoners were released or Sinn Féin entered government.

The elections for the new Assembly on 25 June 1998 indicated the problems that the pro-agreement unionist politicians faced. The UUP's vote slumped to 21.3 per cent of the first preference vote, against the DUP's 18 per cent. For the first time the SDLP outpolled the UUP, receiving 22 per cent of first preference votes, and Sinn Féin secured an impressive 17.7 per cent. After the final results of the election (when votes were transferred under the STV system) the UUP emerged with the largest number of seats, 28. The SDLP won 24, the DUP 20, Sinn Féin 18, UKUP 5, PUP 2, the **Women's Coalition** 2 and there were three (anti-agreement) independent unionists. The UUP result was also slightly more complicated as several of its candidates were far from committed to the agreement. Pro-agreement unionists barely mustered enough support among MLAs to prevent anti-agreement unionists from deadlocking the Assembly. As well as divisions within the unionist community the other notable result of the election was the continuing advance of Sinn Féin.

Women's Coalition: Northern Ireland Women's Coalition, cross-community party formed in 1996.

Declining Protestant support for the Good Friday Agreement

In the referendum campaign only a bare majority of 'Protestants' had supported the GFA while 'Catholics' had overwhelmingly backed it. Opinion polls indicated growing unionist disillusion, as the results of a BBC *Hearts and Minds* poll in 2002 show:

If the referendum was held again today, how would you vote? (Protestant responses)

	Yes	No
1998 (May, referendum result)	55.0%	45.0%
1999 (March)	45.6%	54.4%
2000 (May)	42.8%	57.2%
2001 (September)	42.3%	57.7%
2002 (October)	32.9%	67.1%

Source: BBC *Hearts and Minds* poll, 17 October 2002.

The decline in Protestant support for the agreement reflected the increasing perception that it benefited nationalists more than unionists. In 1999, 59 per cent of Protestants believed this (46 per cent claimed they had benefited 'a lot more', 13 per cent 'a little more') and 32 per cent believed they had benefited 'equally' (only 1 per cent believed unionists had benefited more than nationalists). In contrast, 74 per cent of Catholics felt the two groups had benefited equally and only 5 per cent felt unionists had benefited more, with 11 per cent seeing nationalists as the main beneficiaries. By 2002, 67 per cent of Protestants viewed the GFA as more beneficial to nationalists (55 per cent 'a lot', 12 per cent 'a little') and only 19 per cent believed the two groups had benefited equally (with 1 per cent still believing unionists had benefited most). By then 55 per cent of Catholics still perceived the two as benefiting 'equally', 7 per cent saw unionists as benefitting more than nationalists and 19 per cent saw nationalists as the chief beneficiaries (figures from http://www.ark.ac.uk/nilt/datasets/. For more data and discussion of changing attitudes to the GFA, see Dixon, 2008a, ch. 10). Declining support from unionists was a barrier to implementing the GFA as it limited how far the UUP could go in making concessions to nationalists.

OVERCOMING THE BARRIERS TO IMPLEMENTATION

What then were the barriers that prevented implementation of the agreement and the creation of the devolved institutions? The largest barrier was the refusal of the IRA to decommission weapons, which meant that the UUP would not agree to sit in government with Sinn Féin and so the British would not devolve powers to Northern Ireland. The ambiguity in the agreement over when decommissioning should occur and whether it was linked to Sinn Féin taking seats in government and prisoner releases was important in allowing the deal to be concluded. This ambiguity continued into the referendum campaign. The side-letter that Blair had given to Trimble on the morning of Good Friday had been interpreted by the UUP leader as meaning that decommissioning had to start immediately. Blair encouraged the belief during the referendum campaign that the GFA contained a clear linkage between decommissioning and both prisoner releases and seats in an executive. Once the referendum passed, it became clear that prisoner releases were not linked to decommissioning and, in September 1998, the first loyalist and republican prisoners were released [**Doc. 25, p. 148**]. The two governments zig-zagged between republicans and unionists, first putting pressure on one group, then on the other. In January 1999 Blair argued that decommissioning was required before Sinn Féin entered government as 'people have to know if they are sitting down [in the executive] with people who have given up violence for good' (quoted in Bew and Gillespie, 1999: 389). The next month Bertie Ahern made a similar point: 'being part of a government, or part of an executive, [is not possible] without at least a commencement of decommissioning' (*Sunday Times*, 14 February 1999). Sinn Féin argued, however, that it was simply not possible to get the IRA to decommission. Martin McGuinness told *The Guardian* that he could not ask the IRA to decommission 'at this time'. 'They would chase me out of the room. I can't do it. I can't get the IRA to surrender' (5 February 1999).

The governments sought to put further pressure upon the IRA in April with the Hillsborough Declaration, which suggested that the problem was one of timing. The governments tried to soften the language regarding decommissioning by arguing it was 'not a precondition but is an obligation'. They also sought to acknowledge republicans' concerns, claiming that decommissioning would only occur 'against a background where implementation is actively moving forward'. The declaration claimed that the act of creating the institutions would provide this forward movement and so proposed that the institutions be created but power not be devolved immediately. Within a month 'a collective act of reconciliation will take place. This will see some arms put beyond use on a voluntary basis . . . Around the time of the act of reconciliation, powers will be devolved and the British–Irish agreement will enter into force' (*The Times*, 2 April 1999). While 'around the time' was vague, it was clear that there needed to be an act of decommissioning just before or at the same time as the new institutions came into force. Although the demand was dropped that complete decommissioning needed to take place before Sinn Féin entered into government, it was clear that there had to be some decommissioning. The declaration was favourably received by Trimble and the SDLP but was rejected by the IRA, reportedly because of grass-roots opposition (*The Guardian*, 14 April 1999). Sinn Féin argued that the unionists and the two governments were seeking to rewrite the GFA with their demands over decommissioning. The issue was presented as non-negotiable by McGuinness in an article entitled 'We never agreed to deliver IRA weapons', published shortly after the Hillsborough Declaration was rejected. McGuinness claimed that the decommissioning impasse had 'profound implications for the Good Friday agreement'. 'If the governments do not move away from this, and back to the letter and the spirit of the agreement, then the Good Friday agreement is dead' (*Irish News*, 19 April 1999).

The two governments, having failed to secure movement from republicans, shifted their focus to put pressure on David Trimble to accept Sinn Féin in government before the IRA decommissioned any weapons. Trimble argued that the two governments 'had been spending months trying to push Republicans . . . It hadn't succeeded. So they said, "Oh well, we can't move them, let's turn around and see if we can move the other people"' (*Sunday Telegraph*, 18 July 1999). To this end the rhetoric of the governments altered. In June Ahern argued that it was only possible to get decommissioning 'in the context of a confidence in functioning democratic institutions' (*Irish Times*, 23 June 1999). The governments then published a new blueprint, *The Way Forward*, which was presented to the parties in July 1999. The plan proposed creating the executive before decommissioning occurred, a timetable for IRA decommissioning and that the executive would be suspended if this did not occur. The British Prime Minister increased the pressure on the UUP leader: the 'alternative to this agreement is not decommissioning faster or on different terms, it is no decommissioning at all: ever'. If the UUP rejected the deal it would give 'Sinn Féin the massive propaganda victory of being able to say: we were never even given the chance to get decommissioning but excluded from the Executive. The blame would fall on unionists. It would be a tactical own goal of monumental proportions' that would 'hand the whole high ground to the anti-unionist cause' (*Sunday Times*, 4 July 1999). The UUP refused to accept the proposals on the grounds that suspending the institutions if the IRA refused to decommission penalised all parties; instead they proposed that Sinn Féin be excluded from the institutions, which would continue to function. The SDLP and Irish government were unwilling to accept this proposal.

The decommissioning issue was temporarily overcome after George Mitchell returned to conduct a three-month review from September 1999. An intense period of talks between the parties was conducted at Winfield House, the residence of the US ambassador in London. During the review a greater understanding appeared to emerge between the main parties and a carefully choreographed series of events led the parties into the power-sharing government. On 15 November Trimble announced that he was willing to sit in an executive; Sinn Féin accepted that 'decommissioning is an essential part of the process' but 'can only come about on a voluntary basis'. Three days later an IRA statement asserted it was 'committed unequivocally to the search for freedom, justice and peace in Ireland'. It also announced the appointment of 'a representative to enter into discussions with General John de Chastelain' (Head of the Independent International Commission on Decommissioning (**IICD**)) and described the GFA as 'a significant development' (*Irish Times*, 19 November 1999). Sinn Féin would now enter government *before* decommissioning occurred. Trimble announced that he had 'reluctantly accepted that it was not possible to persuade the IRA to lay down its arms prior to setting up an Executive, nor even to do so on the same day' (*The Times*, 24 November 1999). In order to gain the support of his party for what was a highly controversial move, he lodged a post-dated resignation letter with the party's president. Trimble's resignation was to be triggered if the IRA had not begun decommissioning by February 2000 and the British government refused to suspend the institutions. This was deemed necessary by Trimble as he was asking his party to endorse a move that they had previously argued was unacceptable. Not long before he had told his party, 'Read my lips. No guns, no government' (Millar, 2009: 107) [**Doc. 28, pp. 151–2**]. After his party's ruling council endorsed the deal (by 58 per cent to 42 per cent) Trimble stated that 'We've done our bit. Mr Adams, it's over to you. We've jumped, you follow.' On 2 December 1999 power was devolved to Northern Ireland, for the first time since 1974. At the same time the AIA lapsed as the new British–Irish Agreement came into force, Articles 2 and 3 of the Irish constitution were altered to remove the claim that Northern Ireland was part of the Irish state (it was replaced by an aspiration to unity based upon consent) and the new North–South bodies were created.

IICD: Independent International Commission on Decommissioning, established August 1997 to oversee decommissioning of paramilitary weapons.

POLICING

Decommissioning was not the only contentious issue that needed to be resolved in the post-agreement period. Opinion polls suggested that policing was even more contentious than the constitutional question. Northern Ireland's police force, the RUC, was overwhelmingly Protestant and viewed with suspicion by sections of the nationalist community, while it was a source of pride for unionists, who saw the police as acting professionally and paying a very high price during the conflict (over 300 members of the RUC had been killed and over 8,500 injured).The GFA pledged to bring about the 'development of a police service representative in terms of the make-up of the community as a whole' and stated that an 'independent Commission will be established to make recommendations for future policing arrangements in Northern Ireland'.

The former Northern Ireland minister and Conservative politician Chris Patten headed the Commission, which reported on 9 September 1999. The Commission's report ran to 130 pages and included 175 recommendations. It proposed a fundamental overhaul of how Northern Ireland was policed and also sought to redress the imbalance in membership of the police from the two communities by proposing that 50 per cent of future police recruits must be from the Catholic community until the imbalance was significantly reduced. The report was widely supported by nationalists, but angered unionists who regarded the proposed symbolic changes as a slur on the memory of the RUC. Patten proposed that the RUC be renamed the 'Police Service of Northern Ireland' (**PSNI**), that the existing police badge be replaced, that the Union flag no longer be flown from police stations and that steps be taken to ensure that symbols were 'free from associations with the British or Irish states'. Unionists fought a rearguard action to reverse the decisions on the badge and name but to little avail. In January 2000 the new Secretary of State for Northern Ireland, Peter Mandelson, who had replaced Mo Mowlam in October 1999, announced that virtually all the Patten proposals were to be implemented.

PSNI: Police Service of Northern Ireland, replaced the RUC in November 2001.

The dispute continued and in March 2000 the UUC voted to make involvement in devolved government dependent upon the RUC name being retained. But the unionist leader, according to his biographer, was not prepared to allow this dispute to prevent the return of accountable government (Godson, 2004: 490–93). 'Pan-nationalism' rowed in behind the Patten proposals; Irish nationalists, the Irish government as well as the US House of Representatives and US Vice President (and presidential candidate) Al Gore demanded the full implementation of the Patten Report. The prospects of pro-agreement unionism were damaged both by the Patten Report and by Trimble's climbdown on his 'no guns, no government' slogan and entry into the power-sharing Executive in December 1999.

GUNS AND GOVERNMENT

The IRA had not promised to decommission after the devolution of power on 2 December 1999 but there was an understanding that it would try. On 31 January 2000 the IICD reported that it 'had received no information from the IRA as to when decommissioning will start'. On 11 February 2000 the Secretary of State suspended devolution in order to prevent Trimble's resignation. Irish nationalists and the Irish government opposed suspension, claiming that it broke the terms of the GFA, even though it appeared to be the only way of saving Trimble's leadership.

After further negotiations devolution was restored in May 2000. On 6 May the IRA issued a statement that committed it to decommissioning: 'the IRA leadership will initiate a process that will completely and verifiably put IRA arms beyond use'. It also announced 'a confidence-building measure to confirm that our weapons remain secure. The contents of a number of our arms dumps will be inspected by agreed third parties who will report that they have done so to the Independent International Commission on Decommissioning. The dumps will be re-inspected regularly to ensure that the weapons have remained silent.'

David Trimble secured agreement that the name of the RUC would be included in the 'title' deeds of the PSNI. In return for the IRA's moves the British promised to further demilitarise the North. The UUP leader secured a UUC vote of 53 per cent to 47 per cent in favour of a return to government. By May 2001, however, the IRA had failed to decommission any weapons and Trimble announced that he would resign as First Minister on 1 July if there was no decommissioning by then. This hardline stance may have been designed to shore up the UUP's support in the forthcoming Westminster general election in June 2001. This election clearly illustrated the problems for Trimble and the risks that his strategy of entering government without IRA decommissioning posed for his party. The UUP lost two seats to Sinn Féin and three to the DUP. The UUP's share of the vote dropped from 32.7 per cent in 1997 to 26.8 per cent in 2001, while the DUP's rose from 13.6 per cent to 22.5 per cent. A vote for the UUP was not necessarily a vote for the GFA and the peace process, as anti-agreement voters could vote for anti-agreement UUP candidates. The deteriorating support for the GFA among unionists was, therefore, disguised by these results. Sinn Féin's electoral advance continued and it outpolled the SDLP, becoming for the first time the largest nationalist party in Northern Ireland.

The discontent in the loyalist community contributed to a feud between the pro-agreement UVF, which had two seats in the Assembly, and the UDA (and its associated paramilitary wing the UFF) which was not represented at Stormont. Loyalist paramilitary shootings rose from 33 in 1997/98 to 124 in 2001/02 and loyalists accounted for more assaults than republicans did every year after the GFA was signed. On 10 July 2001 the UFF/UDA announced it was withdrawing its support for the GFA and by October the UFF and smaller **LVF** were no longer considered to be on ceasefire.

LVF: Loyalist Volunteer Force, loyalist paramilitary group formed after a split within the UVF in 1996.

The dispute over the Holy Cross Catholic Girls' primary school in North Belfast between June and November 2001 appeared to symbolise deteriorating inter-communal relations. The school, which was located in what had become a loyalist area, became the focal point for a dispute between local residents. The original dispute, which centred on the display of loyalist flags, soon escalated into an ugly stand-off between the nationalist and Protestant residents. Loyalists picketed the school, while children and mothers had to run the gauntlet of an angry mob and were subjected to missiles and, on occasion, blast-bombs on the way to school – imagery that did little to win support for unionists at home or abroad.

By 1 July 2001, the IRA had not decommissioned and David Trimble resigned as First Minister. The two governments tried to relaunch the peace process with a 'final', 'non-negotiable' plan, which was published in August 2001 after intense all-party talks were held at Weston Park in mid-July. The proposals sought to appeal to republicans by promising demilitarisation, new police legislation to reflect more fully the Patten Report, an international judge to investigate controversial killings, the demolition of British security bases and an undertaking not to pursue on-the-runs (people wanted for offences committed before the IRA called its ceasefire). The proposals argued that decommissioning was 'indispensable' (BBC News Online, 2 August 2001; *The Guardian*, 2 August 2001). After the plan had been published the IICD announced it had received a new proposal from the IRA. Its report (echoing the phrase that the IRA had originally used the year before) stated that 'Based on our discussions with the IRA representative, we believe that this proposal initiates a process that will put IRA arms completely and verifiably beyond use' (BBC News online, 6 August 2001). But the move was not enough to persuade Trimble to return to government and Mandelson later argued that the government's plan 'was basically about conceding and capitulating in a whole number of different ways to republican demands . . . the Sinn Féin shopping list. It was a disaster because it was too much for them' (*The Guardian*, 14 March 2007).

The IRA carried out its first act of decommissioning on 23 October 2001, at a time of increased pressure on republicans. The attacks on the Twin Towers and Pentagon in the US on 11 September had further delegitimised the use of terrorism. In August 2001 three suspected IRA men had been arrested in Colombia, charged with training FARC guerrillas there. This caused anger among Americans who saw FARC as a hostile terrorist organisation second only to Al Qaeda. Gerry Adams was reportedly told by President Bush's Northern Ireland advisor, Richard Haass, in September that 'If any American, service personnel or civilian, is killed in Colombia by the technology the IRA supplied then you can fuck off' (*The Observer*, 28 October 2001). This increased pressure from the US was not the only reason for decommissioning but it may have speeded up the process (*Sunday Tribune*, 28 October 2001).

The IRA's act of decommissioning did not end the controversy over the destruction of weapons as it was not clear that it represented a substantial number of arms. 'Protestants' were also disillusioned by the deceptions that had been perpetrated to drive the peace process forward; according to one opinion poll only 29 per cent of 'Protestants' believed the head of the Independent International Commission on Decommissioning when he stated that a significant act of decommissioning had taken place. Since the GFA the British government, in order to prevent Sinn Féin from being expelled from the political process and to contain the threat from republican dissidents, had turned a blind eye to such IRA activities as so-called 'punishment' beatings and murder. The Labour government acknowledged that the IRA was involved in violent activities but, Tony Blair argued, if the government declared the IRA's ceasefire to be over and suspended the release of prisoners the consequences for the GFA would be 'huge'; this was 'an imperfect peace. However, it is better than no process and no peace at all' (Hansard, HC Deb., 27 January 1999, vol. 324, col. 335). In 1998/99 republican paramilitary groups (not exclusively IRA) inflicted 33 casualties by shootings and 60 through assault; in 2001/02 the figures were 66 shootings and 36 assaults (PSNI, 2006). The British government, in spite of its assurances during the referendum campaign, chose to ignore these activities in the belief that this would keep the peace process moving forward (Powell, 2008: 200–201, 204–5, 253).

The IRA's first act of decommissioning allowed the UUP to return to government. The IRA carried out a second act of decommissioning in April 2002 and Sinn Féin performed very well in the Republic's general election the following month, winning five seats (a gain of four). This more optimistic phase of the peace process was, however, brought to an end by concerns over the apparent continued involvement by republicans in spying and targeting. The IRA was implicated in a break-in at the Special Branch office at Castlereagh police station in March 2002 and on 4 October the PSNI made a high-profile raid on Sinn Féin's offices at Stormont related to allegations that republicans were operating a 'spy-ring'. The head of Sinn Féin's Assembly administration, Denis Donaldson, was arrested. As a result of the raid both the DUP and UUP ministers threatened to resign unless Sinn Féin was excluded from government (the UUP had announced a month earlier that its members would resign in January if the IRA failed to demonstrate it had left violence behind for good). On 14 October the British government suspended the Assembly. The saga had a somewhat bizarre epilogue. In December 2005 it was announced that the prosecutions against Donaldson and two other Sinn Féin members were to be dropped as they were 'no longer in the public interest'. A week later Donaldson was exposed as being a British agent for over 20 years; he was found shot dead in his cottage in Donegal in April 2006. Republicans claimed that 'Stormontgate' was an attempt by the British security services to destabilise the peace process, while unionists saw the failure of republicans to be prosecuted as concessions to keep Sinn Féin in the peace process.

The British and Irish governments now called for clear choices to be made between violence and democracy. In his 'Belfast Harbour' speech on 17 October 2002 Blair argued that rather than 'constructive ambiguity' the peace process now needed clear 'acts of completion' from the IRA [**Doc. 29, pp. 152–3**]. The British government demanded the transparent decommissioning of IRA weapons, a statement from the IRA that it would disband and an end to paramilitary activity. Subsequent attempts to restore devolved government under the leadership of David Trimble failed. Assembly elections were due and the British government wanted to hold these at a time that would improve the UUP leader's chances of retaining his leadership of unionism: probably after a major and transparent act of IRA decommissioning and the restoration of devolution. The election due in May 2003 was postponed. In October 2003 there was an attempt to choreograph a number of moves by the UUP and Sinn Féin that would culminate in a major act of IRA decommissioning and the restoration of devolution. The choreography broke down because David Trimble claimed the statement from the IICD did not go into enough detail about exactly what the IRA had decommissioned. The scheduled election went ahead on 26 November 2003 and the long-expected triumph of the hard-line Sinn Féin and DUP was the outcome. The DUP's vote rose by 7.5 per cent to 25.6 per cent and it secured 30 seats (ten more than in 1998); the UUP vote increased slightly and it elected 27 MLAs. The situation for the UUP deteriorated when three of the party's MLAs, including the long-time critic of Trimble's approach to the peace process and fellow MP Jeffrey Donaldson, left the party and joined the DUP (meaning that Paisley's party had a 33 to 24 seat advantage over Trimble's UUP). Sinn Féin continued its electoral success and asserted its dominance over the SDLP by polling 23.5 per cent against the SDLP's 17 per cent and achieved 24 MLAs to the SDLP's 18.

The 2003 election clearly illustrated the diminishing support among unionists for both the GFA and Trimble's handling of the peace process. Unionists felt they had been deceived over the implications of the GFA in the referendum campaign and led to believe that IRA decommissioning would take place before either paramilitary prisoners were released or Sinn Féin entered an executive. In addition, the Patten Report on policing dealt a further blow to pro-agreement unionism. 'Protestants' perceived that nationalists were benefiting from the GFA more than unionists. The DUP exploited these developments, accusing Trimble of being a delivery boy to the IRA and undermining the Union. This appeal was increasingly attractive to unionists. The decline of the UUP was further evident at the 2005 British general election when it only won a single seat at Westminster. Trimble resigned the leadership after losing his own seat and was succeeded by Sir Reg Empey. One analyst of Trimble's strategy has argued that from the outset of the peace process it was based on his desire 'to end what he saw as the dangerous isolation of unionism, and to secure an agreement that would settle and secure Northern Ireland's place in the United Kingdom' (Millar, 2009: 111). This explains why Trimble was willing to take so many risks to try to achieve devolved government. His problem, and ultimately his party's, was that this strategy was dependent upon the actions of others over whom he had no control. With the IRA's continued failure to decommission, the refusal of the SDLP and Irish government to agree to exclude Sinn Féin, and the British failure to insist there was a link between guns and government, Trimble's position was increasingly exposed to criticisms from more hard-line unionist parties.

The nationalist community was rewarding Sinn Féin and transferring its allegiance to it from the traditionally moderate SDLP. This was not necessarily a move away from moderation: a case can be made that the change in electoral allegiance was the result of Sinn Féin's move towards the moderate ground occupied by the SDLP. On the other hand, if nationalists had wanted to signal their impatience with the continuing existence of the IRA and its activities they could have done this by voting for the SDLP. Whatever the reasons for the advance of Sinn Féin and the decline of the UUP, if devolved government was to be restored after November 2003 a deal would have to be done between Sinn Féin and Paisley's DUP – a deal that Tony Blair had called 'pie in the sky' just six months earlier.

REACHING THE 'PIE IN THE SKY': THE DUP–SINN FÉIN DEAL

The omens for a deal between the DUP and Sinn Féin in the immediate aftermath of the 2003 Assembly elections were not good [**Doc. 30, p. 153**]. The DUP MLA, Ian Paisley Jr, stated that 'It's dead in the water. The Agreement is over – that was the message of this election' (*Independent on Sunday*, 30 November 2003). However, the DUP's position regarding both the agreement and devolved government that included Sinn Féin was more nuanced than its public statements suggested. While the DUP opposed the GFA in the referendum campaign it had been careful to leave open the possibility that it would take up its ministerial posts when power was devolved. Nonetheless, it was a surprise to many when, in December 1999, Peter Robinson (regional development) and Nigel Dodds (social development) became 'ministers in opposition', taking up their ministerial portfolios but refusing to sit around the cabinet table. The DUP's tactical approach to the agreement provoked some disquiet. In January 2000, loyalists in Portavogie spontaneously expressed their outrage at Paisley, who had brought the Agricultural Committee, including its Sinn Féin members, to their town. Subsequently, a 'Policy Review' was established by the DUP leadership in part to explain its approach to the agreement to its restless grass roots. Even before the 2003 Assembly Elections there were reports that the Irish government in particular, but also elements in the British government and Bush administration, had decided that Trimble's position was not 'saveable' and that a deal should be done between the DUP and Sinn Féin (*Irish Times*, 27 September 2000; see also Paul Bew's articles in the *Daily Telegraph*, 22 April 2003 and *The Times*, 26 October 2003). Blair appears to have believed that there was little prospect of an alternative deal between the DUP and Sinn Féin and had placed his faith in the UUP (Campbell, 2007; Powell, 2008) [**Doc. 30, p. 153**].

It was only after the electoral triumph of the DUP that the British government decided that it was 'not going to make Northern Ireland ungovernable by provoking the unionists too far' (Powell, 2008: 254). This seems to have been the point at which it decided to put serious pressure on republicans and insist that they could not engage in both democratic politics and paramilitarism (Powell, 2008: 264). The key here 'was to get the DUP on board, just as in earlier stages of the talks the key aim had been to get the Republicans on board' (Powell, 2008: 287). After the election the government launched a series of talks with the DUP and Sinn Féin to persuade the unionists to be 'suitably pragmatic' and to convince republicans of the necessity for 'acts of completion'. Progress seems to have been made in September 2004 at talks at Leeds Castle in Kent. The DUP demanded photographic evidence of any IRA decommissioning, which republicans saw as an attempt to humiliate them. This perception was perhaps underlined by Paisley's assertion that the IRA needed to wear 'sackcloth and ashes' and that those who had 'sinned in public need to repent in public'. Any hope that a deal was about to be reached was ended by the Northern Bank robbery in Belfast on 20 December 2004 when the IRA was linked to the theft of £26.5 million. A month later members of the IRA were also implicated in the gruesome murder of Robert McCartney after a row in a pub in Belfast. The belief that the IRA used its influence to prevent those responsible being apprehended and removed forensic evidence from the scene damaged the chances of a DUP–Sinn Féin deal. The issue was very damaging for republicans as McCartney's family were Sinn Féin supporters from the Nationalist Short Strand. McCartney's sisters and partner waged a high-profile campaign for justice which increased pressure on Sinn Féin. In a clear snub to Sinn Féin, no members of the organisation were invited to the White House on St Patrick's Day in 2005 but McCartney's family had a brief meeting with President Bush.

In the run-up to the 2005 Westminster general election the DUP appeared to harden its stance, asserting that it would 'never enter any government with IRA/Sinn Féin'. Paisley stated afterwards that the GFA had been buried and that his party would 'not be talking to the IRA now, tomorrow or ever' (*Irish Independent*, 7 May 2005; BBC News Online, 11 May 2005). The DUP saw its vote increase to 34 per cent and nine of its candidates were returned as MPs.

In a surprise move on 28 July 2005 the IRA announced that its 'armed campaign' was over and that it would undertake a final act of decommissioning. According to its statement the IRA had 'formally ordered an end to the armed campaign . . . All IRA units have been ordered to dump arms. All Volunteers have been instructed to assist the development of purely political and democratic programmes through exclusively peaceful means. Volunteers must not engage in any other activities whatsoever' (*The Independent*, 29 July 2005). A month later the IICD confirmed that 'the IRA has met its commitment to put all its arms beyond use'. While there was no photographic proof, the act was witnessed by two clergymen, one Catholic and one Protestant.

The British now sought to put pressure on unionists to reach agreement on power-sharing with Sinn Féin. The new Secretary of State for Northern Ireland, Peter Hain, announced that if the parties did not agree to restore devolved government by 25 November 2006, Britain would introduce 'Plan B'. This threatened the DUP with the extension of British–Irish cooperation towards joint authority. The Labour government also threatened to end academic selection for secondary schools, to introduce water charges, to undertake a radical shake-up of local government, to stop all MLA salaries and bring in a major increase in rates. Hain made it clear that this threat was designed to force the parties to agree on devolution. 'If locally elected politicians don't like all this, the solution lies in their hands: [take] their places at Stormont and, for the first time in over three years, [earn] their salaries by exercising self-government' (*The Guardian*, 6 April 2006). The government had a history of setting 'final' deadlines during the peace process that were subsequently abandoned, but Hain stressed that this time was different. He told the House that 'if anyone thinks that the Government are going to blink, come midnight on 24 November, they could not be more wrong . . . All the parties need to understand that, if midnight on 24 November comes and goes and there is no restoration of the Assembly, the salaries and allowances will stop and the curtain will come down' (Hansard, HC Deb., 26 April 2006, vol. 445, col. 560). Blair insisted that 'This is the last chance for this generation to make the process work' (*The Guardian*, 27 June 2006). As late as July 2006, Ian Paisley announced that no unionist would share power with Sinn Féin [**Doc. 31, p. 153**].

After a series of talks between the parties a breakthrough appeared to have been made at St Andrews in Scotland. The St Andrews Agreement was announced after three days of all-party talks on 13 October 2006. The proposals introduced some relatively minor changes to what had been created under the GFA. Notably, there was a new pledge of office for ministers, which included an oath to support the police, something that Sinn Féin had not agreed to previously. The British government agreed to give up its power to suspend devolution. The agreement was drawn up by the governments and neither the DUP nor Sinn Féin publicly endorsed it (the two parties had not negotiated face-to-face at St Andrews). However, on 24 November Gerry Adams indicated that Martin McGuinness would be the party's nomination for the post of Deputy First Minister and the speaker of the Assembly claimed that Paisley had nominated himself as First Minister, though it was not clear that he had. In January 2007 a special Sinn Féin *ard fheis* (conference) overwhelmingly approved a motion endorsing the PSNI and in support of the rule of law. The DUP did not commit itself to entering into government with Sinn Féin before the Assembly election held on 7 March 2007. The outcome of the elections cemented the dominance of the DUP and Sinn Féin, which received 36 and 28 seats respectively (the UUP achieved 18 seats, the SDLP 16). On 26 March Paisley and Adams met and announced they had agreed to form a power-sharing government. Devolution was restored on 8 May 2007 when Ian Paisley and Martin McGuinness were sworn in as First and Deputy First Ministers. The fantasy had become reality.

CONCLUSION: EXPLAINING THE TRIUMPH OF THE EXTREMES

Why did Sinn Féin and the DUP agree to share power in May 2007? For the DUP, securing Sinn Féin's endorsement of the police was seen as a vital step that went some way to fire-proofing the party against accusations that it was in power with unreconstructed terrorists. The party could also claim that the changes brought in after St Andrews altered the situation and represented a better deal for unionism. However, the significance of these changes, and to what extent St Andrews marked a radical departure from the GFA, are open to debate. A poll in November 2006 indicated that only 42 per cent of DUP supporters favoured the St Andrews Agreement, with 32 per cent against and 22 per cent undecided (BBC *Hearts and Minds* poll, November 2006). Paisley claimed that the threat of Plan B meant he had to do the deal in the interests of the people of Northern Ireland. According to Paisley, 'We were told if we didn't do this then it was going to be curtains for our country . . . How would I have faced my people if I had allowed this country to have the union destroyed and the setting up of a joint government by the south of Ireland?' (BBC News Online, 4 April 2007).

Sinn Féin's decision to enter into a 'partitionist' devolved government was taken in 1998. Although in the early post-GFA period McGuinness had strongly indicated that Sinn Féin would prefer to deal with Trimble than those perceived as more hard-line unionists – McGuinness had argued 'only a lunatic would want to deal with Jeffrey Donaldson' (*The Guardian*, 5 February 1999) – Sinn Féin had not been willing or able to take the steps that might have helped shore up Trimble's support. While polls showed that nationalists favoured power-sharing with the UUP rather than the DUP, by 2003 it was clear that any future deal had to be with the DUP.

9

Conclusion: the peace process and the future of Northern Ireland

The history of the Northern Ireland conflict since 1969, and indeed before, continues to be highly controversial. Nationalists continue to aspire to a united Ireland and republicans argue that substantial progress is being made towards this goal. The Democratic Unionist Party, by contrast, argues that the republicans have been effectively defeated and the Union is secure. The ultimate goal of unionist and nationalist politicians, therefore, has not substantially changed because of the peace process. The transformation has come in the tactics by which nationalists and unionists pursue these objectives. The overwhelming majority of republicans have given up the 'armed struggle' to pursue Irish unity by peaceful and democratic means. The DUP has accepted power-sharing and an Irish dimension as a means of securing unionists a share of power and consolidating the Union. Loyalist paramilitaries are not completely inactive but much progress has been made towards this end.

Different interpretations of the recent peace process lead to different conclusions about the future of Northern Ireland and the prospects for peace. Among those who support the peace process and the GFA, we can simplify the differences into a debate between two perspectives – the *enthusiasts* and the *sceptics* – in order to understand the implication of interpretations of the peace process for the future of Northern Ireland. The enthusiasts are the British and Irish governments, Sinn Féin and the DUP, who champion the outcome of the period since 1998. The sceptics include the more moderate parties, the UUP and SDLP, who lost out electorally in the post-GFA period.

THE ENTHUSIASTS

The enthusiasts argue, with the benefit of hindsight, that the handling of the peace process was ultimately successful and that the peace process can serve as a model of resolution for other conflicts around the world. The governments and parties that achieved the St Andrews Agreement of 2007 are the greatest exponents and enthusiasts of the Northern Ireland model. Tony Blair draws on his Northern Ireland experience in his current involvement in diplomacy to end the conflict in the Middle East. The Irish government has set up a Conflict Resolution Unit within its Department of Foreign Affairs to share some of the lessons of the Irish conflict. Prominent politicians from the DUP and Sinn Féin have been involved in advising parties to conflicts in Iraq and Sri Lanka. These political actors have successfully negotiated the current power-sharing arrangements and may seek to benefit their parties, governments and their own reputations by association with this success. Among the enthusiasts there are different, and often competing, narratives about the conflict in Northern Ireland and the process of its resolution.

The dominant narrative among enthusiasts, certainly internationally, is that of the Labour government championed by ex-ministers and advisers who worked on the peace process (Powell, 2008). The two governments have been strong advocates of the GFA/St Andrews settlement as the best that was available, a view shared to a considerable extent by the Irish government. According to this account the key to the peace process was the British government's decision to reverse its policy and 'talk to terrorists' in the IRA. This represented a major shift in British government thinking from an exclusive process, which concentrated on building agreement among the moderate parties, to an inclusive process, which brought in republican and loyalist paramilitaries. This policy did not originate with the Labour government; the opening stages of the peace process were conducted by the Conservatives. But, given that it was under Labour that the GFA was signed, much of the debate has focused on the Labour government and its actions during the peace process. As Blair's Chief of Staff, Jonathan Powell, has argued, 'It is very difficult for governments in democracies to be seen to be talking to terrorists who are killing their people unjustifiably. But it is precisely your enemies, rather than your friends that you should talk to if you want to resolve a conflict' (Powell, 2008: 313). As well as the risks taken in talking to terrorists, this narrative highlights the intensity of the government's engagement with the issue and the pragmatic approach to the problem as key to the successful negotiation of the GFA and the 'Yes' vote in the referendum campaign. Northern Ireland is seen by enthusiasts as one of the major achievements of the Blair government. Another former Secretary of State for Northern Ireland, John Reid, argued that 'If Tony Blair's Labour government never did anything else but bring to an end the longest-running political dispute in European history and the longest running war probably in world history, on and off, it would be worth having the Labour government just for that' (*The Guardian*, 13 March 2007).

According to the governments' account, during the negotiations and implementation of the GFA great care was taken to ensure 'balance' in the concessions to nationalists, republicans and pro-agreement unionists to keep them in the peace process. This resulted in several substantial periods of devolution. In spite of the best efforts of the two governments, the moderate centre parties – the SDLP and the UUP – went into electoral decline and Sinn Féin and the DUP became dominant. The blame for the decline of the moderates is placed on those parties, on Trimble's failure to sell the GFA aggressively enough to his unionist constituency and on the SDLP leadership's failure to go into government with the UUP without Sinn Féin. What the governments did was to provide the impetus that ensured the process continued. Powell uses the metaphor of the peace process as a bike, which required continual momentum: 'If we ever let the bicycle fall over, we would create a vacuum and that vacuum would be filled by violence' (Powell, 2008: 5). Ultimately, the governments could only encourage the process as best they could; they could not control it. The process may not have concluded as they originally envisaged, due to the triumph of the extremes, but that was an unintended outcome of the process. Indeed the triumph of the extremes could be seen as advantageous. The dominance of the hard-line parties means that they cannot be outflanked and so power-sharing between the DUP and Sinn Féin is far more stable than it could be between the SDLP and the UUP. The problem for the moderate parties was that they were constantly under threat of having their position undermined by their hard-line rivals and therefore took aggressive policy stances in order to minimise electoral damage. Bringing in the extremes leaves no place to go for those who oppose power-sharing. Indeed, some enthusiasts argue that the growing electoral support for the hard-line parties does not indicate a hardening of attitudes among the Northern Irish public. They argue that there has been a symmetrical convergence in attitudes among unionists and nationalists for 'peace' and 'power-sharing' but that voters vote for the hard-line parties as the best protectors of their communal and ethnic interests (Mitchell et al., 2009). For the advocates of this version of the enthusiasts' narrative the Northern Ireland peace process is over and the conflict has been resolved.

An alternative enthusiast's narrative of the peace process is offered by Sinn Féin. According to this view the republican leadership responded to a changing landscape in Northern Ireland by making brave and highly risky moves such as ending its violence, agreeing to support a settlement short of a united Ireland, decommissioning its arms and supporting the justice system in Northern Ireland. These decisions were the result of the successes that republicans, along with other parties in the pan-nationalist front (the SDLP and Irish government, with support from the US) had in forcing the British government and unionists into accepting the legitimacy of their ideals and making structural changes that improved the plight of nationalists in

Northern Ireland. The movement by republicans was not undertaken from a position of weakness or capitulation; it was a tactical adjustment. This adjustment, they argue, was possible due to the changed situation in Northern Ireland, which was largely the result of pressure exerted by republicans on the British state since 1969. This changed situation meant that violence was no longer required to advance the aim of a united Ireland; the more equitable situation in Northern Ireland that they had brought about meant that this end could now be advanced by 'constitutional' politics rather than paramilitary activity. As the IRA's Easter message proclaimed in 2007, 'We believe that Irish republicanism is stronger, more united and more confident than at any time since partition and that we can achieve an end to the partition of our country and the establishment of a free and independent Ireland. We firmly believe that our republican goal of a united Ireland is achievable through purely peaceful and democratic means' (IRA, 2007). While republicans would acknowledge that during the peace process centrist unionists were marginalised by the more extreme DUP, their response would be that this was an unanticipated outcome of what was a complicated process. It was not the role of republicans to try to secure the UUP's future; they had embarked upon the very difficult task of seeking to persuade the republican movement of the viability of the non-violent route to a united Ireland. It was the difficulty of this task that explained the length of time that decommissioning and support for policing took. The fact that along the way the UUP were marginalised was not the fault of republicans but of the failure of Trimble to educate his constituency to the benefits of the peace process in the way that the republican leadership had educated its community. On the eclipse of the SDLP, Sinn Féin would simply argue that this is a reflection of the realisation among nationalists that Sinn Féin was the best defender of nationalism's interests.

The position of the DUP is more problematic given its apparent opposition to the GFA for much of the period after 1998 [**Doc. 31, p. 153**]. However, as a result of the DUP decision to enter into government with Sinn Féin in 2007, it tends to be on the enthusiast's side of the debate. The DUP's version of the narrative would stress that the peace process was largely a 'surrender process' to republicans until it managed to assert its leadership of unionism and secured the 'renegotiation' of the GFA at St Andrews in 2006. Its firm stance on key questions such as decommissioning and the necessity for Sinn Féin to support the justice system in Northern Ireland, and its unwillingness to continue the concessions that had been made to republicans since the early 1990s, forced the IRA to finally abandon violence in a meaningful way. The post-2007 variant of the peace process, which was the result of the actions of the DUP, created a situation that strengthened the Union and the position of unionists in Northern Ireland. The actions of the

DUP in entering government with Sinn Féin also prevented the British government from introducing 'Plan B' and so not only avoided increased taxes for the people of Northern Ireland but, more importantly, thwarted plans to further increase Dublin's role in Northern Ireland. The DUP's argument is that it did not betray its previous stance of not entering into government with the IRA/Sinn Féin but that its actions forced republicans to change, to accept the reality of the Union and no longer carry on their unjustified sectarian campaign. The DUP's firm stance forced republicans to become acceptable partners for the DUP to share government with (although continued vigilance from the DUP remains necessary to ensure that republicans do not seek to reverse the changes that have been forced upon them).

So it was the republicans' position that altered, not the DUP's. According to Paisley, Sinn Féin's claim that there will be a united Ireland is just 'wishful thinking on their part'. 'Everybody knows the very heart of the united Ireland policy was never to give any credence to British rule, and especially Republicans always saw the police as representatives of a foreign power that was keeping them in subjection and out of the Union. Now that they are prepared to take office in a government that is part and parcel of the United Kingdom and also to take the oath of allegiance to the police, I think they have forsworn general Republican thinking'. Asked if he had any regrets over his actions over the last 30 years, he told the *Washington Post* he had 'no real regrets that the line I took was the right line. I think that has now been vindicated by what has happened. We have got a deal we were told we couldn't get. It is quite clear to everybody there is going to be no united Ireland for 100 years, at least' (*Washington Times*, 13 April 2007). The decline of the UUP was seen by the DUP as the inevitable outcome of the actions of Trimble's party. When it became obvious that the UUP was too weak to stand up to republicans, the pan-nationalist front or the untrustworthy British government, the unionist community turned to the DUP to act as the defender of the Union.

THE SCEPTICS

There are different types of sceptics. Unionist and republican opponents of the peace process and the GFA have already been discussed. The sceptical position outlined here is that which is supportive of the peace process and the GFA but critical of the way that process was handled and which argues that the outcome might have been better. This view maintains that the triumph of hardliners in 2007 was not inevitable, that politicians make choices and that better choices may have resulted in a better outcome that would be more just and stable. The result of this is that sceptics are less complacent than enthusiasts about the future of Northern Ireland and more concerned about the levels of segregation, sectarianism and inequality. They argue that further change is necessary to consolidate power-sharing.

The sceptics reject the assertion that a key 'lesson' derived from the Northern Ireland peace process is the importance of 'talking to terrorists'. Sceptics argue that this ignores the *context* in which the British government 'talked to terrorists' and the conditions that were placed on the IRA's movement into democratic politics. These conditions were imposed by British Labour and Conservative governments. The entry of republicans into the peace process was highly conditional – most obviously on a ceasefire before Sinn Féin could enter substantive negotiations with the British government. Suggestions that there were no preconditions to talks are not accurate and misrepresent what happened in Northern Ireland (O'Kane, 2010).

The Good Friday Agreement was an elite-driven compromise that was not propelled by a major shift in attitudes from below. The agreement was remarkable because it represented a major compromise on previously stated public positions. Whether the deal could have been designed more judiciously is open to debate. One sceptical narrative, closely associated with the UUP, argues that an agreement more tilted towards unionism might have had a better chance of being sustained by pro-agreement unionists than the deal that was agreed. The British were aware of the pressure that the moderate unionists were under, which was implicitly acknowledged when Tony Blair deceived unionists in the run-up to the referendum on the GFA, claiming that the agreement entailed decommissioning before either the release of paramilitary prisoners or Sinn Féin's participation in government (Dixon, 2008a). This deception became more obvious as the agreement was implemented, prisoners released and Sinn Féin entered government. The plight of pro-agreement unionism was apparent from the Assembly elections in June 1998 and in subsequent elections and opinion polls. Yet, the Labour government appeared to do little to help the UUP leader shore up his position from the attacks of anti-agreement unionists both within his party and outside it. Blair realised the dire situation of the UUP leader too late to save him (Campbell, 2007: 489; Powell, 2008: 191, 235). It was only after the DUP had triumphed that the Labour government decided to exert more serious pressure on republicans to deliver (Powell, 2008: 254, 264, 287).

The Labour government did have to take into account the very real pressures on the republican leadership and the serious threat of a split in the IRA if republicans were pushed 'too far' in negotiations. There are at least four reasons why it seems that political miscalculation rather than hard constraints explains why pro-agreement unionists were pushed too far:

1. The Labour government, in spite of having informers working within the republican movement, does not seem to have had great insight into the pressures facing the Sinn Féin leadership and therefore no accurate sense of how far it could be pushed. Blair's negotiator, Jonathan Powell, states that they were just making a 'best guess' of the bottom line of republicans and unionists, 'There was no science to the judgment; it was a matter of feel' (2008: 163). Ed Moloney (2007) takes a more sceptical position on this and argues that the republican leadership was bluffing and denies that there was internal dissent to hold up decommissioning.

2. Peter Mandelson, Secretary of State for Northern Ireland 1999–2001, argued (based presumably on the intelligence also available to Blair) that unionism was being pushed 'too far' and should have been faced down (Powell, 2008: 163).

3. After the demise of Trimble, the Labour government decided to exert more pressure on republicans. According to Powell, 'the key prize was to get the DUP on board, just as in earlier stages of the talks the key aim had been to get the Republicans on board' (2008: 287).

4. The rapid shifts in Sinn Féin/the IRA's position ('full' decommissioning, endorsement of policing) after the triumph of the DUP in 2003 seems to suggest that republicans had much more room for manoeuvre than they were claiming (Moloney, 2007).

For its part, the SDLP has complained at the way it was marginalised in the ongoing negotiations by the British government, reinforcing the impression that it was Sinn Féin – backed up by the guns of the IRA – rather than the SDLP who wielded power and had influence. Tony Blair informed the SDLP its problem was that it did not have guns and therefore lacked bargaining power in the peace process. This focus on Sinn Féin and the marginalisation of the SDLP (then the largest nationalist party) in the aftermath of the signing of the GFA undermined the SDLP's standing within the nationalist constituency. Sinn Féin's moderating position meant that the republicans were also increasingly encroaching on SDLP electoral territory.

The two governments designed the GFA to achieve moderate power-sharing and failed in that goal. The narrative has since changed to suggest that the triumph of the hard-line parties, while not intended, may be an even better result for the peace process. Sceptics, by contrast, argue that Sinn Féin–DUP power-sharing is better than no power-sharing at all, and certainly a vast improvement on the violence of the conflict prior to 1994. Nevertheless, moderate power-sharing is preferable to hard-line power-sharing and the two governments could have taken decisions that, at the very least, would have made this outcome more likely. The problem is that elite agreement has been achieved with only limited evidence that this has helped to moderate attitudes and, sceptics argue, plenty of evidence of hardening of public opinion in the post-agreement period among unionists.

Sceptics claim that the rise of the DUP and Sinn Féin is a problem because they are the most hard-line and sectarian parties in Northern Ireland. These were the parties, to paraphrase SDLP leader Mark Durkan, that gave us the worst of our past and so are unlikely to give us the best of our future (*Irish Times*, 8 May 2007).

Sceptics argue that the DUP's history throughout the recent conflict has been strongly antagonistic towards nationalists. During the civil rights period Ian Paisley opposed measures that recognised discrimination against nationalists and the steps that were taken to address legitimate grievances. Some have argued that the DUP inspired violence against nationalists and its rhetoric has, at times, dangerously obscured the distinction between the IRA and ordinary nationalists. The DUP worked with loyalist paramilitary organisations during the UWC strike in 1974 and the loyalist strike in 1977. In order to oppose the AIA, the DUP launched Ulster Resistance in 1986, a paramilitary-style group – although it did not undertake 'military operations' while it was associated with the DUP. The DUP's prescriptions for security policy in Northern Ireland demonstrated little respect for human rights and its commitment has, until very recently, been not so much to democracy as to unionist majority domination. It has little noticeable commitment to integration or equality.

Sceptics also argue that Sinn Féin is the political wing of the IRA, an organisation that was responsible for approximately 1,771 deaths and probably thousands more injured. Gerry Adams and Martin McGuinness have, allegedly, been active in the IRA and in the wider republican movement throughout the recent conflict, a period in which the IRA perpetrated attacks not only on the security forces but also on civilians, bombing shopping areas, pubs and restaurants. Unionists perceive many of these attacks as being on their state and their community and have reason to see sectarianism as part of republican motivation. For example, in 1987 Sinn Féin published *A Scenario for Peace*, which claimed that in a united Ireland loyalists would have constitutional guarantees to protect their minority rights: 'Anyone unwilling to accept a united Ireland and wishing to leave should be offered resettlement grants to permit them to move to Britain or assist them to move to a country of their choice' (*The Guardian*, 2 May 1987).

The record of the DUP and Sinn Féin is such that opinion polls indicate that unionists would prefer to share power with the SDLP and are much more hostile to Sinn Féin. Likewise, nationalists would much prefer to share power with the UUP than with the DUP. The social conservatism of the DUP and the socialism of Sinn Féin do not make them the most natural of partners in government. This has inhibited their ability to work together in government and make significant legislative progress because the governing parties need to manage the expectations of highly contrasting constituencies.

Sceptics are concerned that the elite-negotiated power-sharing deal does not have a strong and stable foundation among the public of Northern Ireland. Sceptics question the enthusiast argument that the increase in voting for hard-line parties actually signifies a symmetrical softening of attitudes among the public and constitutes a vote for 'peace' and 'power-sharing'. Sceptics argue that there is convincing evidence that there was a hardening of attitudes among unionists in the post-GFA period and unionists only endorsed the GFA in the referendum campaign because they were deceived about its implications. Opinion poll evidence suggested increasing unionist disillusionment with the GFA and opposition to it. The rise in support for the DUP and other hard-line unionist parties reflected this disillusion. When the DUP finally did decide to share power with Sinn Féin in May 2007 it did so without giving its electorate a chance to vote on that deal. No referendum was held on the St Andrews Agreement and in the March 2007 Assembly election voters could easily vote for the DUP believing that it was a vote against power-sharing. It would appear that a section of the DUP's base is more sceptical than enthusiastic concerning the peace process. Arguably, the key electoral appeal of the DUP in elections since 1996 was opposition to the peace process and, later, opposition to the GFA. To a large extent, therefore, a vote for the DUP was *against* power-sharing with Sinn Féin.

While the leadership of the DUP can be categorised as enthusiastic concerning the post-2007 variant of the peace process, it is not clear that it has convinced its base that the situation is markedly different from that between 1998 and 2007. There was little evidence until 2004 that there was any chance of power-sharing between Sinn Féin and the DUP and even after then observers had every reason to believe that such a deal was impossible. The announcement of a power-sharing deal at the end of March and the devolution of power on 8 May 2007 represented a truly remarkable about-turn in the DUP's position. A more convincing interpretation of DUP-voting, therefore, backed up by opinion polls, is that it did represent a hardening of public opinion on the unionist side and not a vote for power-sharing.

The hard-line reputation of Ian Paisley gave him the credibility to sell power-sharing with Sinn Féin to unionism. Major shifts in Sinn Féin's position – the 'standing down' of the IRA, the endorsement of the police and the rule of law – probably made power-sharing more palatable for unionists. The DUP leadership did win over a significant section of unionism to accept power-sharing, but the adverse reaction of many unionists suggests that this was probably a bitter pill for many to swallow. The enthusiasts tended to believe that Ian Paisley's dominance over his party enabled him to lead it where he wished, while sceptics pointed to the history of the DUP and the constraints that its supporters have placed on the DUP leadership.

Ian Paisley and the DUP have managed to bring many unionists to acquiesce in the post-2007 power-sharing accommodation. But this has come at some cost to the DUP leadership and the party. The apparently easy relationship that developed between Paisley and McGuinness (their smiling performances at press conferences earned them the nickname 'the Chuckle Brothers') underscored the remarkable about-turn performed in the DUP's stance towards Sinn Féin, and this alienated some DUP supporters. In January 2008, when Ian Paisley stepped down as head of the Free Presbyterian Church, the Church that he had founded, some claimed that this was because of his power-sharing stance. In June 2008, Ian Paisley stepped down as First Minister and was replaced by Peter Robinson, his long-time deputy.

Unionist opposition to Sinn Féin–DUP power-sharing has been rallied by Jim Allister and his party Traditional Unionist Voice (TUV). Allister was the DUP's member of the European Parliament until he resigned from the DUP in protest at power-sharing in May 2007. He then founded TUV in December 2007. TUV performed strongly in the European election of 2009 with Allister attracting over 60,000 votes, although failing to retain his seat. The DUP's share of the first preference vote tumbled from 32 per cent in 2004 to 18.2 per cent in 2009. The enthusiasts' complacency about the dominance of the hard-line parties and belief that they cannot be outflanked was challenged by the rise of the TUV. This rise was, however, somewhat checked in the general election of 2010. Jim Allister failed in his bid to prevent Ian Paisley, Jr from securing his father's seat in North Antrim. The wider impact of the TUV on the election was negligible. The DUP's overall share of the vote did fall from 33.7 per cent to 25 per cent compared with the 2005 election but the party managed to hold eight of its nine seats. In one of the largest upsets of the election its leader Peter Robinson lost the seat he had held since 1979 to the non-sectarian Alliance Party. Robinson's defeat came in the wake of personal and political scandals surrounding his wife's sexual and business affairs, which appear to have caused a backlash against the First Minister. The decline of the UUP continued as it lost its last remaining Westminster seat, when Sylvia Hermon left the party in protest against the UUP's link with the Conservative Party and successfully contested the election as an independent. The UUP's share of the vote fell to 15.2 per cent (from 17.7 per cent in 2005).

Nationalists reacted differently than unionists during the peace process. Nationalists in the North were overwhelmingly supportive of the GFA. 'Catholics' perceived themselves as having gained from the GFA and its implementation and there is a high level of support, both electoral and in public opinion polls, for power-sharing. Nationalists have increasingly been able to vote for Sinn Féin as an endorsement and reward for giving up violence and for its involvement in the peace process. The nationalist vote can more easily be interpreted as a vote for the GFA and the St Andrews Agreement than can the unionist vote. There has been a gradual moderation in Sinn Féin's position over 20 years, which nationalist voters have increasingly rewarded, whereas the DUP's 'moderation' was much more dramatic over a much shorter period of time. The argument of sceptics that the two governments have bolstered the impression of Sinn Féin as the most effective negotiating party for nationalists and have therefore undermined the SDLP has substance. The challenge to republicans comes at the activist level, where republican dissidents attempt to peel off a significant number of members of the IRA to continue with a violent military campaign for a united Ireland. The widespread perception, among both unionists and nationalists, that the GFA represented more of an advance for nationalists than unionists helped Sinn Féin to maintain its electoral and activist support. Sceptics would argue that Sinn Féin has benefitted most from the GFA despite the fact that the SDLP played the larger role in negotiating the deal. (A similar point is made by the UUP in relation to the DUP. The DUP absented itself from the GFA negotiations yet ultimately reaped the benefits of the deal and marginalised the UUP. As Trimble's successor as leader of the UUP, Reg Empey, argued when Paisley agreed to enter into government with Sinn Féin, the DUP had benefitted from 'the heavy lifting' of the UUP (*Sunday Life*, 15 October 2006).) Sinn Féin's electoral advance in the Republic of Ireland reinforced the impression of the republicans marching forward to power in both the North and the South and then to Irish unity. Republican dissidents have been comprehensively rejected at the ballot box but they continue to sustain a level of violence that in March 2009 resulted in the deaths of two soldiers and a policeman. Dissidents have also reportedly threatened to kill Martin McGuinness (*Daily Telegraph*, 24 April 2009). In May 2010 the Independent Monitoring Commission (**IMC**) reported that the dissident groups (and in particular the Real IRA) had 'neither significant local nor international support. While the threat from RIRA is dangerously lethal, it is also politically marginal' (IMC Report, 26 May 2010). As Sinn Féin's electoral advance in the South falters and there appears to be no realistic strategy for achieving a united Ireland the party may come under increased pressure.

IMC: Independent Monitoring Commission, created September 2003 to monitor actions of paramilitary groups in Northern Ireland.

Sceptics argue, therefore, that there has been a hardening of attitudes among unionists during the peace process, and there have been indications of underlying sectarian tensions during the peace process. The conflict over Drumcree was, perhaps, the most serious indicator that the peace process had coincided with the sharpening of some sectarian attitudes. The picketing of a Catholic Church in Harryville and Holy Cross School were depressing reminders of the depth of sectarian tensions. There is also intense conflict over the issue of how to deal with the legacy of the Troubles and the question of compensation for victims and the investigation of murders. During the course of the recent conflict, segregation in Northern Ireland has tended to increase in housing, employment, education and social activities. The Community Relations Council has reported an increase in the number of 'peace walls' separating unionist and nationalist areas in Belfast, from 26 in 1994 to 80 in 2009. It is younger voters who are voting disproportionately for the hard-line parties.

Enthusiasts are relatively unconcerned about segregation because they tend to believe that segregation reflects the wishes of the people of Northern Ireland or will decline as the situation in Northern Ireland stabilises further. They argue that 'good fences make good neighbours' and that segregation reduces the opportunity for contact and, therefore, conflict between different communal groups. The DUP and Sinn Féin have been the most segregation-oriented parties, although the record of the SDLP and the UUP is not much better, and so there is no great pressure from the power-sharing administration for integration. The two governments, relieved to have achieved a devolved government, may choose not to challenge the status quo.

Sceptics argue that the GFA is no longer, as in 2001, 'balanced precariously on still seething reservoirs of hatred between unionists and nationalists' (Dixon, 2008a: 345), but that there is little reason to be complacent about the current political arrangements. The power-sharing, devolved executive that was established in May 2007 has lasted longer than any other period of devolution since the GFA. In March 2009 the politicians in the Assembly unanimously condemned the attacks on soldiers and police. Sceptics are concerned that segregation creates very different life experiences for nationalists and unionists and this creates an environment in which prejudice and violence against 'the other' community can be tolerated and encouraged. However, according to opinion polls the people of Northern Ireland do desire integration, which can be effective in reducing inter-group conflict. Sceptics criticise the Good Friday/St Andrews agreements for reinforcing communal identity with their insistence that MLAs describe themselves as 'nationalist', 'unionist' or 'other'. The checks and balances in the particular design of power-sharing leave it prone to deadlock and no major legislative programme has been passed by the Assembly. The inclusive executive leaves little significant opposition in the Assembly and this leaves it vulnerable to an anti-political, 'a plague on all their houses', backlash. The world economic crisis of 2007–2010 could hit Northern Ireland badly and this could exacerbate sectarian tensions. Sceptics highlight that the elite agreement is built, precariously, on top of public attitudes that are not necessarily supportive. While it is to be hoped power-sharing and the return of power to Northern

Ireland is consolidated, sceptics argue that the peace process is not over and much work still needs to be done.

Both sceptics and enthusiasts agree that Northern Ireland is far more peaceful than it has been since 1969. What remains contested is how secure this peace is. The enthusiasts believe that the conflict has ended and that Northern Ireland is now a model to export to the rest of the world. Sceptics, on the other hand, argue that there are still fundamental problems that remain and the momentum of the peace process needs to be maintained. What is not in doubt is that the conflict in Northern Ireland since 1969 will continue to be disputed, interpreted and reinterpreted in a debate as much over the future as about the past.

Part 2

DOCUMENTS

FROM CIVIL RIGHTS TO CIVIL WAR, 1969–72

Document 1   'THE MEN BEHIND THE WIRE'

The song 'The Men Behind The Wire' was written and composed by Paddy McGuigan in the aftermath of internment, 1971. McGuigan was among those interned.

Chorus

Armoured cars and tanks and guns
Came to take away our sons
But every man will stand behind
The Men Behind the Wire

Through the little streets of Belfast
In the dark of early morn
British soldiers came marauding
Wrecking little homes with scorn.

Heedless of the crying children
Dragging fathers from their beds
Beating sons while helpless mothers
Watched the blood flow from their heads

Chorus

Not for them a judge or jury
Or indeed a crime at all
Being Irish means they're guilty
So we're guilty one and all

Round the world the truth will echo
Cromwell's men are here again
England's name again is sullied
In the eyes of honest men

Chorus

Proudly march behind our banners
Firmly stand behind our men
We will have them free to help us
Build a Nation once again

On the people stand together
Proudly firmly on your way

Never fear, and never falter
Till the boys are home to stay

Chorus

A LOYALIST SONG   **Document 2**

Men Behind The Wire

Twas' [sic] a dark and gray November morn as I left old Belfast town
In a cold and lonely prison van, for Longkesh I was bound
But my spirit was unbroken, and my heart was still on fire
For I knew that soon I would be with the Men Behind The Wire.

When the judge had past [sic] my sentence, and the warders took me down
I cried out No Surrender, bless the red hand and the crown
but grant me just one favour, that is my one desire
Please let me serve my sentence, with the Men Behind The Wire.

There were many faces strange to me, and many more I knew
Whose only crime was loyalty to the old Red, White and Blue
And the love for dear old Ulster, even in the darkest hour
It shined within these loyal men, the Men Behind The Wire

And when this war is over, and our victory is won
Let's not forget the sacrifice, made by these loyal sons
They were staunch and true, for me and you so lift your glasses high
Where would we have been without them the Men Behind The Wire

Source: All Gave Some: Some Gave All – Loyalist Songbook No. 1, n.d.

UK CABINET'S SUB-COMMITTEE MINUTES   **Document 3**

This extract from the minutes of the UK Cabinet's sub-committee on Northern Ireland (GEN (71) 47 5th Meeting, 6 October 1971, 10.30am) suggests that the Conservative government was considering its options, including Irish unity.

In general discussion the Meeting recognised that it was essential to define the main object of the Government's Northern Ireland policy. If this were to maintain the status quo constitutionally, it was probably that the terrorist problem should be overcome as the first priority. On the other hand, if the object were to preserve the option of creating a united Ireland at some time in the future, it might be better to seek first for a political solution in which the minority were persuaded to broaden his Government to include 'non-militant' Republicans, the support for the terrorist campaign might be undermined by political action, rendering more severe military measures unnecessary. But there were few signs of an early political solution. A major new military initiative in the Roman Catholic areas in Belfast and London-derry or on the Border would alienate the Roman Catholics even further than at present without necessarily defeating the Irish Republican Army's (IRA) campaign. It would also place a heavy new burden on the Army. Despite the difficulty of reaching a political or military solution, the Meeting recognised that the continuation of the present trends might well lead to a situation in which direct rule would prove to be inevitable.

Source: The National Archives: Public Record Office.

Document 4   THE DEATH OF BERNARD McGUIGAN ON BLOODY SUNDAY

The book Lost Lives, *from which this extract is taken, describes the death of every victim of the recent conflict in Northern Ireland and represents a moving tribute to the people who died.*

January 30, 1972
Bernard McGuigan, L/Derry City
Civilian, Catholic, 41, married, ex-foreman

From Enniscairn Crescent, Derry, he was the fourth person to be shot on Bloody Sunday. Locals said he was killed as he went to help another man who had been wounded, carrying a white handkerchief. In a statement a 19-year-old member of the Order of Malta Ambulance Corps said: 'There was one man who wanted to try and get across. He stepped out and a soldier came round the corner of the Rossville Street Flats and the person in ques-tion, I found out later, was Mr Barney McGuigan. He raised his hand in the air – right out – and shouted "Don't shoot, don't shoot."

'And seconds later he was just shot in the head and landed in my lap at the alleyway at Rossville Street Flats. I could do nothing but just weep and I called everything to every soldier that was in my head. From the wounds in his head he was definitely dead.'

Another woman said in a statement that an injured man was lying at steps at Fahan Street. She went on: 'Another man was lying at Fahan Street steps.

I could hear him squealing but nobody could get to him because of the shooting. Mr McGuigan said he was going to try to reach him because he didn't want him to die alone. He took two steps forward and was then shot in the head. Mr McGuigan seemed to have been shot from the walls. Myself and some others crawled over to Mr McGuigan to see if we could do anything but he was dead. After this my nerves went and I was taken away in an ambulance.'

Source: D. McKittrick, S. Kelters, B. Feeney, C. Thornton and D. McVea, *Lost Lives*, Edinburgh: Mainstream, 1999, p. 147.

IRA TRAINING MANUAL   **Document 5**

The following extracts are taken from 'The Green Book', an IRA training manual.

Commitment

Commitment to an organisation is belief in that organisation. Commitment to the Army is total belief in the Army, in its aims and objects, in its style of war, in its method of struggle, and in its political foundation. Commitment is dedication to its cause in the good times and the bad. Commitment means standing steadfast to principles when all others condemn those principles and vilify the Army. It means choosing a path because one believes in the righteousness of that course, and having chosen it, to stick by it regardless of all obstacles. Commitment to the Republican Movement is the firm belief that its struggle both military and political is morally justified, that war is morally justified and that the Army is the direct representatives of the 1918 Dail Eireann parliament, and that as such they are the legal and lawful government of the Irish Republic, which has the moral right to pass laws for, and to claim jurisdiction over, the whole geographical fragment of Ireland . . . and all of its people regardless of creed or loyalty. . . .

Confidence in victory and loyalty to the movement

. . . loyalty to the Movement is the most important aspect of being a Volunteer. Loyalty in conjunction with confidence in victory are the essential ingredients in the make up of eventual victory.

Moral superiority

The Irish Republican Army as the legal representatives of the Irish people are morally justified in carrying out a campaign of resistance against foreign occupation forces and domestic collaborators. All volunteers are and must feel morally justified in carrying out the dictates of the legal government, they as the Army are the legal and lawful Army of the Irish Republic which has been forced underground by overwhelming forces. All volunteers must look upon the British Army as an occupying force, must look upon the RUC, the Gardai, the UDR and the Free State Army as illegal armies and illegal forces whose main tasks are treasonable and as such morally wrong, politically unacceptable and ethically inexcusable. . . .

What it means to be a volunteer

All recruits entering the Army declare that they shall obey orders issued to them by their superior officers and by the Army authority. This means what it is supposed to mean literally, that you obey all orders, whether you like them or not . . . It is not an easy thing to take up a gun and go out to kill some person without strong convictions of justification. The Army, its motivating force is based upon strong convictions, convictions of justification. It is these strong convictions which bonds [sic] the Army into one force and before any potential Volunteer decides to join the Army he must have these strong convictions. Convictions which are strong enough to give him confidence to kill someone without hesitation and without regret.

Source: Brendan O'Brien, *The Long War: The IRA and Sinn Féin 1985 to Today*, Dublin: O'Brien Press, 1993, pp. 401–402. Copyright © Brendan O'Brien.

Document 6   THE DEATH OF JEAN McCONVILLE

This is another extract from Lost Lives, *describing the tragic death of Jean McConville.*

December 7, 1972
Jean McConville, West Belfast
Civilian, Catholic, 37, widow, 10 children

Abducted from her home in the Divis area and killed by the IRA, her body has never been found. Because members of her family highlighted the case she is the best known of a group of individuals who came to be referred to as 'the disappeared'. Widowed ten months earlier, she had been taken from her maisonette in the Divis complex on December 6 and was held and beaten for some hours before escaping and returning home. Her daughter Helen, who was 15 at the time, later recalled that in the early evening of the next day her mother asked her to go to the shop to get chips for the children while she had a bath.

'Four girls dragged her from the bathroom at gunpoint,' the daughter, Helen McKendry, recalled when she first went public on the issue in the 1990s. Jean McConville was taken away again and was never again seen by her family . . .

Six weeks after the abduction Helen McKendry told the civil rights movement what had happened and the next day police, journalists and the social services contacted them. The family tried to survive Christmas 1972 on their own, but when news of their situation became known social services moved in and the children were split up. Eight of the family were taken into care. One daughter, who was described as mentally disabled, died in 1992 in Muckamore Abbey . . .

Little is known about what happened to Jean McConville or why. Helen McKendry has suggested that the IRA may have been looking for a woman they believed was involved in the Four Square laundry, an army undercover operation which ended with the death of a soldier, Sapper Ted Stuart. A frequently suggested explanation, however, is that Jean McConville angered the IRA by comforting a soldier who had been seriously injured outside her door. Before the abduction, the McConville family had been living in Divis for only two years. Jean McConville, an east Belfast Protestant by birth, had become a Catholic on marrying her husband. He had served in the army but left in 1964 and became a builder. A mixed couple, they had been intimidated out of their home in the Avoniel area of east Belfast in 1969. He died of cancer less than a year before Jean McConville's disappearance.

Source: D. McKittrick, S. Kelters, B. Feeney, C. Thornton and D. McVea, *Lost Lives*, Edinburgh: Mainstream, 1999, p. 301.

SUNNINGDALE, 1972–74

PROPOSALS OF THE SDLP **Document 7**

The Social Democratic and Labour Party's proposals for the constitutional reform 1972.

Proposals of the Social Democratic and Labour Party (Six Members in the Northern Ireland House of Commons before prorogation. Leader, Mr Gerard Fitt)

(i)   An immediate declaration by the United Kingdom that it would be in the best interest of all sections of the communities in both islands (i.e. Great Britain and Ireland) if Ireland were to become united on terms which would be acceptable to all the people of Ireland, and that the United Kingdom will positively encourage such development.

(ii)   Pending the achievement of unity, the establishment of an interim system of government for Northern Ireland under the joint sovereignty of the United Kingdom and the Irish Republic, who would reserve to themselves all powers relating to foreign affairs, defence, security, police and financial subventions and would be represented in Northern Ireland by Commissioners who would sign all legislation of a Northern Ireland Assembly, or, if one or both considered it necessary, refer it for determination by a joint Constitutional Court.

(iii)   The Assembly to consist of 84 Members elected by the STV system of proportional representation, with power to legislate in all fields including taxation, except those matters reserved to the joint sovereign powers.

(iv)   An executive of 15 Members to be elected from the Assembly by proportional representation and to hold office through the duration of an Assembly except in the case of a 75 per cent adverse vote. A chief executive, elected by the executive, to allocate departmental responsibilities subject to the approval of both Commissioners.

(v)   No representation for Northern Ireland in either the Westminster or the Dublin Parliament.

(vi)   All powers of security to be under the direct control of a department headed by both Commissioners.

(vii)   Creation of a new national Senate for the whole of Ireland, with equal representation from the Dublin Parliament and the Northern Ireland Assembly, the Parties from each being represented according to their strength, to plan the integration of North and South and agree on an acceptable constitution.

Source: John Magee, *Northern Ireland: Crisis and Conflict*, London: Routledge, 1974, pp. 160–161.

Document 8   GREEN PAPER ON THE FUTURE OF NORTHERN IRELAND

The Future of Northern Ireland *is a discussion paper released by the British government in 1972 to stimulate debate over the constitutional future of the region but it also indicates government thinking.*

The United Kingdom interest

74. . . . The United Kingdom Government has three major concerns in Northern Ireland. First, that it should be internally at peace – a divided and strife-ridden Province is bound to disturb and weaken the whole Kingdom. Second, that it should prosper, so as to contribute to and not detract from the prosperity of the whole. Third, that Northern Ireland should not offer a base for any external threat to the security of the United Kingdom. . . .

The Irish Dimension

76. A settlement must also recognise Northern Ireland's position within Ireland as a whole. The guarantee to the people of Northern Ireland that the status of Northern Ireland as part of the United Kingdom will not be changed without their consent is an absolute: this pledge cannot and will not be set aside . . . The problem of accommodating that minority within the political structures of Northern Ireland has to some considerable extent been an aspect of a wider problem within Ireland as a whole. . . .

77. No United Kingdom Government for many years has had any wish to impede the realisation of Irish unity, if it were to come about by genuine and freely given mutual agreement on conditions acceptable to the distinctive communities. Indeed the Act of 1920 itself, which has for so many years been the foundation of Northern Ireland's constitutional status, explicitly provided means to move towards ultimate unity on just such a basis; but the will to work this was never present.

Source: Northern Ireland Office, *The Future of Northern Ireland: A Paper for Discussion* (Green Paper), London: HMSO, 1972.

A UNIONIST VIEW ON THE FUTURE OF NORTHERN IRELAND   **Document 9**

William Craig, the author of the pamphlet from which this extract is taken, was the leader of Vanguard, an important group within the Ulster Unionist Party, which later formed the Vanguard Unionist Party.

The United Kingdom Government's Green Paper entitled 'The Future of Northern Ireland' further confirms the worst fears of Ulster Loyalists who cherish and seek to maintain their British Heritage. Gently, but with great clarity, the United Kingdom Government has declared that it has no interest in maintaining the Union of Great Britain and Northern Ireland and would favour the unification of Ireland as an independent Republic if the Ulster people would or could be prevailed upon to give their consent. The policies favoured in the document appear to be more concerned with weakening the political power of the loyalist majority and sapping their will to resist. . . .

Ulster for sale

. . . THE GREEN PAPER SAYS CLEARLY THAT THE BRITISH GOVERN-MENT DOES NOT STAND IN THE WAY OF THE UNIFICATION OF IRELAND. IT IS ONLY THE LOYALISTS OF NORTHERN IRELAND WHO DO. THE GREEN PAPER ALSO SAYS THAT THE BRITISH GOVERNMENT IS NOT GOING TO HELP THE LOYALISTS OF NORTHERN IRELAND TO MAINTAIN THE UNION OR THEIR BRITISH HERITAGE AND THE MOST THE LOYALISTS CAN EXPECT IS THAT THE GOVERNMENT 'BOUND BY STATUTE AND BY CLEAR AND REPEATED PLEDGES' WILL HONOUR ITS COMMITMENTS FROM A POSITION OF NEUTRALITY WITH A BIAS IN FAVOUR OF THE IRISH REPUBLIC. . . .

The Ulster Decision

. . . Our British Heritage we will preserve. We are opposed to joining an all Ireland Republic and we demand that the power and resources of the State shall be deployed against all efforts to bring about the unification of Ireland. We would prefer to maintain the Union but the desire must be reciprocated and pledges must be accompanied by a powerful Parliament in Northern Ireland to resist all attacks and to defeat the inevitable recurring terrorists [sic] onslaughts virtually guaranteed to take place by the success of the present attack. If there is not to be this strength in the United Kingdom we would prefer to be outside the United Kingdom seeking no special treatment but expecting at least the same consideration as the anti-British South when it opted out of the 1920 Constitution.

Source: William Craig, *The Future of Northern Ireland* [1972?]. Full document available at www.cain.ulst.ac.uk

Document 10   WHITE PAPER ON NORTHERN IRELAND CONSTITUTIONAL PROPOSALS

This White Paper followed the Green Paper (extracted above) and represented the British government's proposals for a constitutional package that was capable of winning the consent of unionists and nationalists.

Conditions for a settlement

Essential conditions

15. In determining the broad nature of a settlement, it has to be constantly borne in mind that the situation in Northern Ireland is complex. Constitutional proposals clearly have a significant part to play in the restoration of stability, because the institutions of government touch at one point or another the lives of all the people, and condition wider attitudes towards authority. Moreover, in Northern Ireland the clash of national aspirations heightens interest in, and concern about, the machinery of government. Yet the problems extend in one way or another into countless aspects of the life of the community – into patterns of education, housing and employment; into general social attitudes and responses; into history and culture and tradition. Thus, the solution to 'the Northern Ireland problem' is not to be found in any set of political proposals or institutions alone. However skilfully and fairly framed, these can do no more than provide opportunities which the people of Northern Ireland themselves may take or fail to take; and even with the utmost goodwill, the patterns of generations cannot be changed overnight.

Relations with the republic of Ireland

. . .

109. It is noteworthy that virtually all the Northern Ireland political parties have envisaged some sort of scheme for institutional arrangements between North and South which many describe as a 'Council of Ireland', although there were different concepts of such a Council, and in some cases an emphasis upon conditions which would have to be met before it could operate successfully.

110. As far as the United Kingdom is concerned, it favours and is prepared to facilitate the formation of such a body. . . .

Conclusion

. . .

118. These proposals are designed to benefit the law-abiding majority in both communities, who may have conflicting views on the ultimate constitutional destiny of Northern Ireland, but who seek to advance those views by peaceful democratic means alone, and have strong mutual interests in making social and economic progress. The proposals provide an opportunity for all such people to stand together against those small but dangerous minorities which would seek to impose their views by violence and coercion,

and which cannot, therefore, be allowed to participate in working institutions they wish to destroy. . . .

122. These, then, are the Government's proposals to Parliament, to the country, and above all to the people of Northern Ireland themselves for a way forward out of the present violence and instability. At every point, they require the co-operation of those people themselves if they are to have any prospect of success. They can be frustrated if interests in Northern Ireland refuse to allow them to be tried or if any section of the community is determined to impose its will on another. It should now be perfectly clear that these are prescriptions for disaster. The Government believes, however, that the majority of the people of Northern Ireland have an overwhelming desire for peace and that they will accept the opportunity which these proposals offer.

Source: Northern Ireland Office, *Northern Ireland Constitutional Proposals* (White Paper), Cmnd 5259, London: HMSO, 1973.

Document 11   HAROLD WILSON'S 'SPONGERS SPEECH'

This text is from a television broadcast made by Harold Wilson on 25 May 1974 during the Ulster Workers' Council Strike. It has become known as the 'Spongers Speech'. Some loyalists pinned bits of sponge to their coats in protest and the speech helped to precipitate the collapse of power-sharing.

As this holiday weekend begins, Northern Ireland faces the gravest crisis in her history. It is a crisis equally for all of us who live on this side of the water. What we are seeing in Northern Ireland is not just an industrial strike. It has nothing to do with wages. It has nothing to do with jobs – except to imperil jobs. It is a deliberate and calculated attempt to use every undemocratic and unparliamentary means for the purpose of bringing down the whole constitution of Northern Ireland so as to set up there a sectarian and undemocratic state, from which one third of the people of Northern Ireland will be excluded. This is not – this has not been at any time over these past few difficult years – a party matter in the House of Commons or in this country at all. Where the political wildcats of Northern Ireland seek to divide and embitter, all the major parties in Britain have sought to heal and to unite. . . .

The people on this side of the water – British parents – have seen their sons vilified and spat upon and murdered. British taxpayers have seen the taxes they have poured out, almost without regard to cost – over £300 million a year this year with the cost of the Army operation on top of that – going into Northern Ireland. They see property destroyed by evil violence and are asked to pick up the bill for rebuilding it. Yet people who benefit from all this now viciously defy Westminster, purporting to act as though they were an elected government; people who spend their lives sponging on Westminster and British democracy and then systematically assault democratic methods. Who do these people think they are?

Source: full text of the speech is available at: http://cain.ulst.ac.uk/events/uwc/docs/ hw25574.htm

SEARCHING FOR SOLUTIONS, 1974–82

IRA 'STAFF REPORT'   **Document 12**

These extracts are taken from an IRA 'Staff Report' seized in 1977.

The three-day and seven-day detention orders are breaking volunteers and it is the Republican Army's fault for not indoctrinating volunteers with the psychological strength to resist interrogation.

Coupled with this factor which is contributing to our defeat we are burdened with an inefficient infra-structure of commands brigades, battalions and companies. This old system with which the Brits and [Special] Branch are familiar has to be changed. We recommend reorganisation and remotivation, the building of a new Irish Republican Army.

We emphasise a return to secrecy and strict discipline. Army men must be in total control of all sections of the movement. . . .

. . . We must gear ourselves towards Long Term Armed Struggle based on putting unknown men and new recruits into a new structure. This new structure shall be a cell system. . . .

Sinn Fein: Sinn Fein should come under Army organisers at all levels. Sinn Fein should employ full-time organisers in big Republican areas.

Sinn Fein should be radicalised (under Army direction) and should agitate around social and economic issues which attack the welfare of the people. S. F. [Sinn Fein] Should be directed to infiltrate other organisations to win support for, and sympathy to, the Movement. S. F. Should be re-educated and have a big role to play in publicity and propaganda departments.

Source: Tim Pat Coogan, *The I.R.A.*, London: Fontana, 1980, pp. 578–81.

Document 13   THE GLOVER REPORT

These extracts are taken from a secret report by Brigadier James Glover of the Defence Intelligence Staff (MOD) entitled 'Northern Ireland: Future Terrorist Trends', dated 2 November 1978.

Introduction

3. In its study of the Threat the same paper ['Future Organisation of Military Intelligence in Northern Ireland'] assessed that the Provisional leadership is deeply committed to a long campaign of attrition. The Provisional IRA (PIRA) has the dedication and the sinews of war to raise violence intermittently to at least the level of early 1978, certainly for the foreseeable future. Even if 'peace' is restored, the motivation for politically inspired violence will remain. Arms will be readily available and there will be many who are able and willing to use them. Any peace will be superficial and brittle. A new campaign may well erupt in the years ahead.

4. In 1977 PIRA adopted the classic terrorist cellular organisation in response to their difficulties. But at other times their tactics and weaponry have changed for reasons that cannot be forecast, such as the influence, often transitory, of individual leaders and the professional ability of key terrorists. Also an isolated incident, such as 'Bloody Sunday', can radically alter support for violence. . . .

Manpower

15. The Provisionals cannot attract the large numbers of active terrorists they had in 1972/73. But they no longer need them. PIRA's organisation is now such that a small number of activists can maintain a disproportionate level of violence. . . .

16. Calibre of Terrorist

a. Leadership. PIRA is essentially a working class organisation based in the ghetto areas of the cities and in the poorer rural areas. Thus if members of the middle class and graduates become more deeply involved they have to forfeit their life style. Many are also deterred by the Provisionals' muddled political thinking. Nevertheless there is a strata of intelligent, astute and experienced terrorists who provide the backbone of the organisation. Although there are only a few of these high grade terrorists there is always the possibility that a new charismatic leader may emerge who would transform PIRA yet again. . . .

c. Rank and File Terrorists. Our evidence of the calibre of rank and file terrorists does not support the view that they are merely mindless hooligans drawn from the unemployed and unemployable. PIRA now trains and uses its members with some care. The Active Service Units (ASUs) are for the most part manned by terrorists tempered by up to ten years of operational experience. . . .

Conclusion

64. The Provisionals' campaign of violence is likely to continue while the British remain in Northern Ireland. During the next 5 years we see little prospect of change in the inter-relationship between the various terrorist groups in Ireland but we expect PIRA may become gradually more influenced by overseas terrorist groups. We see little prospect of political developments of a kind which would seriously undermine the Provisionals' position.

Source: Sean Cronin, *Irish Nationalism: A History of its Roots and Ideology*, London: Pluto Pres, 1980, Appendix XVIII.

IAN PAISLEY CALLS FOR THE EXTERMINATION OF THE IRA   **Document 14**

The following is an extract from a speech made by Ian Paisley on 23 November 1981.

We demand that the IRA be exterminated from Ulster. The aim of the IRA is to destroy the last vestige of Protestantism in our island home. But there is one army the Republic fears and that every other enemy of Ulster fears and that is the army of armed and resolute Protestants.

. . . Here are men willing to do the job of exterminating the IRA. Recruit them under the Crown and they will do it. If you refuse, we will have no other decision to make but to do it ourselves.

Source: Dennis Cooke, *Persecuting Zeal: Portrait of Ian Paisley*, Dingle, Co, Kerry: Brandon, 1996, pp. 191–2.

THE ANGLO-IRISH AGREEMENT 1985

Document 15   THE ANGLO-IRISH AGREEMENT 1985

The following text is taken from the Anglo-Irish Agreement 1985 between the government of the Republic of Ireland and the government of the UK.

A. *Status of Northern Ireland*

Article 1
The two Governments

(a) affirm that any change in the status of Northern Ireland would only come about with the consent of a majority of the people of Northern Ireland;

(b) recognise that the present wish of a majority of the people of Northern Ireland is for no change in the status of Northern Ireland;

(c) declare that, if in the future a majority of the people of Northern Ireland clearly wish for and formally consent to the establishment of a united Ireland, they will introduce and support in the respective Parliaments legislation to give effect to that wish.

B. *The intergovernmental conference*

Article 2
(a) There is hereby established, within the framework of the Anglo-Irish Intergovernmental Council set up after the meeting between the two Heads of Government on 6 November 1981, an Intergovernmental Conference (hereinafter referred to as 'the Conference'), concerned with Northern Ireland and with relations between the two parts of the island of Ireland, to deal, as set out in this Agreement, on a regular basis with
   (i)   political matters;
   (ii) security and related matters;
   (iii) legal matters, including the administration of justice;
   (iv) the promotion of cross-border co-operation.

(b) The United Kingdom Government accept that the Irish Government will put forward views and proposals on matters relating to Northern Ireland within the field of activity of the Conference in so far as those matters are not the responsibility of a devolved administration in

Northern Ireland. In the interest of promoting peace and stability, determined efforts shall be made through the Conference to resolve any differences. The Conference will be mainly concerned with Northern Ireland; but some of the matters under consideration will involve cooperative action in both parts of the island of Ireland, and possibly also in Great Britain. Some of the proposals considered in respect of Northern Ireland may also be found to have application by the Irish Government. There is no derogation from the sovereignty of either the Irish Government or the United Kingdom Government, and each retains responsibility for the decisions and administration of government within its own jurisdiction.

Source: Agreement between the Government of the United Kingdom of Great Britain and Northern Ireland and the Government of the Republic of Ireland (Hillsborough, 15 November 1985) [Anglo-Irish Agreement], Cmnd 9657, London: HMSO, 1985.

A UNIONIST MP ON THE ANGLO-IRISH AGREEMENT   **Document 16**

Extracts from the speech of Harold McCusker, Ulster Unionist MP for Upper Bann, in the debate on the Anglo-Irish Agreement in the House of Commons in November 1985.

I went to Hillsborough on the Friday morning. . . . I stood outside Hillsborough, not waving a Union flag—I doubt whether I will ever wave one again—not singing hymns, saying prayers or protesting, but like a dog and asked the Government to put in my hand the document that sold my birthright. They told me that they would give it to me as soon as possible. Having never consulted me, never sought my opinion or asked my advice, they told the rest of the world what was in store for me.

I stood in the cold outside the gates of Hillsborough castle and waited for them to come out and give me the agreement second-hand. . . .

I had to go home on the Friday night after the Hillsborough agreement and tell my wife that I regretted bringing up our children to believe what hon. Members have brought their children up to believe, because they will have to live with the legacy that I have to live with. It would have been better if they had never looked at the Union flag or thought that they were British or put their trust in the House of Commons than spending the rest of their lives knowing that they are now some sort of semi-British citizen.

Source: Hansard, HC Deb., 27 November 1985, vol. 87, cols 912–13.

Document 17 THE UDA'S ANALYSIS OF THE CONFLICT

Extract from Common Sense – An Agreed Process, *published by the Ulster Political Research Group (attached to the loyalist paramilitary Ulster Defence Association), January 1987.*

How long can this go on?

The stubborn determination of each community not to 'give in' to, nor be beaten by, the other ensures that the conflict could continue indeterminately unless we can produce a settlement which removes the main sources of antagonism to each side. In the quest for proposals which may lead to a social and political solution to the Ulster conflict we must first identify the parameters within which such proposals are realistic. Surely by now we recognise that there are limits beyond which each community will not (under any circumstances) retreat nor indeed be forced. It is not always that which is true which is important, but that which is believed to be true. Each community tends to form its impression of the other from the rhetoric and posturing of the most zealous and vocal sections of that group. The trouble with the silent majority is that it is indeed silent, and therefore makes little impression.

What impression then does each community have of the other?

Ulster 'Protestants' do not fear nor mistrust Ulster 'Catholics' because they are Catholics but because they believe them to be Irish Nationalists – fifth columnists – uncommitted citizens, intent on the destruction of Northern Ireland in pursuit of a united CATHOLIC-GAELIC-IRISH NATIONALIST-REPUBLIC. Loyalists fear that if these Irish Nationalists are allowed any authority or position of 'power' within the political framework of Northern Ireland then they will use that power and authority to undermine, or even overthrow the State to achieve their Nationalist ambitions. For this reason Loyalists have opposed, and will continue to oppose, any proposal or scheme which contains an 'Irish dimension' or which Loyalists believe is contrived by Irish Nationalists to either undermine the 'Union' with Great Britain or bring a United Ireland one step nearer.

Source: full document available at cain.ulst.ac.uk

JOHN HUME CRITICISES SINN FÉIN

Document 18

John Hume's speech at the SDLP Conference, November 1988.

There are also those who are mirror images of traditional unionism. They too believe in 'themselves alone' as the only answer to the problem of a deeply divided society, without the slightest reference, apart from the verbal ritual genuflections and lip service, to the existence of anyone else. Self determination of the Irish people is their objective they say. The Irish people are defined by them, if we judge by their actions and their contempt for the views and opinions of other Irish people, as themselves alone. They are more Irish than the rest of us, they believe. They are the pure master race of Irish. They are the keepers of the holy grail of the nation. That deep-seated attitude, married to their method has all the hallmarks of undiluted fascism. They have also the other hallmark of the fascist – the scapegoat – the Brits are to blame for everything even their own atrocities! They know better than the rest of us. They know so much better that they take unto themselves the right, without consultation with anyone to dispense death and destruction. By destroying Ireland's people, they destroy Ireland.

. . . If I were to lead a civil rights campaign in Northern Ireland today the major target of that campaign would be the IRA. It is they who carry out the greatest infringements of human and civil rights whether it is their murders, their executions without trial, their kneecappings and punishment shootings, their bombings of jobs and people.

Source: Speech by John Hume MP to the SDLP's 18th Annual Conference, 25–27 November 1988, Europa Hotel, Belfast (published by the SDLP), pp. 4–5.

AN SDLP VIEW OF REPUBLICANS

Document 19

Austin Currie was a civil rights activist and founder member of the SDLP. He stood in 1990 as Fine Gael's candidate to become the Irish President.

It took considerable courage to work for the SDLP in these elections [in the 1980s]. Many of the Sinn Fein workers saw the election as an extension of their war campaign, which of course it was ('a ballot paper in one hand and an armalite in the other'), where both intimidation and persuasion were acceptable. There were housing estates where it was advisable, when canvassing, to drive to the far end and face out to minimise the possibility of being trapped. Gangs would follow canvassers from estate to estate, under the guidance of Sinn Fein activists. Posters were systematically pulled down.

On one occasion I travelled part of the way with a team that erected posters every 200 yards on the road from Ballygawley to Enniskillen, over a distance of some fifteen miles – a job which took hours. Returning home after attending a meeting in Enniskillen, we found nearly every poster had been removed; we actually saw the 'patriots' at their work. On another occasion an attempt was made to force the car I was in off the road. I had the satisfaction of seeing the Sinn Fein supporter responsible convicted of the offence.

It was not just during elections that intimidation occurred. Known SDLP members and supporters suffered in various ways. Windows in houses and business premises would be broken and buildings sometimes blown up, or burned down. A stretch of road outside Coalisland was a favourite spot for hijacking cars for use in IRA activities. It was no coincidence that the vehicle hijacked was invariably SDLP-owned. Children of SDLP parents were more likely to be beaten up at discos and other social functions.

Source: Austin Currie, *All Hell Will Break Loose*, Dublin: O'Brien Press, 2004, pp. 329–30. Copyright © Austin Currie.

THE ORIGINS OF THE PEACE PROCESS, 1985–94

Document 20   PETER BROOKE'S 'WHITBREAD SPEECH'

These extracts are from a speech made by Secretary of State for Northern Ireland Peter Brooke to the British Association of Canned Food Importers and Distributors at London's Whitbread Restaurant on November 9, 1990. The speech became known as the 'Whitbread Speech'.

. . . I believe, in particular, that a huge majority of those who would wish to see a united Ireland one day, both in the north and in the whole of Ireland, know in their hearts that a 32 county state in the terms I have used could never be created by force or advanced by putting a union of territories before a union of hearts and minds. A state brought into being by such corrupt methods could never live up to the vision of a united Ireland enjoying the loyalty and protecting the rights of Catholic, Protestant and dissenter. . . .

For what purpose does this [IRA] killing continue? . . .

At the heart of this matter there is the question of the so-called 'British presence' in a part of Ireland. It is to remove that presence that republican terrorism is said to be dedicated. So let us examine, for a moment, just what the 'British presence' actually is.

It has four main aspects. The first . . . is the visible presence and activity of British troops on the streets and in the countryside of Northern Ireland

... The United Kingdom has of course no vested interest in maintaining these high force levels a day longer than is necessary. . . .

The second aspect of the British presence is . . . my own presence in Northern Ireland as Secretary of State . . . But it is the clearly stated policy of this Government to seek to find ways of returning significant responsibilities for the affairs of Northern Ireland to locally elected representatives in a way which would command widespread acceptance within Northern Ireland. . . .

The third main aspect . . . is . . . the transfer from the common Exchequer every year of very large sums of money to enable programmes well beyond the capacity of locally raised taxation to be carried out. This support is not given in furtherance of some strategic interest or in the expectation of some corresponding gain to the people of Great Britain. It seeks no return other than the satisfaction of improving the conditions of life in Northern Ireland.

. . . fourth and most significant aspect of the British presence. Every time I hear that call for 'Brits out', it brings home to me the paramount reality that the heart and core of the British presence is not the British army or British ministers, but the reality of nearly a million people living in a part of the island of Ireland who are, and who certainly regard themselves as, British.

. . . Those who live here [in Great Britain] would not bar the way if at some future time that [Irish unity] were to be the wish of the people of Northern Ireland themselves; indeed the Government has made clear on several occasions, notably in signing the Anglo-Irish Agreement, that if in the future a majority of the people of Northern Ireland clearly wished for and formally consent to the establishment of a united Ireland it would introduce and support in parliament legislation to give effect to that wish. However, we will fully support our fellow-citizens while, by their own free and clearly-expressed wish, they remain our fellow-citizens. Partition is an acknowledge-ment of reality, not an assertion of national self-interest. The border cannot simply be wished away. . . .

Only if violence is abandoned can a true reconciliation be achieved. There is a need for reconciliation at three levels – between the communities in Northern Ireland; within Ireland; and between the peoples on both these islands. The terrorists constitute a major impediment on the road to peace and great understanding and to new political institutions which adequately reflect everyone's interests. The British government has no selfish strategic interest in Northern Ireland: our role is to help, enable and encourage. Britain's purpose, as I have sought to describe it, is not to occupy, oppress or exploit, but to ensure democratic debate and free democratic choice. That is our way.

Source: *Irish Times*, 10 November 1990.

Document 21   THE 'TUAS' DOCUMENT

'TUAS' is a republican document circulated by the leadership to justify the IRA's 1994 ceasefire. The acronym is ambiguous; it stands for 'Totally UnArmed Strategy' or 'Tactical Use of Armed Struggle', the first definition probably for an external audience and the second for rank and file republicans.

The briefing paper of April deals with strategic objectives and events to that date in more detail than this paper. However, a brief summary is helpful.

Our goals have not changed. A united 32 County Democratic Socialist Republic.

The main Strategic Objectives to move us towards that goal can be summarised thus. To construct an Irish nationalist consensus with international support on the basis of the dynamic contained in the Irish peace initiative. This should aim for:

a. The strongest possible political consensus between the Dublin government, Sinn Féin and the SDLP.
b. A common position on practical measures moving us towards our goal.
c. A common nationalist negotiation position.
d. An international dimension in aid of the consensus (mostly U.S.A. and E.U.).

The Strategic Objectives come from prolonged debate but are based on a straightforward logic: that republicans at this time and on their own do not have the strength to achieve the end goal. The struggle needs strengthening most obviously from other nationalist constituencies led by SDLP, Dublin government and the emerging Irish-American lobby, with additional support from other parties in E.U. rowing in behind and accelerating the momentum created.

The aim of any such consensus is to create a dynamic which can:

1. Effect the domestic and international perception of the republican position, i.e. as one which is reasonable.
2. To develop a northern nationalist consensus on the basis of constitutional change.
3. To develop an Irish national consensus on the same basis.
4. To develop Irish-America as a significant player in support of the above.
5. To develop a broader and deeper Irish nationalist consensus at grassroots level.
6. To develop and mobilise an anti-imperialist Irish peace movement.

7. To expose the British government and the unionists as the intransigent parties.

8. To heighten the contradictions between British unionist and 'Ulster Loyalism'.

9. To assist the development of whatever potential exists in Britain to create a mood/climate/party/movement for peace.

10. To maintain the political cohesion and organisational integrity of Sinn Féin so as to remain an effective political force.

. . . After prolonged discussion and assessment the leadership decided that if it could get agreement with the Dublin government, the SDLP and the I.A. [Irish-American] lobby on basic republican principles which would be enough to create the dynamic that would considerably advance the struggle then it would be prepared to use the TUAS option.

We attempted to reach such a consensus on a set of principles which can be summarised briefly thus:

1. Partition has failed.
2. Structures must be changed.
3. No internal settlement within 6 Counties.
4. British rule breaches the principle of N.S.D. [national self-determination].
5. The Irish as a whole have the right to N.S.D. without external impediment.
6. It is up to the Dublin/London governments with all parties to bring about N.S.D. in the shortest time possible.
7. The unionists have no veto over discussions involved or their outcome.
8. A solution requires political and constitutional change.
9. An agreed united and independent Ireland is what republicans desire. However an agreed Ireland needs the allegiance of varied traditions to be viable.

Contact with the other parties involved have been in that context. . . .

It is the first time in 25 years that all the major Irish nationalist parties are rowing in roughly the same direction. These combined circumstances are unlikely to gel again in the foreseeable future.

The leadership has now decided that there is enough agreement to proceed with the Tuas option.

Source: E. Moloney, *A Secret History of the IRA*, London: Penguin, 2002, pp. 498–501.

Document 22   GERRY ADAMS ON DEMANDS FOR IRA DECOMMISSIONING

In an interview with the Irish News *on 8 January 1994 Adams criticised British politicians for repeating their demand for an IRA weapons handover.*

Mr Mayhew goes on to say 'well the exploratory dialogue will be so we can discuss with Sinn Fein how the IRA will hand over their weapons'.

So I say to myself: 'This is what they want. They want the IRA to stop so that Sinn Fein can have the privilege 12 weeks later, having been properly sanitised and come out of quarantine, to have discussions with senior civil servants of how the IRA can hand over their weapons. And then I hear that reiterated again and again; by Douglas Hurd, by John Major, by Patrick Mayhew.'

Source: *Irish News*, 8 January 1994.

CEASEFIRE TO GOOD FRIDAY AGREEMENT, 1994–98

Document 23   THE MITCHELL PRINCIPLES

The Mitchell Principles are named after Senator George Mitchell, who produced the Report of the International Body on Arms Decommissioning, 22 January 1996.

Accordingly, we recommend that the parties to such negotiations affirm their total and absolute commitment:

- To democratic and exclusively peaceful means of resolving political issues;
- To the total disarmament of all paramilitary organisations;
- To agree that such disarmament must be verifiable to the satisfaction of an independent commission;
- To renounce for themselves, and to oppose any effort by others, to use force, or threaten to use force, to influence the course or the outcome of all-party negotiations;
- To agree to abide by the terms of any agreement reached in all-party negotiations and to resort to democratic and exclusively peaceful methods in trying to alter any aspect of that outcome with which they may disagree; and,
- To urge that 'punishment' killings and beatings stop and to take effective steps to prevent such actions.

Source: International Body on Arms Decommissioning, *Report of the International Body on Arms Decommissioning* [Mitchell Report], 22 January 1996.

Extracts from an address by Prime Minister Tony Blair at the Royal Agricultural Society, Belfast on 16 May 1997.

. . . My message is simple. I am committed to Northern Ireland. I am committed to the principle of consent. And I am committed to peace. A settlement is to be negotiated between the parties based on consent. My agenda is not a united Ireland – and I wonder just how many see it as a realistic possibility in the foreseeable future. Northern Ireland will remain part of the United Kingdom as long as a majority here wish.

What I want to see is a settlement which can command the support of nationalists and unionists. That is what the people of Northern Ireland rightly demand of me and of their political leaders. . . .

The union

Northern Ireland is part of the United Kingdom alongside England, Scotland and Wales.

The Union binds the four parts of the United Kingdom together. I believe in the United Kingdom. I value the Union. . . .

But let me make one thing absolutely clear. Northern Ireland is part of the United Kingdom because that is the wish of a majority of the people who live here. It will remain part of the United Kingdom for as long as that remains the case. This principle of consent is and will be at the heart of my Government's policies on Northern Ireland. It is the key principle.

It means that there can be no possibility of a change in the status of Northern Ireland as a part of the United Kingdom without the clear and formal consent of a majority of the people of Northern Ireland. Any settlement must be negotiated not imposed; it must be endorsed by the people of Northern Ireland in a referendum; and it must be endorsed by the British Parliament.

Of course, those who wish to see a united Ireland without coercion can argue for it, not least in the talks. If they succeeded, we would certainly respect that. But none of us in this hall today, even the youngest, is likely to see Northern Ireland as anything but a part of the United Kingdom. That is the reality, because the consent principle is now almost universally accepted.

Democracy and violence

. . . I am ready to make one further effort to proceed with the inclusive talks process. My message to Sinn Fein is clear. The settlement train is leaving.

I want you on that train. But it is leaving anyway, and I will not allow it to wait for you. You cannot hold the process to ransom any longer. So end the violence. Now.

. . . Loyalist terrorism is equally contemptible, equally unacceptable, just as futile and counter-productive . . .

But let us have no illusions. Commitment to democracy means no violence or threat of violence. There can be and will be no double standards.

Source: full text available on cain.ulst.ac.uk

Document 25   THE GOOD FRIDAY AGREEMENT

The decommissioning issue was a source of continuing controversy and this is all the Good Friday Agreement had to say on the matter.

Decommissioning

1. Participants recall their agreement in the Procedural Motion adopted on 24 September 1997 'that the resolution of the decommissioning issue is an indispensable part of the process of negotiation', and also recall the provisions of paragraph 25 of Strand 1 above.
2. They note the progress made by the Independent International Commission on Decommissioning and the Governments in developing schemes which can represent a workable basis for achieving the decommissioning of illegally-held arms in the possession of paramilitary groups.
3. All participants accordingly reaffirm their commitment to the total disarmament of all paramilitary organisations. They also confirm their intention to continue to work constructively and in good faith with the Independent Commission, and to use any influence they may have, to achieve the decommissioning of all paramilitary arms within two years following endorsement in referendums North and South of the agreement and in the context of the implementation of the overall settlement.
4. The Independent Commission will monitor, review and verify progress on decommissioning of illegal arms, and will report to both Governments at regular intervals.

6. Both Governments will take all necessary steps to facilitate the decommissioning process to include bringing the relevant schemes into force by the end of June.

Source: Northern Ireland Office, *The Agreement: Text of the Agreement reached in the Multi-Party Negotiations on Northern Ireland* (10 April 1998) [Good Friday Agreement/ Belfast Agreement], Cmnd. 3883, Belfast: HMSO.

THE ALLIANCE PARTY SETS OUT ITS PRINCIPLES FOR A SETTLEMENT   **Document 26**

The Alliance Party consistently supported power-sharing during the recent conflict. This extract restates its position in the run up to the Good Friday Agreement.

A community government

Our first principle expressed the conviction that, despite the obvious divisions, the people of Northern Ireland form a community. Like any other such community, these people have the right to determine their own future, and participate directly in their own governance. For this reason it is very strongly our view that a provincial or regional government is necessary, to provide a common focus of identity, and an opportunity to share in self-government. This is not an exclusively Northern Ireland requirement, but is being recognised increasingly throughout Europe where regional government is the norm. More recently the people of Scotland and Wales, when given the opportunity, have expressed their desire to have regional government, and the enabling legislation will soon begin its route through parliament. The taking of responsibility through self-government is a positive and enabling principle.

On the more negative side, uncertainty and ambiguity provoke anxiety and give encouragement to those who thrive on fear. Any settlement must therefore remove negative uncertainties. The acknowledgement by the two governments of the principle of consent is a clear statement of the right of the Northern Ireland community to self-determination, and a tacit acknowledgement that the present wish of that community as a whole is to remain within the United Kingdom. This principle must also be enshrined in any settlement, and, since it has been a fundamental matter of dispute, it must form part of fundamental law in all the jurisdictions which participate in these talks. Fear thrives not only on uncertainty, but also on ignorance, confusion, and unnecessary complexity. Openness and transparency, [sic] are the enemies of the fears fed by ignorance and confusion. These must also be key principles in the establishing of any settlement, and indeed of this Talk Process.

Given that there are, as in every community, different identities, and particularly since at least some of these distinctions have, in Northern Ireland, been pushed to the point of division, it is necessary to create common institutions and instruments of government in which all can participate and with which all can identify. We take the view that an elected assembly, with legislative as well as executive functions in an extensive range of areas (giving significant socio-economic autonomy), including relationships with the Republic of Ireland is the minimum necessary to provide this unifying factor. It would be Profoundly [sic] counter-productive if in the construction of such structures the very divisions which they were established to heal were institutionalised by the forms of protection they used. For this reason setting out two separate sets of mirroring rights, with parity of esteem between only two traditions, and insisting on always dividing people into Protestant and Catholic, and unionist and nationalist (and assuming also that these divisions are contiguous), would not be a healing of the divisions but an institutionalising of them. Instead we should recognise one set of rights that applies to everyone, one community with a number of rich, overlapping strands of culture and tradition, and recognition of an inclusive pluralism of religious and political thought and adherence which does not marginalise the partners and children of mixed marriages, the values of integrated education, and inter-denominational religious activities, and political liberals who do not espouse nationalism of one kind or another. Everyone must be able to be confident of equality of treatment.

Source: The Alliance Party of Northern Ireland, *The Principles and Realities of a Settlement: An Alliance Paper*, 13 October 1997. Full version available at: http://www.allianceparty.org/resources/index/4-Peace%20Process/1997%20Multi-Party%20Talks

IMPLEMENTING THE AGREEMENT, 1998–2007

Document 27   LOYALISTS CLASH: THE DUP AND THE PUP

David McKittrick describes an exchange of views at a meeting on the Shankhill Road in Belfast between Mrs Iris Robinson of the DUP and Billy Hutchinson of the Progressive Unionist Party, the political wing of the UVF.

[Iris Robinson asks] '. . . Why should Mr Paisley sit down with Gerry Adams, who has the blood of so many hundreds of people on his hands?'

Hutchinson . . . challenged her.

'She's sitting there saying you can't talk to murderers, but here on the Shankhill Road thousands of young men and women have been to prison for fighting the IRA and republicanism. Now she's calling these people murderers.'

Mrs Robinson replied: 'As a born-again Christian I cannot support anyone who murders. That has always been my stand.' 'Then why do you keep saying that there's going to be civil war?' asked Mr Hutchinson. 'Because you read the writing on the wall,' came her response.

Hutchinson called out: 'You and your husband and your party have cried to the people out there to get out on the streets and fight republicanism. You can't deny them now, you have to stand by them.'

'No,' said Mrs Robinson. 'I say to you use your numbers to fight through the ballot box. I've never asked anyone to come on the streets.' Hutchinson, referring to the days when Mr Paisley and Mr Robinson took to the streets in recruitment rallies for a shadowy organisation, Ulster Resistance, responded: 'When you wear red berets and march in ranks it's a statement of militarism, and you scare the life out of young men who then think they have to go out and fight. This is hypocrisy.'

Source: David McKittrick, 'Ulstermen march to a new drum', *The Independent*, 14 October 1994; reprinted in D. McKittrick, *The Nervous Peace*, Belfast: Blackstaff Press, 1996, pp. 38–41.

DAVID TRIMBLE ON PEACEMAKING, NOBEL PEACE PRIZE SPEECH **Document 28**

The Nobel Peace Prize for 1998 was awarded jointly to John Hume and David Trimble 'for their efforts to find a peaceful solution to the conflict in Northern Ireland'. These are the Unionist Party leader's reflections on the politics of peacemaking.

[Edmund] Burke is the best model for what might be called politicians of the possible. Politicians who seek to make a working peace, not in some perfect world, that never was, but in this, the flawed world, which is our only workshop.

Because he is the philosopher of practical politics, not of visionary vapours, because his beliefs correspond to empirical experience, he may be a good general guide to the practical politics of peacemaking. . . .

But the realisation of peace needs more than magnanimity. It requires a certain political prudence, and a willingness at times not to be too precise or pedantic. Burke says, 'It is the nature of greatness not to be exact.' Amos Oz agrees, 'Inconsistency is the basis of coexistence. The heroes of tragedy driven by consistency and by righteousness, destroy each other. He who seeks total supreme justice seeks death.'

Again the warning not to aim for abstract perfection. Heaven knows, in Ulster, what I have looked for is a peace within the realms of the possible. We could only have started from where we actually were, not from where we would have liked to be. . . .

. . . Ulster Unionists, fearful of being isolated on the island, built a solid house, but it was a cold house for catholics. And northern nationalists, although they had a roof over their heads, seemed to us as if they meant to burn the house down.

None of us are entirely innocent.

Source: David Trimble's Nobel Peace Prize Speech, Oslo, 10 December 1998. Full version available at: http://nobelprize.org/nobel_prizes/peace/laureates/1998/trimble-lecture.html

Document 29   TONY BLAIR'S 'BELFAST HARBOUR SPEECH'

This is an extract from British Prime Minister Tony Blair's pivotal speech to the Belfast Harbour Commissioners, 17 October 2002 in which he called on the IRA to complete its transition away from violence.

. . . one hangover from this history remains. Even when republicans realised they were not going to get Britain to give up Northern Ireland by terror, they still thought it had another tactical purpose. It gave them negotiating leverage. . . .

. . . the problem is that the very thing republicans used to think gave them negotiating leverage, doesn't do it anymore. It no longer acts to remove Unionist intransigence, but to sustain it; it no longer pushes the British Government forward, but delays us. It doesn't any longer justify David Trimble's engagement; it thwarts it. . . .

But the crunch is the crunch. There is no parallel track left. The fork in the road has finally come. Whatever guarantees we need to give that we will implement the Agreement, we will. Whatever commitment to the end we all want to see, of a normalised Northern Ireland, I will make. But we cannot carry on with the IRA half in, half out of this process. Not just because it isn't right any more. It won't work anymore.

Remove the threat of violence and the peace process is on an unstoppable path. That threat, no matter how damped down, is no longer reinforcing the political, it is actually destroying it. . . .

It's time for acts of completion.

Source: Belfast Telegraph, 18 October 2002.

TONY BLAIR'S SCEPTICISM THAT THE DUP WANT POWER-SHARING   **Document 30**

The British government's decision on 1 May to suspend the Assembly elections scheduled for 29 May 2003 was a set-back for those who championed the idea of a Sinn Féin–DUP deal. Tony Blair, the British Prime Minister, was explicit in arguing that there was no point in holding elections if no Executive was to be formed after an election.

. . . There is no possibility at the moment of having an elected government out of it [an election to the Assembly], and if anyone believes that the DUP would offer an elected government, that is complete pie in the sky. They have made it absolutely clear that they want fundamentally to destroy the Good Friday Agreement, which is really what they mean when they talk about renegotiating it, and they say they will have nothing whatever to do with the Republic of Ireland Government. Well that is a recipe for complete and total chaos.

Source: www.number-10.gov.uk/print/page3569.asp

IAN PAISLEY DECLARES HE WILL NOT SHARE POWER WITH REPUBLICANS   **Document 31**

Extract from Ian Paisley's speech to the Orange parades, July 2006.

No unionist who is a unionist will go into partnership with IRA–Sinn Fein. They are not fit to be in partnership with decent people. They are not fit to be in the government of Northern Ireland. And it will be over our dead bodies that they will ever get there . . . Ulster has surely learned that weak, pushover unionism is a halfway house to republicanism. There is no discharge in this war . . . Compromise, accommodation and the least surrender are the roads to final and irreversible disaster. There can be no compromise.

Source: Irish Times, 13 July 2006.

Guide to further reading

Northern Ireland is one of the most studied areas in the world and authors frequently apologise for adding to the shelves of books on the subject. The purpose of this section is to guide the reader to the key books and articles on the history and politics of Northern Ireland since 1969. This literature does not just include academic work. Northern Ireland has been blessed by some superb journalists who have greatly added to the understanding of the conflict. The memoirs of political activists have also added colour to the debate over the conflict.

The Northern Ireland conflict: overviews

Paul Dixon's book *Northern Ireland: The Politics of War and Peace* (Palgrave, 2nd edn, 2008b) does offer a more in-depth analysis of the conflict and is the logical next step for readers of this book. *Northern Ireland: The Politics of War and Peace* focuses on the attempt of British and Irish politicians during the recent conflict to 'bridge the gap' between nationalists and unionists to create a sustainable power-sharing settlement and the obstacles these political actors encountered.

A more nationalist perspective is offered by Brendan O'Leary and John McGarry's *The Politics of Antagonism: Understanding Northern Ireland* (Athlone, 1st edn, 1994; 2nd edn, 1996).

Sydney Elliott and William Flackes have produced an invaluable dictionary to the conflict: *Northern Ireland: A Political Directory* (Blackstaff Press, 1999). This is packed with information including dictionary, chronology, election results, systems of government, office holders, the security system and security statistics. Paul Bew and Gordon Gillespie's *Northern Ireland: A Chronology of the Troubles 1968–1999* (Gill and Macmillan, 1999) is a useful guide and contains some good short essays on key moments during the Troubles. Every death as a result of the conflict is listed in David McKittrick *et al.*'s depressing but important *Lost Lives: The Stories of the Men, Women and*

Children who Died as a Result of the Northern Ireland Troubles (Mainstream, 2004). The journalist Kevin Myers's *Watching the Door* (Atlantic Books, 2008) is a colourful account of living in Belfast and covering the early days of the Troubles. The book is an entertaining and often very humorous read but serves to illustrate the randomness of the violence and the dangers of the city in the early 1970s.

The history of Northern Ireland

Michael Farrell's classic republican socialist *Northern Ireland: The Orange State* (Pluto Press, 1976) emphasised the repressive nature of the unionist-dominated state. In 1979 Paul Bew, Peter Gibbon and Henry Patterson published *The State in Northern Ireland, 1921–72* (Manchester University Press, 1979). This was a revisionist socialist repost to Farrell's book which paid closer attention to the tensions within unionism and the challenge of the Northern Ireland Labour Party, an early champion of civil rights in Northern Ireland. Bew *et al.*'s work has stood the test of time and continues to be revised, updated and republished as *Northern Ireland 1921–2001: Political Forces and Social Classes* (Serif, 2002). More recently Patterson has published *Ireland Since 1939* (Penguin, 2007), which successfully plunders the archives to revise our understanding of politics North and South. Professor (Lord) Bew has published *Ireland: The Politics of Enmity 1789–2006* (Oxford University Press, 2007). While this book covers a much wider time span than the Troubles period, it contains an excellent and accessible chapter on the period since 1969. Joseph Ruane and Jennifer Todd's *The Dynamics of Conflict in Northern Ireland: Power, Conflict and Emancipation* (Cambridge University Press, 2nd edn, 2007) is an interesting socio-historical analysis that emphasises the broader historical constraints that have shaped the conflict. In *Northern Ireland 1968–2008: The Politics of Entrenchment* (Palgrave, 2010), Cillian McGrattan provides a radical new analysis of the conflict.

There are some important studies of the conflict since 1969. Niall Ó Dochartaigh's *From Civil Rights to Armalites: Derry and the Birth of the Irish Troubles* (Cork University Press, 1997) is an excellent, fair-minded account of an important period in the conflict. The historian Tom Hennessey has trawled the archives to produce *Northern Ireland: The Origins of the Troubles* (Gill and Macmillan, 2005) and *The Evolution of the Troubles 1970–72* (Irish Academic Press, 2007). Eamonn McCann's *War and an Irish Town* (Penguin, 1974) is the classic account of an activist in the civil rights movement in Derry. Aaron Edwards' *A History of the Northern Ireland Labour Party: Democratic Socialism and Sectarianism* (Manchester University Press, 2009) covers a much neglected topic.

Interpreting the conflict

John Whyte's book *Interpreting Northern Ireland* (Clarendon Press, 1990) is a clearly written and magisterial overview of the various interpretations of the conflict. John McGarry and Brendan O'Leary's *Explaining Northern Ireland* (Blackwell, 1995) is a useful review of various perspectives and their edited collection *The Future of Northern Ireland* (Clarendon Press, 1990) presents a range of proposed 'solutions' including chapters on Irish unity, repartition (favoured by the editors), joint authority and independence. Ironically, none of the essays discusses power-sharing with an Irish dimension, which was to become the basis of the Good Friday Agreement.

Padraig O'Malley's *Uncivil Wars: Ireland Today* (Blackstaff Press, 1983) is a fascinating snapshot and critical analysis of the political stances of key political actors, parties and governments. In *Questions of Nuance* (Blackstaff Press, 1990), O'Malley returned to Northern Ireland to update his work at a particularly gloomy post-Anglo-Irish Agreement period and again interviewed key actors.

Adrian Little's *Democracy and Northern Ireland: Beyond the Liberal Paradigm?* (Palgrave, 2004) is an excellent survey of the debates among political theorists on Northern Ireland. John D. Cash's *Identity, Ideology and Conflict: The Structuration of Politics in Northern Ireland* (Cambridge University Press, 1996) is a difficult but rewarding analysis, which takes ideology and the politics of identity seriously. Cathal McCall's *Identity in Northern Ireland* (Palgrave, 1999) takes up postmodern themes and applies them to the conflict. Celia Davis *et al.*'s *Gender, Democracy and Inclusion in Northern Ireland* (Palgrave, 2000) studies women's involvement in grass-roots organisations in Northern Ireland in order to illuminate how democracy works. Marysia Zalewski and John Barry have edited a challenging but absorbing collection of articles in *Intervening in Northern Ireland: Critically Re-thinking Representations of Conflict* (Routledge, 2006).

Unionism and loyalism

In more recent years the literature on unionism has ballooned. Unionism is probably more difficult for outsiders to understand than nationalism and republicanism, but giant strides have been taken to both understand unionism and articulate its perspective more effectively. Alan F. Parkinson has produced an interesting study on *Ulster Loyalism and the British Media* (Four Courts Press, 1998) which suggests that the media tends to ignore unionism and its grievances.

Sarah Nelson's *Ulster's Uncertain Defenders* (Appletree, 1984) is a brilliant, participant-observation study of Protestant politics in the mid-1970s. Arthur

Aughey's *Under Siege: Ulster Unionism and the Anglo-Irish Agreement* (Blackstaff Press, 1989) is a meticulous study of an important period in unionist politics and examines the tension between integrationists and devolutionists within unionism. Feargal Cochrane's *Unionist Politics and the Politics of Unionism since the Anglo-Irish Agreement* (Cork University Press, 2nd rev. edn, 2001) is a more hostile interpretation of unionism but is a rich source of material on unionism. The once dominant Ulster Unionist Party has been the subject of two books: Graham Walker's *A History of the Ulster Unionist Party: Protest, Pragmatism and Pessimism* (Manchester University Press, 2004), which has a chapter on the period 1972–2002, and Henry Patterson and Eric Kaufmann's *Unionism and Orangeism in Northern Ireland Since 1945* (Manchester University Press, 2007). Christopher Farrington's *Ulster Unionism and the Peace Process in Northern Ireland* (Palgrave, 2006) focuses on more recent developments in unionism. Two interesting edited collections of essays are Peter Shirlow and Mark McGovern's *Who are 'the People': Unionism, Protestantism and Loyalism in Northern Ireland* (Pluto, 1997) and Richard English and Graham Walker's *Unionism in Modern Ireland* (Macmillan, 1996). Dean Godson's biography of David Trimble, the UUP leader, *Himself Alone: David Trimble and the Ordeal of Unionism* (HarperCollins, 2004) is an exhaustive account of Trimble's career but also a major study of the peace process. This should be read alongside Frank Millar's *David Trimble: The Price of Peace* (Liffey Press, 2004), which provides a subtle analysis of the UUP leader's role and strategy during the peace process.

The Democratic Unionist Party has little sympathy among academics and journalists and this may help to explain the lack of work on the now dominant party among unionists. Steve Bruce's book *God Save Ulster! The Religion and Politics of Paisleyism* (Oxford University Press, 1986), which was updated in 2007 as *Paisley: Religion and Politics in Northern Ireland* (Oxford University Press, 2007), is a notable exception and is a sympathetic, well-argued study of the leader of the Democratic Unionist Party. This should be contrasted with Ed Moloney's more critical biography, *Paisley: From Demagogue to Democrat?* (Poolbeg, 2008). The trials and tribulations of the DUP post-2007 are covered in David Gordon's excellent *The Fall of the House of Paisley* (Gill and Macmillan, 2010).

The loyalist paramilitaries were little researched until Bruce's ground-breaking study *The Red Hand: Protestant Paramilitaries in Northern Ireland* (Oxford University Press, 1992). Since then two journalists, Jim Cusack and Henry MacDonald, have produced books on the *UDA* (Penguin, 2004) and *UVF* (Poolbeg, 1997; rev. edn, 2008), Colin Crawford has published *Inside the UDA* (Pluto Press, 2003) and Ian S. Wood has published *Crimes of Loyalty: A History of the UDA* (Edinburgh University Press, 2006). Graham Spencer in *The State of Loyalism in Northern Ireland* (Palgrave, 2008) traces the role of the loyalist paramilitaries in the peace process, discussing their little known role in the behind the scenes negotiations that brought about an IRA ceasefire and their on-going involvement in the peace process.

The rise and fall of the Orange Order in Northern Ireland has attracted considerable attention of late. The pick is Eric Kaufmann's *The Orange Order: A Contemporary Northern Irish History* (Oxford University Press, 2007), which draws on the Order's archives and uses statistics to chart the segmentation of the Order. Brian Kennaway's *The Orange Order: A Tradition Betrayed* (Methuen, 2006) is a critical insider account of the way the Order has become identified with a bigoted and unyielding unionism. Mervyn Jess' *The Orange Order* (O'Brien, 2007) and Ruth Dudley Edwards' *The Faithful Tribe: An Intimate Portrait of the Loyal Institutions* (HarperCollins, 2000) are two useful journalistic accounts of the Order.

On unionist ideology, Norman Porter's *Rethinking Unionism: An Alternative Vision for Northern Ireland* (Blackstaff Press, 1996) divides unionism into cultural, liberal and civic varieties and makes the case for a more progressive, civic unionism. John D. Cash's *Identity, Ideology and Conflict* (Cambridge University Press, 1996) is an impressive, if difficult, study with several perceptive chapters on unionism.

The Alliance Party is the only party in Northern Ireland that attracts significant cross-community support and seeks to overcome 'tribal' politics. Jon Tonge discusses the prospects for the centre ground and strategies for overcoming 'tribalism' in *The New Northern Irish Politics?* (Palgrave, 2005).

Nationalism and republicanism

While the IRA's violence has brought it plenty of interest, the more moderate nationalism of the Social Democratic and Labour Party has – for a considerable period of the conflict – been overlooked. Gerard Murray has addressed this deficiency in the literature with *John Hume and the SDLP* (Irish Academic Press, 1998), which draws on the party's archive. Fionnuala O Connor's *In Search of a State: Catholics in Northern Ireland* (Blackstaff Press, 1993) is a very well-written, subtle and perceptive analysis of Catholic attitudes in Northern Ireland. Gerard Murray reprises some of this work in his book co-authored with Jonathan Tonge, *Sinn Féin and the SDLP: From Alienation to Participation* (Hurst, 2005), which sets the evolution of the two nationalist/republican parties side by side. Ian McAllister's *The Northern Ireland Social Democratic and Labour Party* (Macmillan, 1977) is a valuable and detailed study of the emergence of the SDLP in its early years.

The Provisional republican movement has attracted some excellent studies. The outstanding book on the IRA was published by the journalist Ed

Moloney. *A Secret History of the IRA* (Penguin, 2nd edn, 2007) is based on extensive interviews with key members of the republican movement, both named and unnamed, and other key actors in the conflict. Moloney presents a highly critical analysis of the Sinn Féin/IRA leadership but from a perspective that republican critics of the peace process would have some sympathy for. M.L.R. Smith's *Fighting for Ireland? The Military Strategy of the Irish Republican Movement* (Routledge, 1995), Henry Patterson's *The Politics of Illusion: A Political History of the IRA* (Serif, 1997) and Richard English's *Armed Struggle* (Macmillan, 2003) are based on more publicly available sources and they complement Moloney's work. Malachi O'Doherty's *The Trouble With Guns: Republican Strategy and the Provisional IRA* (Blackstaff Press, 1998) is also a stimulating read from a critical source. Jon Tonge's *Northern Ireland* (Polity, 2006) has five useful, up-to-date chapters on republicans and republican dissidents. Kevin Bean's *The New Politics of Sinn Féin* (Liverpool 2007) is an interesting and illuminating examination of the evolution of Sinn Féin from war to peace by a close observer of the republican movement.

Eamonn Collins' *Killing Rage* (Granta, 1998) is a brilliant insider account of the IRA that reads like a thriller. Gerry Adams has published a number of books and collections of his journalism; his *Hope and History: Making Peace in Ireland* (Brandon, 2004) presents his perspective on the peace process. The best biography of Gerry Adams is *Gerry Adams: Man of War, Man of Peace* (Pan, 1998) by two journalists, David Sharrock and Mark Devenport. Liam Clarke and Kathryn Johnston have profiled Martin McGuinness in *Martin McGuinness: From Guns to Government* (Mainstream, 2001).

The classic socialist republican text is Michael Farrell's *Northern Ireland: The Orange State* (Pluto, 1976). A more sophisticated analysis followed with Liam O'Dowd *et al.*'s edited collection *Northern Ireland: Between Civil Rights and Civil War* (CSE Books, 1980) and *Rethinking Northern Ireland: Culture, Ideology and Colonialism* (Longman, 1998), edited by David Miller.

British policy towards Northern Ireland

British policy towards the conflict in Northern Ireland has been a strangely neglected topic. Paul Dixon's *Northern Ireland: The Politics of War and Peace* (Palgrave, 2nd edition, 2008b) contains an analysis of British policy that emphasises the continuity and tactical adjustments made by British governments that were largely constrained to follow a bipartisan approach. There is a review of different interpretations of British policy in Dixon's '"A tragedy beyond words": interpretations of British government policy and the Northern Ireland peace process' in Aaron Edwards and Stephen Bloomer's *Transforming* the *Peace Process in Northern Ireland: From Terrorism to Democratic Politics* (Irish Academic Press, 2008). Eamonn O'Kane's *Britain, Ireland and Northern Ireland Since 1980* (Routledge, 2007) examines the development of British policy since 1980 and draws on interviews with many of the key British policymakers. Michael Cunningham's *British Government Policy in Northern Ireland 1969–2000* (Manchester University Press, 2nd edn, 2001) is a very good survey of British government policy and should be considered alongside the first edition, which has more information on the earlier period of British policy. Peter Neumann draws on the archives in his *Britain's Long War: British Strategy in the Northern Ireland Conflict, 1969–98* (Palgrave, 2003) and portrays British policy in a more favourable light. D.G. Boyce's *The Irish Question and British Politics: 1868–1996* (Macmillan, 1996) is a brief survey by a knowledgeable and fine historian.

In the meantime the outstanding book on security policy is the journalist Mark Urban's *Big Boys' Rules: The SAS and the Secret Struggle against the IRA* (Faber and Faber, 1992). Another journalist, Desmond Hamill, published *Pig in the Middle: The Army in Northern Ireland 1969–85* (Methuen, 1985), which although it is short on references and analysis is useful because of his wide access to sources within the army. Chris Ryder has produced books on the Northern Ireland recruited security forces: *The Ulster Defence Regiment: An Instrument of Peace?* (Mandarin, 1992) and *The RUC: A Force Under Fire* (Mandarin, 1997).

Anthony Jenning's edited collection *Justice Under Fire: The Abuse of Civil Liberties in Northern Ireland* (Pluto, 1988) is dated but raises important legal issues about human rights. On the British state's 'dirty war' in Northern Ireland, Martin Ingram and Greg Harkin's *Stakeknife: Britain's Secret Agents in Ireland* (O'Brien, 2004) and Justin O'Brien's *Killing Finucane: Murder in Defence of the Realm* (Gill and Macmillan, 2005) make fascinating if also disturbing reading. Jon Moran's *Policing the Peace in Northern Ireland: Politics, Crime and Security after the Belfast Agreement* (Manchester University Press, 2008) reviews the reform of the RUC into the PSNI and other changes after the Good Friday Agreement.

Republic of Ireland attitudes towards Northern Ireland

There is a gap in the literature on the South's attitude and policy towards Northern Ireland. One of the fullest accounts of the recent attitude of the South towards Northern Ireland can be found in Eamonn O'Kane's *Britain, Ireland and Northern Ireland Since 1980* (Routledge, 2007). The book examines the cooperation and competition between the Irish and British governments and their relationships with the major parties in Northern Ireland. Catherine O'Donnell's *Fianna Fail, Irish Republicanism and the Northern Ireland Troubles 1968–2005* (Irish Academic Press, 2007) and Henry Patterson's *Ireland Since 1939* (Penguin, 2007) also cover southern attitudes.

The international dimension and comparative perspectives

Adrian Guelke's *Northern Ireland: The International Perspective* (Gill and Macmillan, 1988) is an outstanding study on the impact of the international on the conflict. Michael Cox has argued for the importance of the international in explaining the peace process while Paul Dixon has claimed that the impact of the international has been deliberately exaggerated and had a malign effect on unionist opinion. This debate is available in M. Cox *et al.* (eds) *A Farewell to Arms? Beyond the Good Friday Agreement* (Manchester, 2nd edn, 2006) along with important chapters on Europe and the US dimension. On the US, see also Andrew J. Wilson's *Irish America and the Ulster Conflict 1968–1995* (Blackstaff Press, 1995) and Conor O'Clery's *The Greening of the White House* (Gill and Macmillan, 1996).

Two important approaches to conflict management in Northern Ireland are the consociational and civil society approaches. Paul Dixon's 'Paths to peace in Northern Ireland (I): civil society and consociational approaches', *Democratization*, 4, 2 (Summer 1997) provides a brief overview and critique of these contrasting theories.

The media

David Miller's *Don't Mention the War: Northern Ireland, Propaganda and the Media* (Pluto Press, 1994) is a valuable republican analysis of the British state's propaganda machine in Northern Ireland and is supplemented by Bill Rolston and D. Miller's edited collection *The Northern Ireland Media Reader* (Beyond the Pale, 1996). These authors have little to say about the reporting of unionism so should be read alongside Alan F. Parkinson's fascinating study of *Ulster Loyalism and the British Media* (Four Courts Press, 1998) and David Butler's *The Trouble with Reporting Northern Ireland* (Avebury, 1995). Graham Spencer's *Disturbing the Peace? Politics, Television News and the Northern Ireland Peace Process* (Avebury, 2000) contains excellent interview material and should be read alongside his numerous journal articles that interrogate the role of the media in the conflict.

The peace process

Paul Dixon's *Northern Ireland: The Politics of War and Peace* (Palgrave, 2nd edn, 2008b) is the best place to start for an overview of the peace process. Eamonn O'Kane's *Britain Ireland and Northern Ireland Since 1980* (Routledge, 2007) has a detailed examination of the origins and development of the peace process and the reasons for the apparent changes in the position of the key parties to the conflict in the early 1990s. O'Kane's book also offers an extensive discussion of the problems in implementing the GFA. The important issue of decommissioning is examined in O'Kane's article, 'Decommissioning and the peace process: where did it come from and why did it stay so long?', *Irish Political Studies*, 22, 1 (2007).

An excellent, blow-by-blow account of the peace process is Deaglun de Breadun's *The Far Side of Revenge: Making Peace in Northern Ireland* (Collins Press, 2008). Tom Hennessey's *The Northern Ireland Peace Process* (Gill and Macmillan, 2000) is a useful and detailed account reproducing some key documents. Roger MacGinty and John Darby's *Guns and Government: The Management of the Northern Ireland Peace Process* (Palgrave, 2002) is an account from a 'conflict resolution theory' perspective. Two journalists, Eamonn Mallie and David McKittrick, have used their contacts with politicians to gain access to some important sources on the peace process. Their two books, *The Fight for Peace: The Secret Story of the Irish Peace Process* (Heinemann, 1996) and *Endgame in Ireland* (Hodder and Stoughton, 2001), give a nationalist perspective. Aaron Edwards and Stephen Bloomer's *Transforming the Peace Process in Northern Ireland: From Terrorism to Democratic Politics* (Irish Academic Press, 2008) and Michael Cox et al.'s *A Farewell to Arms? Beyond the Good Friday Agreement* (Manchester University Press, 2nd edn, 2006) are both useful collections of articles on the peace process. On the Good Friday Agreement itself, see Rick Wilford (ed.), *Aspects of the Agreement* (Oxford University Press, 2001) and J. Ruane and J. Todd (eds), *After the Good Friday Agreement* (UCD Press, 1999). Jon Tonge's *The New Northern Irish Politics?* (Palgrave, 2005) surveys the political scene after the Good Friday Agreement. A more unionist perspective on the peace process is offered in Brian Barton and Patrick J. Roche's *The Northern Ireland Question: Peace Process and the Belfast Agreement* (Palgrave, 2009).

See the above entries on 'Unionism and Loyalism' and 'Nationalism and Republicanism' for the perspectives of political actors on the peace process. For British perspectives on the peace process, see Anthony Seldon's biography of the British Prime Minister *John Major* (Weidenfeld and Nicolson, 1997) and John Major's own memoirs, *John Major: The Autobiography* (Harper-Collins, 1999). On the Labour government's approach, see the memoirs of Secretary of State for Northern Ireland 1997–99 Mo Mowlam, *Momentum*

(Hodder and Stoughton, 2002). Jonathan Powell was Tony Blair's key adviser on Northern Ireland and he defends the Labour government's handling of the peace process in *Great Hatred, Little Room* (Bodley Head, 2008).

On republican 'dissidents', see Jon Tonge's 'Republican ultras' in his book *Northern Ireland* (Polity, 2006), Ed Moloney's *A Secret History of the IRA* (Penguin, 2nd edn, 2007) and Anthony McIntyre's *Good Friday: The Death of Irish Republicanism* (Ausubo Press, 2008).

Some journalism and web sources

A daily selection of journalism about Northern Ireland is available from http://www.irishcentral.com/news/nuzhound/ and the blog by 'Slugger O'Toole' 'Notes on Northern Ireland Politics and Culture' hosts lively debate: http://www.sluggerotoole.com/. *Fortnight* magazine is an award-winning Northern Ireland monthly (despite its title) political magazine that has been running since 1970 and features articles by commentators from a diversity of perspectives. The Conflict Archive on the Internet (CAIN) has collected an impressive array of source material and information and a detailed chronology up to 2001, http://cain.ulst.ac.uk. The Access Research Knowledge (ARK) web site, http://www.ark.ac.uk, hosts information on Northern Irish elections and surveys. For an index of Northern Ireland Politics, go to http://www.nidex.com/politics.htm. The web sites of key players in the conflict can be found here: the Government of Northern Ireland: http://www.nics.gov.uk/; the British Northern Ireland Office: http://www.nio.gov.uk/; the Irish Government: www.irlgov.ie/iveagh; the UUP: www.uup.org; the DUP: www.dup.org.uk/; Traditional Unionist Voice: http://www.tuv.org.uk/; the Alliance Party: www.allianceparty.org; the SDLP: www.sdlp.ie; and Sinn Féin: www.sinnFéin.ie.

References

Arnold, B. (1993) *Unlucky Deeds: Life and Times of Charles J. Haughey*, London: HarperCollins.

Bew, P. (2007) *Ireland: The Politics of Enmity 1789–2006*, Oxford: Oxford University Press.
Bew, P. and Gillespie, G. (1996) *The Northern Ireland Peace Process 1993–1996: A Chronology*, London: Serif.
Bew, P. and Gillespie, G. (1999) *Northern Ireland: A Chronology of the Troubles 1968–99*, Dublin: Gill and Macmillan.
Bew, P., Gibbon, P. and Patterson, H. (1995) *Northern Ireland 1921–94: Political Forces and Social Classes*, London: Serif.

Campbell, A. (2007) *The Blair Years*, London: Hutchinson.
Cox, M. (1997) 'Bringing in the "international": the IRA ceasefire and the end of the Cold War', *International Affairs*, 73, 4, pp. 671–93.
Cox, M., Guelka, A. and Stephen, F. (eds) (2006) *A Farewell to Arms? Beyond the Good Friday Agreement*, 2nd edn, Manchester: Manchester University Press.
Cunliffe, B. (ed.) (2001) *The Penguin Atlas of British and Irish History*, Harmondsworth: Penguin.

Dixon, P. (2002) 'Political skills or lying and manipulation? The choreography of the Northern Ireland peace process', *Political Studies*, 50, 3, pp. 725–41.
Dixon, P. (2006) 'Performing the Northern Ireland peace process on the world stage', *Political Science Quarterly*, 121, 1, pp. 61–91.
Dixon, P. (2008a) 'Whatever you say, say nothing: truth and lies in the Northern Ireland peace process', PSA Swansea, April 2008.
Dixon, P. (2008b) *Northern Ireland: The Politics of War and Peace*, 2nd edn, Basingstoke: Palgrave Macmillan.

Donoughue, B. (1987) *Prime Minister – The Conduct of Policy under Harold Wilson and James Callaghan*, London: Jonathan Cape.

Duffy, S. (ed.) (1997) *Atlas of Irish History*, Dublin: Gill and Macmillan.

Edwards, Aaron (2009) *A History of the Northern Ireland Labour Party: Democratic Socialism and Sectarianism*, Manchester: Manchester University Press.

English, R. (2004) *Armed Struggle: The History of the IRA*, London: Pan Books.

Finlay, F. (1998) *Snakes and Ladders*, Dublin: New Island Books.

Fitzgerald, G. (1991) *All in a Life*, Dublin: Gill and Macmillan.

Godson, D. (2004) *Himself Alone: David Trimble and the Ordeal of Unionism*, London: HarperCollins.

Hennessey, T. (2000) *The Northern Ireland Peace Process*, Dublin: Gill and Macmillan.

Howe, G. (1994) *Conflict of Loyalty*, London: Pan.

ICBH (Institute for Contemporary British History) (1997) Anglo-Irish Agreement Witness Seminar, 11 June, London: ICBH.

IRA (2007) 'Text of IRA Easter statement (released 5 April 2007)', at http://cain.ulst.ac.uk/othelem/organ/ira/ira050407.htm

Kenny, A. (1986) *The Road to Hillsborough*, Oxford: Pergamon.

Loughlin, J. (1995) *Ulster Unionism and British National Identity Since 1885*, London: Pinter.

McCann, E. (1974) *War and an Irish Town*, Harmondsworth: Penguin.

McKittrick, D., Kelters, S., Feeney, B., Thornton, C. and McVea, D. (1999) *Lost Lives*, Edinburgh: Mainstream.

Major, J. (1999) *John Major: The Autobiography*, London: HarperCollins.

Mallie, E. and McKittrick, D. (1996) *The Fight for Peace: The Secret Story of the Irish Peace Process*, London: Heinemann.

Mallie, E. and McKittrick, D. (2001) *Endgame in Ireland*, Hodder & Stoughton: London.

Millar, F. (2009) *Northern Ireland: A Triumph of Politics*, Cork: Irish Academic Press.

Mitchell, G. (1999) *Making Peace: The Inside Story of the Making of the Good Friday Agreement*, London: Heinemann.

Mitchell, P., Evans, G. and O'Leary, B. (2009) 'Extremist outbidding in ethnic party systems is not inevitable: tribune parties in Northern Ireland' *Political Studies*, 57, 2, pp. 397–421.

Moloney, E. (2002) *A Secret History of the IRA*, London: Penguin.

Moloney, E. (2007) *A Secret History of the IRA*, 2nd edn, London: Penguin.

Needham, R. (1998) *Battling for Peace*, Belfast: Blackstaff Press.

O'Brien, B. (1993) *The Long War: The IRA and Sinn Féin 1985 to Today*, Dublin: O'Brien Press.

O'Clery, C. (1996) *The Greening of the White House*, Dublin: Gill and Macmillan.

Ó Dochartaigh, N. (1997) *From Civil Rights to Armalites: Derry and the Birth of the Irish Troubles*, Cork: Cork University Press.

O'Donnell, C. (2007) *Fianna Fail, Irish Republicanism and the Northern Ireland Troubles 1968–2005*, Dublin: Irish Academic Press.

O'Kane, E. (2007) *Britain, Ireland and Northern Ireland since 1980: The Totality of Relationships*, Abingdon: Routledge.

O'Kane, E. (2010) 'Learning from Northern Ireland: the uses and abuses of the Irish "model"', *British Journal of Politics and International Relations*, 12, 2, pp. 239–56.

O'Rawe, R. (2005) *Blanketmen: An Untold Story of the H-Block Hunger Strikes*, Dublin: New Island.

Owen, E.A. (1994) *The Anglo-Irish Agreement: The First Three Years*, Cardiff: University of Wales Press.

Patterson, H. (1997) *The Politics of Illusion: A Political History of the IRA*, London: Serif.

Patterson, H. (2002) *Ireland Since 1939*, Oxford: Oxford University Press.

Powell, J. (2008) *Great Hatred, Little Room: Making Peace in Northern Ireland*, London: Bodley Head.

PSNI (2006) PSNI Annual Statistics available from http://www.psni.police.uk/index/updates/updates_statistics.htm

Rees, M. (1985) *Northern Ireland: A Personal Perspective*, London: Methuen.

Rose, R., McAllister, I. and Mair, P. (1978) 'Is there a concurring majority about Northern Ireland?', Studies in Public Policy, 22, University of Strathclyde.

Shepherd, R. (1997) *Enoch Powell*, Pimlico: Hutchinson.

Sinn Féin (1993) *Setting the Record Straight*, Sinn Féin: Belfast.

Sunday Times Insight Team (1972) *Ulster*, Harmondsworth: Penguin.

Thatcher, M. (1993) *Downing Street Years*, London: HarperCollins.

White, B. (1984) *John Hume: Statesman of the Troubles*, Belfast: Blackstaff Press.

Whyte, J. (1983) 'How much discrimination was there under the Unionist Regime, 1921–68?', in T. Gallagher and J. O'Connell (eds), *Contemporary Irish Studies*, Manchester: Manchester University Press, pp. 1–36.

Index